Painting

WITH LIGHT

JOHN ALTON

Introduction by Todd McCarthy

UNIVERSITY OF CALIFORNIA PRESS
Berkeley   Los Angeles   London

The publisher gratefully acknowledges the contribution provided by the General Endowment Fund of the Associates of the University of California Press.

University of California Press
Berkeley and Los Angeles, California

University of California Press
London, England

Library of Congress Cataloging-in-Publication Data
Alton, John.
    Painting with light / John Alton.
        p.   cm.
    Originally published: New York: Macmillan, 1949. With new
    introductory material and filmography.
    Includes index.
    Filmography: p.
    ISBN 978-0-520-08949-5 (alk. paper: pbk.)
    1. Cinematography—Lighting.   2. Alton, John.   I. Title.
TR891.A48   1995
779.5′343—dc20   94-44121
                                                              CIP

Printed in the United States of America

13   12   11
16   15   14   13   12

The paper used in this publication meets the minimum requirements of ANSI/NISO Z39.48-1992 (R 1997) (*Permanence of Paper*). ∞

TO MY DEAR WIFE *Rozalia*

whose infinite patience and encouragement made

this book possible.

Life is short, but long enough to get what's coming to you.

THE AUTHOR

CONTENTS

THROUGH A LENS DARKLY:
THE LIFE AND FILMS OF JOHN ALTON

Todd McCarthy

"Black and white are colors," John Alton has stated, and no cinematographer in film history has more deeply explored the value of those colors, or the nature of the violent contrast between them, than has John Alton. "I could see more in the dark than I could in color," he claimed, "I could see in the dark." His remarkable talent lay in the way he enabled audiences to do the same.

At the same time, Alton displayed a remarkable ability—intentional or not—to enshroud his career in mystery. He was the Greta Garbo of Hollywood cameramen, an Austro-Hungarian nearly as illustrious in his own field as the great Swede was in hers and, as the years passed, possibly even more mysterious and elusive. After he abruptly quit the industry in 1960 at age 59, he was rumored to have abandoned cinema for painting, and to be living in Switzerland, Patagonia, or even Hollywood. He refused all requests for interviews or to be a guest at film festivals. The image grew of a ferocious artistic purist who would tolerate no intrusion upon his privacy or the sanctity of his vision.

As it happens, Alton is decidedly an artistic purist, but is ferocious only in the tenaciousness with which he expresses his ideals and opinions. A Middle European charmer and bon vivant even at 92, Alton has proven to be the most disarming and congenial of guests since, in 1993, he finally reemerged into the public eye at film festivals and special screenings. This process of reacquaintance with cinephiles now continues with the long-overdue republication of his classic 1949 book, *Painting With Light,* the first book on the art of cinematography ever written by a leading Hollywood cameraman. This event, along with the groundswell of attention Alton has been receiving, represents a happy confirmation of this volume's original epigraph: "Life is short, but long enough to get what's coming to you."

For too many years, Alton was one of the private pet obsessions of a handful of film buffs and critics; those who even knew his name and could cite a few of his credits belonged to a sort of secret society, a shadowy inner circle within the already exclusive coterie of specialists in film noir. Yet, over time, such films as *T-Men, Raw Deal, He Walked by Night, Border Incident,* and *The Big Combo* gradually developed wider followings and their striking style began asserting an influence on contemporary filmmakers. Recognition started with the cults surrounding Anthony Mann and Joseph H. Lewis, but finally it became clear that even these directors' other films didn't look like this, that the essence, and ultimate example, of film noir style was, logically enough, created by a cinematographer, not a director.

Considerable academic study has been devoted to film noir in an attempt to define it, describe its parameters, and explain it sociologically, historically, and artistically. But no matter whom one credits with having set the tone for noir—hard-boiled crime writers such as

Chandler, Cain, and Hammett; expressionistic-minded, predominantly Germanic émigré directors, including Lang, Wilder, Siodmak, and Preminger; economy-minded executives and producers looking for tough, timely material that could be done on the cheap; or the politicians of the postwar, Red Scare era who helped foster a paranoid cultural climate—there can be no doubt that John Alton pushed film noir to its most exciting visual extremes. In the definitive noir period, roughly 1946–1951, no one's blacks were blacker, shadows longer, contrasts stronger, or focus deeper than John Alton's. In fashioning the nocturnal world inhabited by noir's desperate characters, Alton was ever consistent and imaginative in forging his signature, illuminating scenes with single lamps, slanted and fragmented beams and pools of light, all separated by intense darkness in which the source of all fear could fester and finally thrive. Alton's films are paradoxically filled with violent killings and relatively absent of kinetic action, largely because his sculpted style demanded a choreography of shots different, and more static, than the norm. Very often, the brightest object in the frame would be located at the furthest distance from the camera, in order to channel viewer concentration; often, the light would just manage to catch the rim of a hat, the edge of a gun, the smoke from a cigarette. Actors' faces, normally the object of any cameraman's most ardent attention, were often invisible or obscured, with characters from *T-Men* to, perhaps most memorably, *The Big Combo* playing out their fates in silhouette against a witheringly blank, impassive background. Few, if any other, cinematographers' styles could be said to express a philosophy, a concrete view of the world, but Alton's certainly represents the purest visual correlative for fatalistic existentialism yet seen in motion pictures.

I came to know John Alton as a result of my work on the documentary *Visions of Light: The Art of Cinematography*. Unable to locate Alton to interview him, my collaborators and I none-theless devoted a section of the film to Alton's work. When he heard about the film, he wanted to see it, and since then I have had the privilege of spending considerable time with him at private screenings of his own pictures, many of which he was seeing for the first time in decades; at the Telluride Film Festival, where I helped present the first tribute to Alton's work attended by the artist himself (Fig. 1); and at his apartment in Beverly Hills—which is dominated by a few of his own paintings, some photographs, and his Oscar for *An American in Paris*—where he patiently and vigorously answered my many questions about his life and career.

John Alton began his long, accomplished, and exceedingly well-traveled life on October 5, 1901, in Sopron, a Hungarian village near what is now the Austrian border. The family name at the time was the German Altman, although Herr Altman's father undoubtedly had a different surname before moving to Vienna from Russia. John's father Sam Altman, who was born in 1872, and his brother Emile emigrated in the 1880s to the United States, where they changed their names to Alton and became U.S. citizens, thereby giving John Alton an American connection long before he was born. Emile stayed, but in time Sam returned to Vienna, where he reclaimed the Altman name and became a brandy, wine, and champagne maker and exporter. For a time, he worked for the wealthy Szecheny family, and it was in the Szecheny castle, where the Altmans had rooms, that John (or Jacob in German, or Janos in Hungarian) was born.

The family had a strong Jewish identity. Sam's wife, whom he had met through a traditional matchmaker, was a Sephardic Jew named Eva Lipschutz, a descendant of a prominent family that had fled Spain for Austria during the Inquisition. For his part, Sam was an adherent of the Austro-Hungarian Zionist leader Theodor Herzl. "My father was a Zionist all his life, on the religious end," Alton recalled. "He was Orthodox, and I didn't agree with all that. He

Fig. 1 *Filmmaker Bertrand Tavernier, John Alton, and Todd McCarthy during audience discussion at 1993 Telluride Film Festival. Photograph © Wendy H. Smith, courtesy of Telluride Film Festival.*

spoke Hebrew as a boy, so when he got to Palestine he was able to start making speeches right away."

John's native language was "Viennese dialect" German, but he also grew up learning Hungarian and Romanian (a list to which he later added English, Spanish, French, Italian, and a smattering of other tongues). When the boy was four, the family moved to Transylvania, and subsequently Sam opened his own winery in Romania. A precocious kid, John displayed an artistic bent, taking up photography at age five, learning to develop his own film, and drawing constantly. "In school, I was very bad in most subjects, but very good in drawing and art," Alton said. There were six Altman children. The eldest son Michael "was artistically inclined, but my father killed the artist in him, so he

became a bookworm and was not very successful," John recalled. "My father caught the bug of money in America, and he tried for the rest of his life to make everyone American." The second son, Bernard, "was the smartest and most educated of the children. He studied philosophy and was in the German Army in World War I. But later he stayed too long and the Nazis got him and killed him." A daughter, Anna, was next, followed by John, son Harry, and daughter Esther.

Just young enough to miss military service in World War I, Alton attended college for two years. But, as he put it, "I didn't see my future in Hungary." Feeling there were few opportunities for Jews in top professions, and always fascinated by the stories of America told by his father and uncle, he decided to take a chance and go to New York, which he did by freighter in 1919. His mother had died in surgery in Vienna in 1914, and after leaving for America, Alton never saw any of his family again except for his younger sister Esther, whom he visited at her home in Israel last year.

Initially welcomed by Uncle Emile, who by this time was the wealthy owner of a Second Avenue furnishings company, Alton enrolled in school (he has remembered it on different occasions as New York University and City College), where he studied photo-chemistry, among other things. It was during this period that John Alton had his first contact with the professional motion picture industry. Living in the Yorkville section in the East 80s, Alton was "on the bus on Second Avenue when it passed the Cosmopolitan Studios owned by Hearst. I decided to look into it and skip a couple of days of school. So I got off the bus and went up and the man at the gate said, 'You're just the man we're looking for,' and put me in a coat before I could turn my head. After three days, they gave me a check for $10.50. Suddenly, I felt rich. Comes the end of the day, and they read the roll of who's going to be called the next day. I felt I had to go back to school, but then I decided, school can wait. In a few days, we went on location. I had to ride a horse—I'd never ridden a horse, except for a merry-go-round horse. I ended up working for 41 days in a row on location, and I pulled in so much money I thought I had it made." Alton could only recall the film as a Marion Davies silent, but the experience was pivotal: "I fell so in love with the possibilities of what I saw in motion pictures."

Alton's windfall didn't last forever, and Emile, a hard-nosed businessman, was not impressed with his nephew's intellectual interest in the fine arts or his vague career ideas, and refused to help him financially. "Every time we sat down to lunch, he was telling me how much money he had made that week, and I didn't care for it." Finally, they clashed irrevocably, and the young man moved out.

Forced to fend for himself, Alton got his first real job at the Paramount Studios lab in Long Island City. When he had earned enough money, he bought a car and, in the winter of 1923–1924, caravaned with five friends across the country. After their arrival in Los Angeles, Alton remembered, they attended the premiere of Douglas Fairbanks' *The Thief of Bagdad*, which opened at the Egyptian Theater in Hollywood on July 10, 1924. "When I saw it, I started to dream about pictures again, although I had no idea I was going to be a cameraman. There was a fortune-teller for everyone who bought a ticket. She told all the others to go back where they came from. But when I got there, she looked at my palm and said, 'You're going to be a success in pictures.' The rest of them did go back.

"I went to MGM and got a job in the lab, based on the experience I had in New York. When I was there, I gave them ideas, and whenever I gave them ideas, I was fired. But what they forgot was that, in the afternoon, I worked in a different department at the same studio." Despite his occasional run-ins with superiors, Alton gained in-depth experience in various areas that proved tremendously valuable to him when he finally became a cinematographer. In the lab, he became intimately acquainted with the fine points of printing. Transferred to the camera department, he became a loader, and later a first assistant (although he was never an operator). Particularly memorable to him was the opportunity to observe Erich von Stroheim throughout the production of *The Merry Widow*. However, far more influential on Alton's own later work habits was director Woody S. Van Dyke, for whom he toiled on numerous Tim McCoy Westerns in 1926–1927 as assistant to cameraman Clyde de Vinna. Van Dyke, whom Alton liked enormously, taught him how to shoot quickly and work economically, traits that bcame Alton's bread and butter fifteen years later.

Feeling he was ready to be a first cameraman, Alton said that he went to Louis B. Mayer to ask for his promotion. Although his claim seems highly questionable given the fact that most cinematographers at the time were U.S.-born, Alton's version of the meeting is amusing. "Mayer said that all the top cameramen had European accents, and that as long as I had my Brooklyn accent, I'd never become a camera-man. So I worked at recultivating my old accent so that, when I came back, I could get a job."

Instead, studio manager Joe Cohn gave the 26-year-old Alton the enviable assignment of accompanying Ernst Lubitsch and another cam-eraman, Al Lane, to Europe to shoot back-grounds for *Old Heidelberg*, which subsequently became *The Student Prince.* When he returned to Culver City, he discovered that this job had caused resentment among some of his camera department colleagues, something that was to plague him at MGM throughout his career. Al-ton said that Cohn shortly sent him back to Europe to take footage of the 1928 Winter Olympics in Switzerland for potential use in a Garbo picture, although the truth of this is impossible to confirm since no Garbo film fea-tures such a backdrop. Similarly questionable is Alton's recollection of a job with director George Hill shooting location material in Al-geria and Morocco; none of Hill's subsequent films had desert settings.

Landing in Paris in 1928, Alton claims to have made a discovery that did neither him nor MGM any good, but which proved highly fortu-itous for his friend Lubitsch and the history of musicals. In a club in Pigalle, Alton was vastly entertained by a young singer by the name of Maurice Chevalier, who was already known in France but not in the United States. Alton enthused to Irving Thalberg, who happened to be in Paris on his honeymoon with Norma Shearer, and asked permission to make a test. "Thalberg said, 'Go ahead,' so I did, and it turned out pretty well. I sent it to Thalberg at his hotel, and he said, 'This guy hasn't got any-thing.' I had some friends at Paramount, and Paramount looked at it, signed him up, and made a fortune."

Over the next couple of years, heading the

camera department of the Joinville Studios in Paris, Alton shot shorts and other material for MGM and Paramount throughout Europe, in Turkey, and Asia Minor, as well as foreign ver-sions of films in different languages.

To make sure that his colleagues in Holly-wood knew that he was gainfully employed and brimming with ideas and ambition, Alton be-gan contributing regularly to the journal *Inter-national Photographer* in 1930. A letter from Stamboul announced his forthcoming location trip to Syria, Palestine, and Egypt, and later dispatches related his experiences working on such 1931 productions as E. W. Emo's *Better To Laugh,* A. Mitler's *Port Said,* and Curtis Bern-hardt's *Der Mann, Der Den Mord Beging (The Man Who Murdered*), on which he shot exteri-ors in Istanbul and experienced an increasing estrangement from the director.

At the beginning of the sound era, the Ar-gentine film industry, which had enjoyed boom years for a decade after World War I, had come to a total standstill. Technically behind the United States and Europe in producing talk-ing pictures, the country needed experienced hands. Strangely enough, John Alton was their man. "I met some Argentine millionaires"—one of whom was the chief financier of the Buenos Aires opera and other theatrical interests—"who were planning to build a studio in Argentina," Alton recalled. "They asked me to come design it for them, so I asked for one-year leave-of-absence from Joinville. I went to Argentina, we built a studio and I made one film. But in the meantime I got married."

Thus began the most curious, and least known, episode in Alton's life. In 1932, Al-ton sailed for Buenos Aires and, on five acres thirty miles outside the city in the town of San Ysidro, he supervised the construction of the S.A. Radio-Cinematografica Lumiton (Light and Sound) Studio. He stayed on to train the crew as part of his deal. "I did everything. They didn't know what a propman was, so I had to show them. I had to set up the lab." Alton no doubt remained in Argentina so much longer than he originally planned in large part because of his marriage to Rozalia Kiss. A writer for the newspaper La Nacion and a college-educated former beauty contest winner, Kiss interviewed the eminent visitor on board his boat upon its arrival after a 31-day voyage from France. They had dinner that night, and after two weeks were planning a wedding, which took place on November 5, 1932. Originally from an Austrian Jewish family, Kiss was also an early Argentine aviator, but after one hair-raising flight with her through the Andes to Chile, Alton asked Kiss to give up her hobby. They remained married until her death 55 years later.

Late in 1932, Alton photographed what appears to have been the first Argentine talkie, Los Tres Berretines (The Three Buddies), for Lumiton. Directed by Enrique T. Susini, this energetic, carefree comic drama about numerous young people, some of whom are musicians, begins with strikingly evocative street footage of contemporary Buenos Aires to the accompaniment of a wonderful jazz score. As the aspiring working class characters make the rounds through the mostly natural locations of parks, a music conservatory, cafes, a soccer stadium, and other hangouts, one is reminded by turns of Renoir's early 1930s naturalistic human dramas and the speedy, topical, common-people quickies Warner Brothers was turning out at the same time (even including an exceedingly limp-wristed Franklin Pangbornesque gay character). On the outdoor locations, Alton's work is simple and lovely, as he makes his newly adopted city look like a bygone urban paradise, a Paris or Rome in a more tropical setting. Some of his interiors are stunning: At this early date, he was already using slatted and pooled lighting and out-of-the-ordinary facial sculpting; the film's best single shot has a pianist at a grand piano silhouetted in the foreground with several female dancers practicing in the background and bathed in white light. Another scene employs a startlingly noir-like setup as two characters interrogate a third person with a single bulb illuminating them from overhead.

Over the next six years, Alton, by his own estimate, photographed 25 films in Argentina, although it remains difficult to verify the number as a reliable and comprehensive history of the South American film industry has yet to be written. The Fundacion Cinemateca Argentina has been able to authenticate no more than a dozen titles that were definitely shot by Alton, and possesses prints of just six (the Argentine industry and government having been lamentably lax in preserving their output). In addition, Alton directed, coproduced, and/or cowrote a few more.

In 1932, Alton also turned out his first effort as a director, El Hijo de Papa (Papa's Boy), on which he was also tecnico de luz, or lighting technician. This "gaucho film" performed extremely well commercially, although no prints exist because leading man Luis Sandrini so disliked the picture that he bought the negative and all prints and destroyed them. Unlike most people in film, Alton was not seduced by the notion of a directorial career and, in an article for the July 1934 issue of International Photographer entitled "The Cameraman as Director," he made some apt points about the differences between the two jobs. Stating that the camera department is "a place where there is more directorial talent hidden than any other place in the world," Alton, writing from Argentina, noted that, "Many of the few cameramen here have been given a megaphone and failed as directors. But why? They failed because they remained cameramen. They kept on worrying about the photography, ordering lights, etc., thereby driving both cameraman and the gaffer absolutely crazy. The result? That the picture was neither photographed nor directed.

"It is contrary to reason to photograph and direct simultaneously. The new director must forget that he ever was a cameraman. . . . It is for the director to see that the author's mind, spirit, and thought are faithfully reflected upon the mind of the audience. This is an extremely difficult task and far from what the cameraman should concentrate upon." Or, as he elaborated the different roles in *Painting With Light,* "The director sees it as a picture, divided into sequences and scenes, creating in his mind the characters and the dialogue, and worrying about music, sound, and editing . . . The director of photography visualizes the picture purely from a photographic point of view, as determined by lights and the moods of individual sequences and scenes. In other words, how to use angles, set-ups, lights, and camera as means to tell the story." In 1994, Alton simply stated that, "I didn't become a director because every time I looked at a scene, I saw the light on the actors' faces, and didn't hear what they were saying, so I knew I wasn't going to be a good director."

Lumiton was on its way, and remained one of the country's principal studios as the local industry boomed through the 1930s. But Alton, having put it on its feet, accepted an invitation to set up another studio, Argentina Sono Film. By 1939, a year during which some 50 films were being produced in Argentina, Sono had become the country's leading film company, with Alton as its number one cinematographer.

In addition to *Los Tres Berretines,* I have been able to see four other films Alton shot in Argentina. *Amalia,* directed by Luis Moglia Barth in 1936, with cinematographer "Juan Alton" receiving a huge credit onscreen, is a mostly stiff drawing room costumer set in 1840. Still, if one were given only one guess as to who photographed the dazzlingly dark night scenes that open the picture, one would have to venture Alton's name. The first sequence features several sinister-looking caped figures skulking out of a minimally lit doorway. They then head into a forest, where, in some extremely dramatic high-contrast images, most of them are killed in a violent sword fight with some soldiers. Overall, the film resembles a routine stage-bound Hollywood period drama of the era—not well directed but competently shot.

The film *12 Mujeres (12 Women),* also directed by Moglia Barth, in 1939, is a trivial story about the travails of students at a girls' school, graced only by some crisply attractive

night scenes. *El Matrero (The Outlaw),* a gaucho musical, or Argentine Western, directed by Orestes Caviglia, is also of little interest. It tiresomely follows the format of routine American Westerns, and Alton's work is in an atypically pastoral mode.

Still, in 1939, *El Matrero* was considered one of the most accomplished Argentine pictures yet made and was released in the United States (in Harlem in New York). The same treatment was accorded *Puerta Cerrada (Behind Closed Doors),* also made in 1939, which is a lavishly appointed costume picture that demonstrates that Alton could easily have passed muster as a cameraman for MGM at the time. A sort of *Stella Dallas* with songs about a singer whose baby is taken away by the authorities and adopted while she is imprisoned, this is a predictable, glossy affair directed by prominent actor-director Luis Saslavsky. One highlight is a flashback to the singer's love affair in which the visuals strikingly resemble Lee Garmes' gorgeously romantic work in Henry Hathaway's 1935 *Peter Ibbetson,* with the characters in a park or forest surrounded by petals and trees, all appearing within images that have their edges smudged to heighten the intoxicated atmosphere.

Prior to this, in 1937–1938, Alton had made a trip to Hollywood to purchase equipment to take back to Argentina. He stayed long enough to shoot a Spanish-language version of *La Boheme* in 10 days for Columbia. "If I were to give myself an award for the most artistic black-and-white photography, this would be it," Alton said. Starring Gilbert Roland and Rosita Diaz under the direction of Joseph Berne, *La Vida Bohemia,* which happily still exists in 35mm nitrate prints, doesn't quite bear out Alton's memory of it, but the lovely, nuanced lighting and compositions of several scenes testify to an exceptional talent behind the camera. In fact, the film is indicative of a tendency found in many of the low-budget, tightly scheduled films Alton was to shoot over the next 10 years: Unavoidably, the majority of scenes have a flat, perfunctory, B-movie feel to them, but one can tell that Alton put a tremendous amount of attention, ingenuity, and care into a handful of particularly important sequences, which are so visually powerful that they alone lift the entire film up to a higher level than the norm. In other words, Alton was flexing his muscles and showing what he could do in chosen moments in the subterranean reaches of the world film industry, but mainly because he couldn't help himself—it was his nature to be imaginative and bold.

Looking at *La Vida Bohemia* again, 45 years after he shot it, Alton still expressed satisfaction with it, although one can intuit that he loves the film as much for its subject as for the quality of his own contributions. "*La Boheme* is one of my favorite stories about the old days because it's about artists, their struggles, their work," he confessed. Very simply, it's about the kind of person Alton is, and the same could be said of other films he shot, from *Los Tres Berretines* to *An American in Paris*. Into his 90s, Alton habitually wears a beret and has the air of a Continental bohemian of the 1920s.

An important fact about Alton, which bears considerably upon his career, is that he was an intellectual among cameramen at a time when this was neither common nor fashionable. Or, as cinematographer John Bailey put it, "He created an aura of the artistic temperament." Although many of the great cinematographers of the studio era, particularly those who came from Europe, were refined and highly knowledgeable about the arts, the accepted personality for a cameraman was to be a tough, gruff, macho boss of a large crew of union technicians and strong men. Alton could be all this, and was certainly forceful in getting what he wanted, but he either would not or could not hide his elevated artistic sensibility, nor his belief that he was more capable than most of his peers. He dressed in an elegant, dapper manner; ate special lunches, prepared for him by his wife; left the studio promptly every evening to join her rather than go out with the boys; and was open about visiting museums and soaking up the lessons of the masters. "Rembrandt was a big influence. Rembrandt's genius was pictorial, and his ideas could be easily adapted to motion pictures. But I learned something from all of them," he recalled.

The one remaining Argentine film shot by Alton that is known to exist is *Cadetes de San Martin* (*The Cadets of San Martin*), directed by Mario Soffici in 1937. Among the other missing titles are *Crimen a las Tres* (*Crime at 3 O'clock*), directed by Saslavsky, and *Escala en la Cuidad,* directed by Alberto de Zavalia, both in 1935; *Goal,* directed by Luis Moglia Barth in 1936; the particularly highly praised *Macheselva* (*Honeysuckle*), directed by Luis C. Amadori in 1938 and, the following year, the same director's *Caminito de Gloria,* which was coshot by Jose Maria Beltran. There was also Saslavsky's 1937 drama *La Fuga* (*The Flight*), which may have been shot either by Alton or a German named Gerardo Huttula, but which is known because film critic Jose Luis Borges praised it for its pleasing way of avoiding picture-postcard clichés in its depiction of Buenos Aires and the countryside.

Finally, in 1939, Alton and his wife decided to pull up stakes in Buenos Aires and move to Hollywood, an event heralded in the pages of the November 1939 issue of *American Cinematographer* with an article entitled "John Alton Returns to Hollywood from Abroad." With the single exception of *La Vida Bohemia,* Alton had not worked in the United States in more than a decade.

Just prior to this, with war looming in Europe, Sam Altman, his son Michael, and daughters Anna and Esther got out just in time and moved to Palestine, where Sam continued in the spirits business. John's older brothers Harry and Bernard decided to stay in Romania; eventually, Harry escaped, joined the family in Palestine and later enlisted in the army and was killed. Bernard, blindly confident that the Nazis wouldn't bother him because he was a German Army veteran, remained behind and died at Dachau.

With Hollywood in a boom time, and Louis B. Mayer's vague promises still in the back of his mind, Alton hoped to be able to rejoin MGM upon his return. But he had made a number of enemies at Metro back in the 1920s, one of whom, John Arnold, was now in charge of the studio's camera department. As it happened, Arnold would plague Alton's career for the next 15 years, and effectively block any chance Alton might have had of starting at the top in Hollywood.

Instead, Alton was hired at RKO at the personal request of director Bernard Vorhaus, who was impressed with the South American work Alton showed him. Their first assignment together, starting in January 1940, was on *The Courageous Dr. Christian,* the second in a successful series of films that starred the venerable Jean Hersholt as a wise rural doctor. These pictures were decent B-movies made in 12 days, and Alton ended up shooting four of the six entries, also including *Dr. Christian Meets the Women, Remedy for Riches* and *Melody for Three.* Vorhaus also became one of his most frequent collaborators, as they worked together eight times before Vorhaus was blacklisted and moved to England. (Alton has stated that Vorhaus was named by Ronald Reagan, a close friend of Vorhaus's during the 1940s, a charge Vorhaus now deflects in gentlemanly fashion.)

Vorhaus singled out two main reasons that he loved working with Alton: his speed and his ingenuity. "From a practical point of view, he was incredibly fast," Vorhaus recalled in 1994 from his home in London. "When he shot his first film for Metro, they didn't believe he'd used enough light for exposure, and they went around checking up on him. On *The Courageous Dr. Christian* we had a crazy schedule, as usual, with one day on the studio lot to shoot all the exteriors. It was getting late and I was afraid we were going to lose the light before we finished everything we needed. But John said, 'As long as we don't show the sky, we can shoot it after dark, it won't matter.' And we did it at dusk and it looked just like the stuff we'd shot in sunlight.

That was the first time anyone ever said anything like that to me.

"He was so imaginative, he was very innovative, quite remarkable. I've never known anyone like him. He was so good at getting meaningful effects and dramatic lighting," said Vorhaus, who remembered with affection a greenhouse scene in his 1942 *Affairs of Jimmy Valentine* into which Alton introduced striking slatted lighing effects.

Alton himself retains one vivid memory of Vorhaus's *Three Faces West,* a film that is somewhat interesting for its premise—modern cowboy John Wayne leads Austrian refugees to safety away from the Nazis in the American West. Rather than eating in studio commissaries, Alton always had his lunches packed for him by his wife, and he had the habit of eating whenever he happened to get hungry. As he recalled 50 years later, midafternoon one day, he decided to eat his sandwich, and Wayne remarked that it looked good and asked for some. Not giving it a thought, Alton handed it to the actor, who took a bite, only to discover that it was a garlic sandwich. Unfortunately, Wayne was in the midst of shooting a love scene with Sigrid Gurie, who slapped him for his lack of consideration. Wayne was furious with Alton, and never spoke to him again.

Alton worked briefly at Paramount for William Pine and William C. Thomas, B-producers so tight with a buck that they were known as the "Dollar Bills." Their pictures were generally shot in 10 days for under $100,000, but Alton kept thriving under this sort of pressure and furthered his reputation as a cameraman who could make a B-picture look like an A production. As *American Cinematographer* noted of his work on a 1941 quickie, *Power Dive,* "Alton's treatment of his principals is excellent. His set-lightings are far more pictorial than we usually see on pictures made on any such schedule as this . . . In a word, he has not only distinguished himself, but has set a mark for other men who photograph films of this class to shoot at—and envy."

At the end of that year, the same publication commented that Alton's work on John H. Auer's *The Devil Pays Off* was "by far the best camerawork we've seen emerge from the Republic Studios," that it was "definitely major studio calibre, combining fine photographic quality with dramatic feeling and pictorial effectiveness." Throughout his tenure in B-pictures, Alton often saw his contributions to otherwise forgettable films singled out for special mention in the Hollywood trade press.

With such praise coming his way, it is unclear exactly why Alton didn't quickly make the jump to major studio work, or at least remain on the level where he started the 1940s, shooting second-level productions at RKO and Paramount, until being promoted. Instead, Alton's professional standing mysteriously diminished. He signed with Republic in late 1941 but was loaned out to lowly Monogram two years later on pictures such as *The Sultan's Daughter* and the infamous Dr. Goebbels biopic, *Enemy of Woman* (renamed *Mad Lover*).

Alton had an interesting military career during World War II. A blurb in *American Cinematographer* in February 1943 identified him as "Captain John Alton—serving as liaison officer between the Commanding General's office and the Signal Photographic Laboratories, and his former Commander, Lt.-Col. Edward J. Hardy, under whose command Alton received his basic military training." Hardy was commanding officer of the First Signal Corps Photographic Laboratory, and Alton worked in the lab rather than shooting footage for the government. Certain aspects of his military service remain mysterious: Alton has variously stated that he was stationed throughout most of the war at Fort Bliss in Texas, that he served with General Omar Bradley in Europe, and that he was in demand as a linguist, notably in Egypt and Greece toward the end of hostilities. One report maintains that he was discharged in 1944 for having enlisted when overage, another that he was let go for medical reasons. But Alton's most memorable duties were as "a special

courier. I was sent around the world with special confidential mail that they didn't trust to send any other way. It was a great job. I had special planes and special treatment of every kind. I was sent to Rio when the Americans were contemplating an invasion there to combat all the German influence, to Peru, North Africa, Egypt, and the Asiatic countries. And I met some of the big stars and producers everywhere. No matter where I went, all over the world, I met people from Hollywood."

Along with his army service, Alton managed to continue his career apace during the war, lensing five films in 1942, just one in 1943, five in 1944, and three in 1945. He particularly enjoyed shooting *The Lady and the Monster* (renamed *Donovan's Brain*) because it starred Erich von Stroheim and because director George Sherman was almost as fast as he was. Of greater significance, however, was Republic's decision early on to place its recently signed new director, Anthony Mann, in Alton's hands to learn the ropes of filmmaking, a move that would prove of tremendous significance to both men a few years later, even if it never benefited the studio that introduced them.

For seven years, or as long as he had spent in Argentina, Alton bided his time in the B-movies, working well, if anonymously, on films that attracted little interest at the time and have no reputations today. The executives and producers at B-studios liked Alton because of his speed and his ability to give a distinguished look to a cheap product. "I knew in order to exist in this business, I couldn't rely on art," Alton said, "because the producers were not artists. My first job was to win over the man who paid me. So I figured out how. I got $1,500 per week, when others were getting $250, because of my speed, because they made money with me."

The turning point in Alton's career came in 1947. Early in the year, he photographed W. Lee Wilder's crime drama *The Pretender,* which at least one critic, Spencer Selby, in his book *Dark City: The Film Noir,* considers to be

Alton's first noir; to accommodate Alton's expressionistic intentions and deep-focus lenses, special sets were built with forced perspective. Then Anthony Mann, who had been lurching along in B-movies since 1942, signed on with Eagle-Lion, a small company formed in 1946 and run by future industry titans Arthur Krim and Robert Benjamin. Heading production was Bryan Foy, former chief of the B-unit at Warner Brothers, who had a sharp eye for talent that nicely balanced his commercial instincts. For his new film *T-Men* (Fig. 2), Mann specifically asked for Alton, who was loaned out by Republic for the job. A hard-boiled crime story about Treasury Department agents trying to bust up a counterfeit ring, the film begins in the semidocumentary manner made fashionable at the time by *The House on 92nd Street*. But it very quickly plunges into deep noir and

stylization through the use of what Alton at the time called "almost 100 percent natural photography." Creating tremendously dramatic images and tense moments by enshrouding much of the action in utter blackness, Alton and Mann didn't invent film noir, but they created some of the most indelible examples of it, pushing the style further than anyone had dared up to that time. "I found a director in Tony Mann who thought like I did," Alton explained. "He not only accepted what I did, he demanded it.

"Other cameramen illuminated for exposure. They'd put a lot of light in it so the audience could see everything. I used light for mood. All my pictures looked different. That's what made my name, that's what set me apart. People asked for me. I gambled. In most cases, the studios objected. They had the idea that the audience should be able to see everything. But

Fig. 2 *A scene from* T-Men. *Print courtesy of the Museum of Modern Art Film Stills Archive.*

when I started making dark pictures, the audience saw there was a purpose to it."

In the case of *T-Men,* audiences responded in droves, giving Eagle-Lion a major hit on its small investment and making the names of the director and cinematographer in the film industry. Always employable on a certain level, Alton was suddenly in heavy demand. In 1947, he photographed nine films, and the following year he shot five pictures, all examples of film noir in its prime: Crane Wilbur's *Canon City,* Vorhaus's *The Spiritualist* (renamed *The Amazing Mr. X*), Mann's *Raw Deal,* Alfred Werker's (and Mann's) *He Walked by Night,* and Steve Sekely's (and Paul Henreid's) *Hollow Triumph* (renamed *The Scar*).

Another semidocumentary crime entry, *Canon City* was filmed only three months after the Colorado prison break that inspired it (Figs. 3 and 4). The sequences shot on location in the penitentiary are arresting, as Alton took no electricians with him and used only existing light fixtures boosted by stronger than usual bulbs. Unfortunately, the film splinters into a succession of decreasingly effective scenes depicting the assorted escapees hiding out in various families' homes, although Alton's high-contrast touch is readily apparent. Still, the film, which was shot in 19 days, did very well, and was held up as a fine example of what could be done on a low budget.

The Spiritualist, starring Turhan Bey as a phony seer, is a film of modest virtues, but Alton's work in several scenes is remarkable, notably in the dreamily ethereal opening and in the intense mood-setting of Bey's gazes into

Fig. 3 *A scene from* Canon City. *Print courtesy of the Museum of Modern Art Film Stills Archive.*

Fig. 4 *A scene from* Canon City. *Print courtesy of the Museum of Modern Art Film Stills Archive.*

characters' personalities and futures, including clairvoyance sessions in which the light emanates directly from Bey's crystal ball. Once again impressed with Alton's daring, Vorhaus recalled that, for a beach scene near the beginning, "We were shooting day for night, and I said to John, 'Suppose we shoot right into the sun and get some glare,' and he said, 'Why not?' It was taboo at that time."

Raw Deal made a worthy, if less dramatically satisfying, companion piece to *T-Men,* a bleak study of crime and duplicity that features much definitive noir iconography, topped by Raymond Burr's fiery, vertiginous demise (Fig. 5). Less seen today, *He Walked by Night* was received by critics at the time as the high point of the Eagle-Lion crime cycle. Starring Richard Basehart as a brainy killer on the loose in Los Angeles, the film was coscripted by John C. Higgins, who wrote *T-Men* and cowrote *Raw Deal.* Some way into the shooting, the original director, Alfred Werker, was replaced by Mann, and it's not hard to tell what Mann shot: all the night exteriors featuring Basehart, and the astonishing climax in which the killer attempts to elude the enclosing police by slipping through the city's storm water drainage system. Never were Alton's images darker, sharper, or more glistening; his talent for visually conjuring up the unbearable claustrophobia so essential to film noir was at its peak, as was his natural ability for creating compositions that instantly de-

Fig. 5 *John Alton, left, on the set of* Raw Deal. *Print courtesy of the Museum of Modern Art Film Stills Archive.*

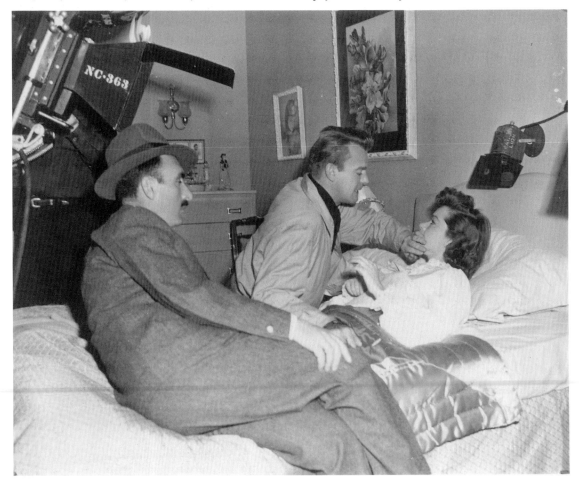

lineated the tension and violent dynamics between characters.

Rounding out this extraordinary year was *Hollow Triumph,* later retitled *The Scar.* Daniel Fuchs' script concerned a low-life former medical student who murders and assumes the identity of a psychiatrist to shed his gambling debts, and the original director was Steve Sekely, a fellow Hungarian Alton had known years before in Europe who made some films of passing interest. But partway into the shoot, no one felt that the results were living up to expectations, so, as Paul Henreid explained in his memoirs, the producer-star took over the direction. In any event, Alton added some quintessential images to the noir canon, including a deftly contrasted hotel-room scene between Henreid and his brother, and a chase on foot through downtown Los Angeles that ends up on the late, lamented Angel's Flight tram, one of the key cityscape icons of hard-boiled fiction.

Alton continued working at full throttle, shooting five films in 1949 and six pictures the following year. So pervasive was the cameraman's credit that *American Cinematographer* felt compelled to report that, "John Alton's life is just one picture after another." In 1949, he lensed one neglected noir, *The Crooked Way,* a rather low-key crime film directed by ex-cinematographer Robert Florey that is fully up to the contemporaneous Alton standard, as well as his first work in color, *Red Stallion in the Rockies,* for director Ralph Murphy at Eagle-Lion. Mann's *Reign of Terror* (later retitled *The Black Book*) was a bizarre oddity, a drama of the French Revolution shot in all-out noir style. Although it didn't do well, the film represented a triumph of sorts in the way Mann, Alton, and designer William Cameron Menzies overcame extremely limited means through diabolical ingenuity, making cramped sets look resplendent and 30 extras look like 300. Even more crucially, Dore Schary, the former head of production at RKO, visited the set of *Reign of Terror* at Eagle-Lion and was impressed with the methods of the key creative team. When Schary

assumed the production reins at MGM, the first people he hired were Mann and Alton. As it happened, they were in active preparation for *Border Incident* at the time, and Eagle-Lion, then cash-strapped, was happy to unload the whole project, which accounts for how the harshest, darkest, and most uncharacteristic film ever made at MGM ended up at Hollywood's most prestigious studio.

It also explains how Alton came full circle to wind up as a leading cameraman at the same studio he had left with Lubitsch more than twenty years earlier and which had shunned him when he arrived from South America ten years before. Still, a differing account of the reason for the move was given by studio vice-president Joe Cohn, who was mightily impressed by *T-Men* and claimed he hired Alton for $800 per week, "more money than I was paying any other cameraman. I gave him that salary because I wanted to hire him and he wouldn't work for less, and I wanted to shake up the other cameramen. I thought our cameramen had become too complacent, and I felt we needed a cameraman who would shake the hell out of the place, and I thought Alton could do that for me. In lighting, he saved a lot of time by lighting only from the floor. This made him very unpopular with the other cameramen."

Border Incident, a violent look at illegal immigration from Mexico, was one of Mann and Alton's top achievements, as was the unjustly neglected *Devil's Doorway,* one of the very first righteously pro-Indian Westerns that suffers today only from the sight of Robert Taylor (in an uncharacteristically fierce performance) playing a half-breed. Mann specifically requested Alton for the picture, and their last collaboration paid off: the cameraman imbued even the expansive exteriors with a sinister quality. A confrontation and fight scene in a barroom also sizzles with low-lit, deep-focus tension within the frame.

Alton continued to contribute to noirish dramas atypical for MGM, such as two John

Sturges films, *Mystery Street* and *The People Against O'Hara*. Because of his on-going dispute with the head of MGM's camera department, John Arnold, Alton was repeatedly leaving and returning to Metro. Alton has described Arnold as the chief nemesis of his career, and he was a bad enemy for a cinematographer to have. A New Yorker who had started his career in the engineering department of the Thomas Edison Company, Arnold then worked for Vitagraph, Biograph, and other companies before joining Metro in 1915. The definition of a company man and an establishment figure, Arnold had been with MGM since its inception in 1924, shot *The Big Parade* for King Vidor the following year, was chairman of the photographic section of the Academy of Motion Picture Arts and Sciences' technical branch, and was the first and long-term president of the American Society of Cinematographers, which Alton had joined in 1937 but quit (an almost unheard-of act for this honorary group) in 1944 "when Arnold started to be rough with me." This act, Alton admitted, "didn't do me any good later." At MGM, Arnold was referred to as "the policeman" who watched over studio's cinematographers to make sure they didn't deviate from the way things had always been done. Alton, whose style ran so completely contrary to the bright, expensive, highly polished look favored at Metro, claimed that Arnold "hated my guts because I succeeded more than he did. I had made him look bad. Because he was head of the department, he stopped me. He fought me. He tried to fire me every time. I lost pictures for a couple of years because of him, so finally I quit. They had difficulty with my ideas. One day they'd fire me, then I'd go off to do an independent picture to pay the rent, then MGM would hire me again." In the end, Alton outlasted Arnold at MGM. "Joe Cohn said to him, 'You use Alton or you're out of here.' Finally, he came to a bad end at MGM, and I was there longer than he was." While both men were at the studio, Alton's trump card was that, no matter what Arnold thought, Alton was not only a favorite of pro-

ducers for his speed, but he became the preferred cinematographer of two of Metro's top directors during the 1950s, Vincente Minnelli and Richard Brooks. Alton acknowledged that, "I always fought with the studio and producers, but I was okay when the directors were somewhat artistic and stood up for me," which these two did at MGM. Minnelli asked for Alton on *Father of the Bride* in 1950 specifically so that he could shoot Spencer Tracy's surrealistic nightmare sequence.

Alton claimed that he turned down Minnelli's next, *An American in Paris,* but later agreed to shoot the ballet because the painterly inspiration of the extravagant 20-minute sequence inspired his imagination (Fig. 6). The contentious feelings other people at Metro had about John Alton are amply evident in Donald Knox's little-known book *The Magic Factory: How MGM Made "An American in Paris."* Published in 1973, the volume includes oral history testimonies from every key surviving member of the film's creative team—25 in all—except Alton. Minnelli began by pointing out that he wasn't happy with the work of Albert Gilks, who shot the narrative body of the picture, because he considered it terribly overlit. For the ballet, then, "I insisted on using another cameraman . . . He was disliked, however, by the other cameramen because he had written a book called *Painting With Light*. They all thought he was egotistical. But he was so fast and used so few lights. I got along just wonderfully with him. I felt that the ballet needed someone who would live dangerously. We had to take chances because in the ballet there is nothing that was done afterwards in the lab; everything you see was done on the set. So I decided it needed John Alton."

Seconding Minnelli's assessment of Alton was Gene Kelly. "Vincente suggested a lot of the light effects. We'd say, 'Wouldn't this be great?' but often they took a lot of time, because cameramen can get very stubborn. But we found Alton willing to try anything. We'd say, 'Can you do this?' He'd say, 'Yeah, that's

Fig. 6 *Ballet sequence from* An American in Paris. *Print courtesy of the Museum of Modern Art Film Stills Archive.*

easy. Yeah.' And for the first few days we were sort of worried because we'd been used to a lot of cameramen saying, 'You guys are nuts. You can't do that.' It seemed that about every picture we'd try something new and the person with whom we'd be working would say, 'No, you can't do that,' because they had never done it before."

The old-line, anti-Alton view was expressed by the film's art director Preston Ames. Describing how difficult it was to create the right look for the ballet's "Van Gogh" set, Ames recalled that, "John Alton, one day, set yellow light filters on all the lights, and he said to Vincente, 'This is the only way you can shoot this thing, you know.' And I looked at him, and I said, 'What are you doing?' And he said, 'Oh,

this is the only way it can be done.' So I had to get a hold of Kelly and say, 'Kelly, do you want a bright yellow face when you're dancing?' And I said to [costume designer Irene] Sharaff, 'Do you want this bright yellow light all over your costumes?' She was furious, and there was a battle royal about it, you know: 'Rip those lousy goddamn things off,' and that's what happened. He started to get smart. He was working his way and not our way, and our way had been studied. He just came on the scene and thought this was very clever. He did the same thing on the next set; he put some purple filters on the Toulouse-Lautrec thing. It was horrible. It was just horrible. But he was painting with light. He loved to use that expression. This fellow was doing a petty thing, and he was destroying everything we had worked months to get, which was the perfect matching of everybody's thing clicking and working together. All of a sudden, he was saying, 'I'm going to show you really how it should be done,' and he loused it up, but royally. We corrected it, and in spite of everything it came out all right, but you had to be very careful that somebody didn't pull a fast one on you and really do things wrong. You just couldn't let them."

Putting some perspective on Alton's position at MGM was the studio's production department head Walter Strohm, who admitted of Alton that, "Most people hated him. They said, 'How can Minnelli put Alton on the ballet?' I said, 'Because he knows how to light.' Believe me, he knew how to light! I'll tell you a director who's difficult to get along with but who was crazy about Alton: Richard Brooks. He thought Alton was just great. Alton had a technique for a production man—and now I'm talking about my side of it—that was very helpful. I know why they didn't like him, and that was the thing that we liked about him most: He had none of this old studio technique. Some cameramen used the same lighting technique every time to light a set, because, the more units they had up there to light with, the more electricians it gave jobs to. Alton didn't give a damn about any of that. He was interested in getting an effect, and he could get an effect like that. He was very fast. Of course, that killed them; he was too fast for them. They didn't like that. He was ready, and the director was left holding the set. He just said to the director, 'I'm ready.' The director wanted to take two hours while they rehearsed and fussed around, and Alton said, 'No, I'm ready. Anytime you want to.'"

No doubt the most ambitious, dramatic, and complex musical number ever staged for an MGM musical, the *An American in Paris* ballet is a swirling, surprising, constantly changing, beautifully designed, and somewhat overripe 20-minute piece that clearly benefited from Alton's bold, unconventional lighting schemes. Very proud of his work on the film, Alton said,

"The ballet had nothing to do with the story and a lot to do with lighting. Minnelli helped me a lot with the lighting. I tried out fluctuations of light within the shots. I shot in color, but with black-and-white lighting." Ironically, Alfred Gilks, whom Minnelli had come to hate, and Alton shared the 1951 Academy Award for best cinematography for this movie. After Gilks delivered brief thanks at the Oscar ceremony, Alton had only this to say to the audience: "I wish to thank Mr. Vincente Minnelli for his confidence in our work. Thank you."

In fact, Alton and Minnelli had worked together on another picture immediately prior to filming the ballet, *Father's Little Dividend,* which, thanks in large measure to the cameraman, was finished in a tight six weeks, an unusually short shoot for Minnelli. Through 1957 they were to collaborate twice more, on the color and Cinemascope *Tea and Sympathy* and *Designing Woman.* Alton adored Minnelli. "Somehow we saw things similarly. He was a designer, and he had New York stage experience, which complemented my motion picture experience."

Despite his Oscar and inside track with producer Arthur Freed and Gene Kelly, Alton didn't fare well on his next assignment. Flush from *An American in Paris,* Alton was hired to shoot *Singin' in the Rain* for Freed and directors Gene Kelly and Stanley Donen. But his work on this film satisfied no one and, after two weeks, he was fired, accused of shooting in a way that would not permit the colors to match and cut together shot-to-shot and scene-to-scene. Much of his material was reshot.

As punishment, Alton was assigned to *Talk about a Stranger,* a small feature being directed by a young Dore Schary protégé, David Bradley, who, up until then, had only made amateur versions of classic texts back in Chicago but had also discovered Charlton Heston (Figs. 7 and 8). Bradley had observed Alton at work on the ballet sequence, and was both thrilled and terrified at the prospect of working with the famous cameraman. "I was warned that he'd eat

Fig. 7 *Director David Bradley, without shirt, and John Alton, with hat, on the set of* Talk about a Stranger. *Print courtesy of David Bradley.*

me up, but we were introduced and he was so charming, just fantastic. I liked his style very, very much, he was awfully good. This was supposed to be a big humiliation for him, this great man, pulled down and given to me. But nothing was too much trouble, nothing was impossible, it was perfect. We seemed to be like one person, and it became almost like father-son, even though I was going out with John Arnold's daughter."

Given this close perspective on and exposure to both sides in the conflict, Bradley was able to observe the pitched battle going on at MGM in the early 1950s from an informed vantage point. "John Arnold went all the way back at MGM to *The Big Parade,* and that's the way he still thought things should be. When

Dore Schary started making lower-budget Bs at MGM, Arnold didn't like it, and he didn't like John Alton and all his dark stuff. There was a lot of friction around MGM between the Schary camp and the Mayer camp, a lot of relatives and friends who had embedded themselves at the studio and didn't want to change their ways." *Talk about a Stranger* turned out to be a modest little thriller with one striking, if very brief, visual sequence depicting a nocturnal chase through an orange grove lit entirely by smudge pots.

As for Richard Brooks, Alton first teamed with him on *Battle Circus* in 1953, and subsequently shot *Take the High Ground, A Catered Affair,* and *The Brothers Karamazov* for him at MGM. The latter film is quite rich visually, but

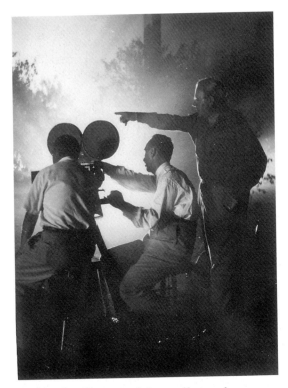

Fig. 8 *John Alton, seated, during filming of* Talk about a Stranger. *Print courtesy of David Bradley.*

does provide some telltale clues as to what his dissatisfied collaborators on *Singin' in the Rain* might have been complaining about: numerous scenes, particularly the interiors, are lit in utterly unrealistic ways, with lighting sources remaining quite unjustified and odd colors, notably purple, green, and yellow, bouncing off ceilings or bathing the characters in back light. The effects are sumptuous, glamorize the cast, and wouldn't be noticed by most viewers, but are a bit odd if you think about them. The affection and respect between director and cameraman was mutual. "I loved to work with Richard Brooks," Alton remembered. "He was so good."

By contrast, Alton retains less fond feelings for Allan Dwan, a veteran director whose long film career had started in 1909. They had worked together once at Republic, on the Western *Driftwood* in 1947, but during some of Alton's periodic vacations from MGM during the mid-1950s, they were paired seven times at RKO. Of Dwan, Alton said, "He was a big director at the beginning of the motion picture industry, but he didn't change, he didn't care or bring anything new to it, so that's why he fell off. But he was a good director." Although their overall quality ranges from excellent to mediocre, the first six of their 1950s films—*Silver Lode, Passion, Cattle Queen of Montana, Escape to Burma* (Fig. 9), *Pearl of the South Pacific,* and *Tennessee's Partner*—are suprisingly undistinguished visually coming from Alton. The last, however, *Slightly Scarlet,* in 1956, is a major noir, and arguably the best ever shot in color and widescreen (RKO's short-lived Superscope process). Saturated in reds (including the hair color of the two female leads) and blacks, the film features scenes of confrontation and violence that nearly match the tension and power of those Alton helped create in the late 1940s. Alton masterfully organized his pools of light to separate the characters and their competing interests. For examples of how Alton still sometimes seemed to put special effort into particular scenes, one need only look at the early sequence featuring mobster Ted de Corsia and his hoods, the follow-up scene between de Corsia and John Payne, and the climactic shoot-out.

Another notable loan-out during this period was for the Mickey Spillane thriller *I, The Jury,* whose single distinction is that it is the only film noir shot in 3-D (Fig. 10). Alton's signature lighting is clearly evident, but Harry Essex's direction is so inept, and takes so little advantage of the action's three-dimensional possibilities, that even a climactic fight on the exposed interior stairway of Los Angeles' Bradbury Building proves more laughable than exciting.

Still, Alton's crowning post-Oscar achievement was, ironically enough, a low-budget, down-and-dirty film noir. Arriving toward the end of the noir cycle in 1955, Joseph H. Lewis's *The Big Combo* was not seen as anything other than a cheap Allied Artists crime programmer at the time, but is now ranked by buffs

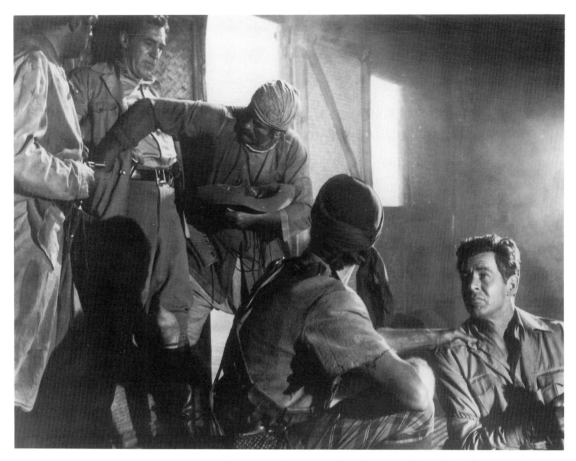

Fig. 9 *Scene from* Escape to Burma. *Print courtesy of Museum of Modern Art Film Stills Archive.*

and specialists as one of the top half-dozen or so noirs ever made (Fig. 11). One last time, Alton pushed his impulse toward severe black-and-white contrasts and silhouetting of characters to the limit. Many scenes are clearly lit with only one source, and the final shot, with the figures of a man and woman outlined in a warehouse against a foggy nightscape and illuminated by a single beacon, makes one of the quintessentially anti-sentimental noir statements about the place of humanity in the existential void. Perhaps the first scholarly American critic to single out Alton's work, Paul Schrader, in his 1971 essay *Notes on Film Noir*, argued that the cinematography of *The Big Combo* "is so nearly identical" to that of *T-Men* "that one has momentary doubts about the directorial differ-

ences between Mann and Lewis. In each film light only enters the scene in odd slants, jagged slices and verticle or horizontal stripes." *The Big Combo* has influenced numerous contemporary directors and cinematographers, notably John Bailey and Allen Daviau. Bertrand Tavernier recalled that, "French critics in Cahiers du Cinéma and Positif, who had praised Alton since *T-Men,* now cited him as among Hollywood's greatest talents."

In 1958, Alton photographed Vincent J. Donehue's *Lonelyhearts* and Brooks's *The Brothers Karamozov*. In June 1959, he jumped back into the low-budget field to shoot a two-bit black-and-white science-fiction entry, *12 to the Moon,* for his friend David Bradley. "John's enticement to work on it was my enthusiasm," Bradley

Fig. 10 *Scene from* I, the Jury. *Print courtesy of Museum of Modern Art Film Stills Archive.*

recalled, "plus the fact that we paid him much more than we would have anyone else. John was very interested in considering the light that would be on the moon, and he had never done a space picture." The patently artificial sets defeated any attempt Alton might have made to create uniquely lunar illumination, but the memorable opening sequence, which introduces the dozen international astronauts walking out of the fog toward their spacecraft, virtually picks up where the final shot of *The Big Combo* left off.

Alton immediately returned to the big time on *Elmer Gantry,* which shot through the fall of 1959. His splendid widescreen work on that picture, which was released the following summer, turned out to be his last. Reunited with Burt Lancaster, Alton started shooting *Birdman*

of Alcatraz for British director Charles Crichton on November 7, 1960. After one week of shooting, Lancaster and producer Harold Hecht replaced Crichton with John Frankenheimer, but retained Alton. However, Frankenheimer could tell from the first moment that he and Alton were incompatible. "It lasted a day, or a day-and-a-half at the most," the director recalled. "It was just a conflict of personalities from the first day. It was just not my kind of shooting. He was used to working with directors who perhaps were not so specific as I was about how to shoot a scene, who let him do what he wanted. I knew I wanted a gritty, semi-documentary look, and he was lighting a lot of things that weren't even going to be in the shots. It was painful because I had great respect for him and I'm sorry it didn't work out.

Fig. 11 *Scene from* The Big Combo. *Print courtesy of Museum of Modern Art Film Stills Archive.*

But I find that, if it doesn't work at the beginning, it's not going to get better." With this, John Alton had worked as a cinematographer for the last time, and none of his and Crichton's footage remains in the picture.

"He said what he wanted to do was go to Europe, to the Alps, and paint," said David Bradley, who kept up with Alton during this time. "That he'd done what he wanted to do, and he wanted to paint with brushes, not with light. He wanted to retire early. I'd see him when he came back to Hollywood once a year to keep up his citizenship standing."

Alton isn't entirely specific about why he quit his profession for good in 1960—his remarks about the years are marked by a mixture of pride, defiance, and bitterness, as well as satisfaction about the work he did. "I disappeared. I started traveling. I had a lot of money, about one million, and no children. I had three houses in Hollywood, and we sold one. My wife and I traveled, all through Europe, South America, the Amazon, Africa, and Asia. We never told anybody where we were, even the family." He did paint, "but I never had an ambition to be a professional painter. I always give them away to friends. If you have a toothache, as soon as you start painting, it stops. When you paint, you lose all pain through the concentration."

Still, from a professional point of view, his departure had to be painful. "The only mistake I made was quitting when I was 59," he confessed at a different moment. "The producers in those days were so shortsighted. I wanted to do quality. I thought about coming back later, but I found that the industry had changed."

So John Alton's abrupt exit from filmmaking, even if intended as temporary, turned into a permanent retirement, and thus did the mystery and legend begin. Critically and historically neglected, save for the odd noir specialist such as Schrader, through most of the 1960s and 1970s, Alton was still "a bit of a legend with some of us at USC [University of Southern California] in the late 1960s," according to John Bailey. "It was the artistic stance he seemed to take toward his work. He created an aura of the artistic temperament. Like Gordon Willis in this generation, who thinks like an artist and isn't afraid to speak of himself that way, it was clear that here was a man who didn't consider himself just another worker bee in the studio system. Just as Gordon's work is so dramatic and different and so polarized generational feelings, so did John's. There were other wonderful cameramen who were doing excellent work in noir, such as Nicholas Musuraca, but I don't think they had quite the presentation, or personality, that John had. John's work didn't just call attention to itself, it did so aggressively. The style was more stark, more uncompromisingly severe than those of other people working around the same artistic area. If there's an Alton legacy, it's of the journey, and his own uncompromising aesthetic."

In 1979, Tom Luddy, codirector of the Telluride Film Festival, approached Alton to be the subject of a career tribute at that year's festival. Alton sent back a letter thanking him for the invitation to the Colorado festival but declined it due to "previous, uncancelable commitments" and unpredictable travel plans. "After I finished *Elmer Gantry*, I decided to take a well-earned vacation. This was in 1959, and am still enjoying it," Alton wrote.

Luddy and his Pacific Film Archive colleague Sally Armstrong tried again the following year, and Alton responded to the latter that, while in South America in 1979, "I became very ill, and was forced to return home. I am still very ill, and my condition was diagnosed as 'FUO,' (a jungle fever of unknown origin)." Writing to Luddy twice more in 1980, Alton elaborated on his many health problems, mused upon what

Darwin would make of the world today (he would write a book called *The Decadence of the Species,* he speculated), and begged off a festival appearance by saying that, "At present I seem to have more important priorities. I have my own 'Energy Problem,' that is, to regain my energy."

In this, Alton was to succeed tremendously. Although his wife Rozalia died without warning of heart failure in 1987, Alton met and married another woman, Billie Roberts, the following year. A year younger than Alton, she died in 1992.

Alton finally emerged into the public eye in February 1993. While making our documentary *Visions of Light: The Art of Cinematography,* my colleagues Arnold Glassman and Stuart Samuels and I had been frustrated in our attempts to secure an interview with Alton, but still included some examples of his work with Anthony Mann. Two days before the Los Angeles premiere, I received a call from Darren Weinstock, Alton's step-grandson, who informed me that Alton had read about the film in the *Los Angeles Times* and wanted to know if he could come see it. And so it was that John Alton received an ovation from a packed house in the presence of Conrad Hall, Haskell Wexler, Vilmos Zsigmond, Laszlo Kovacs, and about a dozen other luminaries in his field. (At the screening, Alton happened to sit across the aisle from an old Hungarian compatriot, director Andre de Toth; they had not seen each other since dining at the Little Prague restaurant in Hollywood more than fifty years before.)

Over Labor Day Weekend 1993, John Alton finally made the trip to the Telluride Film Festival, where audiences can only be said to have responded rapturously to the dazzling excerpts from his work and to his charming, somewhat mischievous personality. Slight and ever the bohemian in his ever-present beret, Alton held forth at two public question-and-answer sessions before hundreds of people, as well as at a smaller group discussion, and was approachable for more casual encounters throughout the weekend. He said that the mountain air and altitude made him feel more vigorous than usual, and he clearly thrived on the attention. After all, it was the first time in his life that he was in front of the public answering questions about his life's work. After avoiding it for so long, he loved it.

A month later, Alton flew to Austria to attend the Vienna Film Festival, which organized an impressive symposium on the enormous contributions of Viennese exiles to Hollywood, then proceeded to Israel, where he spent many weeks with his surviving sister, Esther. In January 1994, he received the Lifetime Achievement Award voted him by the Los Angeles Film Critics Association, and at the ceremonies met Steven Spielberg, who enthused at length about the veteran cinematographer's work. The San Francisco Film Festival held an Alton tribute in May, and the following month Alton traveled to New York to launch an extensive retrospective of his work at the Museum of the Moving Image in Queens. Alton has observed that, no matter where he goes, "It's a strange thing that, when I travel to all these festivals, they show all the small, dark pictures we made in 12 days, not the big pictures we took months to shoot."

Painting with Light began as a series of articles Alton began writing for *International Photographer* magazine in 1945. After many revisions and excisions, the book was bought by Macmillan and published in 1949 to good critical reception and sales. Still, the book may not have done Alton a lot of good within the industry, as it was offered as evidence that he held himself above others in his field, that he was a self-ordained expert on all matters photographic. As a proponent of using little light, he set himself up for attack from establishment traditionalists who regarded Alton's methods as crude, unsophisticated, even amateurish. *American Cinematographer,* which had spotlighted Alton so frequently over the years, took eight years to review the book, and even then

Fig. 12 *John Alton, left, during filming of* Talk about a Stranger. *Print courtesy of David Bradley.*

granted it only a qualified endorsement. The volume, the magazine stated in 1957, is of "interest to the student cinematographer, but unfortunately it falls far short of the mark set by its title because the author has kept his text so concise as to be almost an abridgement" (Fig. 12).

In its 14 brief chapters, the book takes the reader through both the basics and refinements of motion picture photography, from elementary lessons about light sources to sophisticated notions about how to create very precise effects for specific artistic ends. The described means to achieve them, of course, are rooted in 1940s technology, and discussions of the equipment available are linked with the period when Alton was doing his most memorable work. As such, the book represents a trip back in time, a master class as taught by the industry's foremost iconoclast just as he was about to vault from successful obscurity to great renown within his profession. Recalling the profound impact *Painting with Light* had upon him as a student, Allen Daviau noted, "At the time the book came out, no one was going to tell you any secrets about cinematography, and he had instructions! It was the only case of an insider telling you what he did. It was a basic book from a master, and that was so important. This was the one and only book at the time that had some 'how to' to it.

You just learned a lot of the tricks of the trade. The influence the book had on a whole group of us was tremendous—we studied cinematography through *Painting with Light*. Later, I enjoyed watching him break his own rules in some of his films. But because of the influence of the book, I've always looked at Alton as this teacher who also did these great films. So his impact as a cinematographer was doubled or tripled by the fact of this book."

For a contemporary student of cinematography, *Painting with Light* may be outdated in spots as far as the *how* is concerned; today, film is faster, cameras are smaller and more mobile, lenses are sharper, and, in the professional arena, there are not as many rules. But the *what* and the *why* are universal and not influenced by changing technology. Such issues as emotion and dramatic effect represent the essence of motion pictures, and Alton very clearly lays out how to master them strictly through the use of light and lens. The book is a lesson in basic, objective photographic wisdom, couched in a personal, idiosyncratic expression of principles and priorities. As such, it is to be treasured by anyone with even a passing interest in motion picture lighting and photography.

Looking back at 92, Alton observed, "As far as my life is concerned, if I had it to do all over again, I'd do it exactly the same. There are very few people that have the kind of success that I've had. When you enjoy your work, you live. I was very happy in what I did. In the morning, I always felt like a kid, going to the studio. It's what made my life a very fascinating life" (Fig. 13).

Fig. 13 *John Alton at 1993 Telluride Film Festival. Print courtesy of Telluride Film Festival.*

FILMOGRAPHY

ARGENTINE PERIOD
by Todd McCarthy

Alton claims to have shot approximately 25 Spanish-language films, all but one of which was produced in Argentina, and some of which he also directed or had a hand in writing or producing. However, the titles that follow are the only ones that can be verified:

1932 *Los Tres Berretines (The Three Buddies)*
   S.A. Radio-Cinematografica Lumiton Studio
   Directed by Enrique T. Susini

   El Hijo de Papa (Papa's Boy)
   Directed by John Alton

1935 *Crimen a Las Tres (Crime at Three O'clock)*
   Directed by Luis Saslavsky

   Escala en la Cuidad
   Directed by Alberto de Zavalia

1936 *Goal*
   Directed by Luis Moglia Barth

   Amalia
   Directed by Luis Moglia Barth

1937 *Cadetes de San Martin (The Cadets of San Martin)*
   Directed by Mario Soffici

   La Fuga (The Flight)
   (Camera credit disputed; either shot by Alton or Gerardo Huttula)
   Directed by Luis Saslavsky

1938 *La Vida Bohemia (La Vie de Boheme)*
   (Shot in Hollywood)
   Directed by Joseph Berne
   Columbia

   Macheselva (Honeysuckle)
   Directed by Luis C. Amadori

1939 *12 Mujeres (12 Women)*
   Directed by Luis Moglia Barth

   El Matrero (The Outlaw)
   Directed by Orestes Caviglia

   Puerta Cerrada (Behind Closed Doors)
   Directed by Luis Saslavsky

   Caminito de Gloria
   (Cophotographed by Jose Maria Beltran)
   Directed by Luis C. Amadori

AMERICAN PERIOD
by Dennis Jakob

1940 *The Courageous Dr. Christian*
   Directed by Bernard Vorhaus
   RKO
   67 minutes

   Dr. Christian Meets the Women
   Directed by William McGann
   RKO
   70 minutes

   Three Faces West
   Directed by Bernard Vorhaus
   Republic
   83 minutes

   Remedy for Riches
   Directed by Erle C. Kenton
   RKO (William Stephens Production)
   67 minutes

1941 *Power Dive*
   Directed by James Hogan
   Paramount
   69 minutes

   Forced Landing
   Directed by Gordon Wiles
   Paramount
   65 minutes

The Devil Pays Off
Directed by John H. Auer
RKO
70 minutes

Mr. District Attorney
Directed by William Morgan
Republic
69 minutes

Melody for Three
Directed by Erle C. Kenton
RKO
67 minutes

1942 *Pardon My Stripes*
Directed by John H. Auer
Republic
65 minutes

Moonlight Masquerade
Directed by John H. Auer
Republic
68 minutes

Ice Capades Revue
Directed by Bernard Vorhaus
Republic
79 minutes

Affairs of Jimmy Valentine
Directed by Bernard Vorhaus
Republic

1943 *Johnny Doughboy*
Directed by John H. Auer
Republic
64 minutes

The Sultan's Daughter
Directed by Arthur Dreifuss
Monogram
64 minutes

1944 *The Lady and the Monster*
Directed by George Sherman
Republic
86 minutes

Enemy of Women (Mad Lover)
Directed by Alfred Zeisler
Monogram (W. R. Frank Production)
84 minutes

Storm Over Lisbon
Directed by George Sherman
Republic
86 minutes

Atlantic City
Directed by Ray McCarey
Republic
87 minutes

Lake Placid Serenade
Directed by Steve Sekely
Republic
85 minutes

1945 *Love, Honor and Goodbye*
Directed by Albert S. Rogell
Republic
87 minutes

Girls of the Big House
Directed by George Archainbaud
Republic
71 minutes

Song of Mexico
(co-photographed by George Stahl)
Directed by Pablo Marin
Republic
57 minutes

1946 *The Affairs of Geraldine*
Directed by George Blair
Republic
68 minutes

The Madonna's Secret
Directed by William Thiele
Republic
79 minutes

Murder in the Music Hall
Directed by John English
Republic
84 minutes

A Guy Could Change
Directed by William K. Howard
Republic
65 minutes

One Exciting Week
Directed by William Beaudine
RKO
69 minutes

1947 *The Magnificent Rogue*
Directed by Albert S. Rogell
Republic
74 minutes

Driftwood
Directed by Allan Dwan
Republic
90 minutes

T-Men
Directed by Anthony Mann
Eagle-Lion (Edward Small Production)
96 minutes

Wyoming
Directed by Joseph Kane
Republic
84 minutes

The Trespasser
Directed by George Blair
Republic
71 minutes

The Pretender
Directed by W. Lee Wilder
Republic
68 minutes

Bury Me Dead
Directed by Bernard Vorhaus
Eagle-Lion
68 minutes

The Ghost Goes Wild
Directed by George Blair
Republic

Winter Wonderland
Directed by Bernard Vorhaus
Republic
74 minutes

Hit Parade of 1947
Directed by Frank McDonald
Republic
90 minutes

1948   *Canon City*
(co-photographed by Walter Strenge)
Directed by Crane Wilbur
Eagle-Lion
82 minutes

The Spiritualist (The Amazing Mr. X)
Directed by Bernard Vorhaus
Eagle-Lion
79 minutes

Raw Deal
Directed by Anthony Mann
Eagle-Lion (Edward Small Production)
78 minutes

He Walked by Night
Directed by Alfred Werker
Eagle-Lion (Bryan Foy Production)
80 minutes

Hollow Triumph (The Scar)
Directed by Steve Sekely
Eagle-Lion
83 minutes

1949   *Captain China*
Directed by Lewis R. Foster
Paramount
97 minutes

The Crooked Way
Directed by Robert Florey
United Artists (Benedict Bogeaus Production)
80 minutes

Border Incident
Directed by Anthony Mann
MGM (Nicholas Nayfack Production)
92 minutes

Red Stallion in the Rockies
Directed by Ralph Murphy
Eagle-Lion
85 minutes

Reign of Terror (The Black Book)
Directed by Anthony Mann
Eagle-Lion
89 minutes

1950   *Grounds for Marriage*
Directed by Robert Z. Leonard
MGM
89 minutes

Father of the Bride
Directed by Vincente Minnelli
MGM
93 minutes

Mystery Street
Directed by John Sturges
MGM
92 minutes

Devil's Doorway
Directed by Anthony Mann
MGM
84 minutes

It's a Big Country
(co-photographed by Ray June and William
   Mellor)
Directed by Richard Thorpe, Don Weis, John
   Sturges, Don Hartman, William Wellmann,
   and Charles Vidor
MGM (Robert Sisk Production)
88 minutes

1951   *Father's Little Dividend*
       Directed by Vincente Minnelli
       MGM
       82 minutes

       The People Against O'Hara
       Directed by John Sturges
       MGM
       101 minutes

       An American in Paris (ballet sequence only)
       Directed by Vincente Minnelli
       MGM
       113 minutes

1952   *Apache War Smoke*
       Directed by Harold F. Kress
       MGM
       67 minutes

       Washington Story (Target for Scandal)
       Directed by Robert Pirosh
       MGM
       81 minutes

       Talk About a Stranger
       Directed by David Bradley
       MGM
       65 minutes

1953   *Battle Circus*
       Directed by Richard Brooks
       MGM (Pandro S. Berman Production)
       89 minutes

       Count the Hours (Every Minute Counts)
       Directed by Don Siegel
       RKO (Benedict Bogeaus Production)
       74 minutes

       I, the Jury
       Directed by Harry Essex
       United Artists (Victor Saville Production)
       87 minutes

       Take the High Ground
       Directed by Richard Brooks
       MGM (Dore Schary Production)
       100 minutes

1954   *The Steel Cage*
       Directed by Walter Doniger
       United Artists
       80 minutes

       Duffy of San Quentin (Men Behind Bars)
       Directed by Walter Doniger
       Warner Brothers (Berman Swartz-Walter
         Doniger Production)
       76 minutes

       Witness to Murder
       Directed by Roy Rowland
       United Artists (Erskine Productions)
       81 minutes

       Silver Lode
       Directed by Allan Dwan
       RKO (Benedict Bogeaus Production)
       80 minutes

       Passion
       Directed by Allan Dwan
       RKO (Benedict Bogeaus Production)
       84 minutes

       Cattle Queen of Montana
       Directed by Allan Dwan
       RKO (Benedict Bogeaus Production)
       88 minutes

1955   *Escape to Burma*
       Directed by Allan Dwan
       RKO (Benedict Bogeaus Production)
       86 minutes

       Pearl of the South Pacific
       Directed by Allan Dwan
       RKO (Benedict Bogeaus Production)
       85 minutes

       Tennessee's Partner
       Directed by Allan Dwan
       RKO (Benedict Bogeaus Production)
       87 minutes

       The Big Combo
       Directed by Joseph H. Lewis
       Allied Artists (Sidney Harmon Production)
       86 minutes

1956   *Tea and Sympathy*
       Directed by Vincente Minnelli
       MGM (Pandro S. Berman Production)
       122 minutes

       Slightly Scarlet
       Directed by Allan Dwan
       RKO (Benedict Bogeaus Production)
       91 minutes

       The Catered Affair (Wedding Breakfast)
       Directed by Richard Brooks
       MGM (Sam Zimbalist Production)
       92 minutes

       Teahouse of the August Moon
       Directed by Daniel Mann
       MGM (Jack Cummings Production)
       123 minutes

1957   *Designing Woman*
Directed by Vincente Minnelli
MGM (Dore Schary Production)
117 minutes

1958   *Lonelyhearts*
Directed by Vincent J. Donehue
United Artists (Dore Schary Production)
103 minutes

The Brothers Karamazov
Directed by Richard Brooks
MGM (Pandro S. Berman Production)
149 minutes

1960   *12 to the Moon*
Directed by David Bradley
Columbia (Fred Gebhardt Production)
74 minutes

Elmer Gantry
Directed by Richard Brooks
United Artists (Bernard Smith Production)
146 minutes

PREFACE

This book was written on the assumption that photographic lighting as exemplified in Hollywood motion pictures is perhaps somewhat in advance of the lighting techniques as generally applied in other branches of photography. Almost without exception every lighting effect achieved in motion pictures can be accomplished equally well in still photography when the operator has the know-how. To acquaint the reader with certain new methods and materials, the author has reproduced 295 photographs and line cuts illustrating every application and technique mentioned in the text matter of this book; every tool, gadget, and trick of the Hollywood lighting experts mentioned in this book is illustrated and discussed in detail.

Special sections of the book treat other significant aspects of lighting such as the best means of achieving maximum effects in personal lighting in the home and elsewhere. Display lighting of all kinds is also covered.

If there is a philosophy in this book, it might be thought of in terms of the author's sincere desire to share the fruits of his experience with kindred souls who also delight in capturing bits of light at rest on things of beauty.

J. A.

Hollywood

My deepest appreciation to:

Mr. Aubrey Schenck, Executive Producer of the Eagle Lion Studios, who placed the facilities of the entire plant at my disposal.

Mr. Leslie Vaughn and his Still Department.

Mr. Robert Jones and his Electrical Department.

Mr. Harry Strainge and his Grip Department, all of whom were helpful in getting the necessary industrial illustrations.

Credits: Kodachromes by Ted Weisbarth.

Production stills by George Hommel and Ted Weisbarth.

All other pictorial illustrations by the author, unless otherwise indicated.

CHAPTER 1 ⸻

HOLLYWOOD PHOTOGRAPHY

The City of Geniuses

There is hardly another place where there are as many directors as in a motion picture studio in Geniucity, Hollywood.

Visiting the studio, as we arrive at the gate we meet the first director, who claims that without him there would be no shooting. How right he is; as the gateman, he holds the keys to the studio. They call him *Traffic Director,* who directs all the tourists to the different stages.

He shows us the bench on which people wait for the bus. It is called *The Board of Directors.* "That is nothing," he claims, "wait till you see the canteen, it is named *The Directorate.*" The word *payroll* has been replaced by *Directory*—so appropriate. As we proceed, we meet the *First Assistant Director, Second Assistant Director, Art Director, Musical Director, Director of Orchestra, Dialogue Director, Process Director, Sound Director, In-Director,* who has it "in" for the man who directs the picture, *The Director.*

But the man whose work interests us most is the *Director of Photography.*

Production of a motion picture involves the work of hundreds, and in many cases thousands, of people. Into a motion picture go the dream of the writer, careful planning, scheduling, and budgeting by the production department, design of production and construction of sets by the art department, fashion design and costumes by the wardrobe department, rigging and illumination by the electrical department, and film development and

printing by the laboratory. The photographing of a film is not unlike a concert. Every instrument is important by itself, but a conductor is required to coordinate them all, and this is accomplished through the efforts of the *director of photography,* or *first cameraman.* The work of many artists results in a series of pictures impressed on a narrow strip of film; that is *motion picture photography.*

The Photographic Staff

A large staff is necessary to assist in the photography of a picture. It consists of separate little departments, each with its own peculiar functions. Most of these skilled artists and technicians have their own department heads, but on the set they work under the supervision of the cameraman.

The different crews are the following:
1. Camera crew
2. Electrical crew
3. Grip and his department
4. Process department
5. Special effects department
6. Green department
7. Stand-by painter
8. Stage make-up artists and hairdressers
9. Stage wardrobe men and women
10. Stand-ins
11. Laboratory contact man.

THE CAMERA CREW

The camera crew, under the direction of the *first cameraman,* consists of the *second,* or *operative cameraman,* the *technician,* the *as-*

sistant cameraman, and the *filmloader*. They handle the cameras, lenses, and the loading and unloading of the film. The second cameraman operates the camera during the shooting and does the panning and tilting, while the technician follows focus. The assistant holds the number slate and keeps the report of scenes shot. Thus is handled the mechanical end of the photographing of the picture.

On larger sets, or on scenes such as fights, accidents, aeroplane take-offs, fires, explosions, etc., which can be photographed only once, there may be more than one camera with the necessary operative cameramen, and the corresponding assistants for each camera.

THE ELECTRICAL CREW

The really important function of the director of photography is *illumination*. In this difficult task his right-hand man is the chief electrician, or *gaffer*, who is in charge of the electrical crew on the set. Under the gaffer's orders are the *rigging gaffer* and his crew who do the preliminary work of placing the reflectors in their predesignated places. For the actual illumination the gaffer has his regular crew, consisting of the *best boy, dimmer man, generator man, juicers, spot men*, operators, and other helpers

THE GRIP AND HIS DEPARTMENT

Another important assistant to the director of photography is the *key-grip* and his specially trained assistants who do all the incidental construction, breaking down of sets, minor emergency carpenter work, and with the thousand beautifying contraptions help to glamorize the stars. They also operate the crane or boom, and the camera dolly. The key-grip has his best boy, or assistant, the *boom operator*, and other helpers, assistants, and laborers.

THE PROCESS DEPARTMENT

It is sometimes impossible to take entire production crews and cast on certain distant or difficult locations. This problem has been solved by *process photography*. In most Hollywood studios, one particular large stage is set aside for background process scenes, but there are also portable background machines which can be brought on to any set. In some studios the *director of process* is in charge, but in others the director of photography supervises the *front illumination*, and the process department takes care of the balance.

THE SPECIAL EFFECTS DEPARTMENT

If a scene calls for artificial reproduction of rain, snow, fog, windstorm, lightning, smoke, earthquake, or any other activities of the elements, the *special effects man* with his million tricks is called in.

THE GREEN DEPARTMENT

Nature is beautiful, but sometimes we need a garden or any other exterior to suit our action, and we call in the landscape artist who heads a special *green department*. In his work he is assisted by the *greenman*.

Some studios have their own green departments; others have their work done by outside landscape artists who own huge nurseries and glass houses, and have ready any specimen of tree, plant, flower, of any country of the world the script may call for.

The green department can also reproduce a jungle or a forest right on the stage. If a required tree or plant is not available, the greenman constructs it of cardboard or plaster. Each company, when shooting, has its own greenman and his assistants, the number depending upon the size of the set to be photographed. They stand by to dress (shine) the greens of the set, to move bushes, or to do any other "green" duty.

THE STAND–BY PAINTER

No matter how perfect a set, or how beautiful a countryside, a street, or any other location, changes may be required when actually shooting. There are problems that may be solved by a slight spray of black paint, a touch of eggshell to bring out a highlight, or by the change of a color. For this work each production unit has a *stand-by painter* on the set.

STAGE MAKE-UP

Make-ups do not endure under adverse weather conditions. Kisses ruin the lip make-up and leave rouge marks on cheeks, the hair gets mussed up, or a backlight accentuates one single hair standing up against a dark background. Hair styles must match, faces must be kept clean and fresh, and at times tears must be created right on the spot. For these purposes the *make-up artists* and *hairdressers* are always on the set. On sets where there are dancers, skaters, or other artists with parts of their bodies exposed, male and female *body make-up artists* are also required.

WARDROBE

The wardrobes of the artists are selected previous to production. However, minor changes often are required on the set. A dress is torn, coffee is spilled on a shirt front, a button is missing, or pants need to be pressed. Any one of a thousand other minor inconveniences may arise which would cause a serious delay in production if not attended to immediately. Hence, when shooting, the presence of a *wardrobe man* or *woman* is required on the set at all times.

The Outstanding Stand-ins

The lighting of artists, whether in a long shot or a close-up, necessarily takes time. Winter pictures sometimes are made in the summertime (why, I don't know), and it is not very pleasant to be constantly exposed to the terrific heat of the powerful lights needed for modern motion picture photography. Especially is this true when heavy fur coats must be worn. Furthermore, the time required for lighting can be utilized by rehearsal of lines,

change of wardrobe, make-up, or hairdress, making of stills, and all the other requirements of production. Therefore each star and featured player is entitled to have someone similar in type, stature, figure, color of hair, etc., to stand in for him or her. Hence the name *stand-in*, or *second team*. The stand-ins just stand or sit, as the case may be, or mechanically go through the different actions the scene calls for, dress exactly like the *first team* or at least in similar tone. They stand in until the lights are ready, and walk through the scene a few times to check the light. When all is ready for the actual photography, the principals are paged. Some stand-ins have made the grade and have become famous stars.

The Laboratory Contact Man

With lighting alone we still do not have photography. An important part is the processing of the film in the laboratory. The director of photography has no time to be present while the processing is going on. For this purpose a *laboratory contact man* is appointed, who sees to it that all of the cameraman's instructions are carefully carried out.

Tools of Motion Picture Photography

Just as the painter must have brushes of different properties, paints of many colors, canvas, an easel, and other equipment to paint a picture, so must his fellow artist, the director of photography, have his implements to make a painting of as many as possible of the hundreds of setups required for a feature length motion picture.

CAMERA EQUIPMENT

The camera is a familiar apparatus, consisting of the box itself, a magazine with one compartment for unexposed film and another for exposed film, the inside mechanism, and the lenses. Figure 1 shows a Mitchell BNC studio camera; in front of the lens is the matte box used to shade the lens and to hold diffusion disks, filters, gauzes, or other gadgets that individual cinematographers may have developed. Figure 2 shows a Bell and Howell Eyemo camera designed for greater portability than the studio camera.

LENSES

The lenses most widely used are the following:

24 mm or 25 mm lens, used as a wide-angle lens

28 mm lens, narrower in angle, but producing less distortion

30 mm lens, used for long shots with depth

35 mm lens

40 mm lens, used for long shots

50 mm lens, for an angle of view nearest to that of the human eye

75 mm lens ⎫
80 mm lens ⎬ for portraits, close-up, and telephoto shots
100 mm lens ⎭

On some cameras three of these lenses are mounted on a turret on the front of the cam-

Fig. 1 *Mitchell "BNC" 35 mm Studio Camera. (Merriman Photo.)*

Fig. 2 *Bell & Howell "Eyemo" Camera with Filter Holders*

era. On a camera of the latest model, only one lens is mounted at one time, but all are interchangeable by means of a bayonet fitting.

FILTERS

When photographing exteriors we sometimes would like to accentuate clouds, darken blue skies, make night shots in the daytime, or emphasize certain parts of the landscape. For these purposes we add *filters,* which may be either of glass or of gelatin.

THE FILTROSCOPE

To select the filter best fitted for the effect in mind, we use an instrument called the *filtroscope* (Fig. 3). This invention of the author's is similar in form to a slide rule, and has different filters mounted on it, each over a round hole. Over the filters slides a special

Fig. 3   *The Filtroscope*

type of blue glass; the combination of filter and blue glass gives the photographer an idea of how the use of any filter will change the picture.

DIFFUSERS

Because the camera does not lie, corrections must be made by adding beautifying gadgets called *diffusers.* The most frequently used are glass disks which come in different grades, the choice depending upon the degree of diffusion desired. Besides these commercially available beautifiers, each director of photography has developed his own glamorizers such as gauzes of different densities and colors.

EXPOSURE METERS

There was a time when the cameraman, when in doubt about exposure on exteriors, merely stopped down to f:5.6 and blamed the laboratory for the rest. With modern laboratories came chemical engineers, and with them came science; today photography is based on science. If we want a good negative we must expose the film correctly. The human eye is not entirely reliable when subject to light changes, and is far from being as accurate as the photoelectric cell in an *exposure meter.* The meters used by Hollywood photographers are the Weston, the General Electric, and the Norwood. Technicolor has developed a special meter for use in its process of color photography.

NUMBER SLATE

Each scene must be numbered to enable the film editor to select the best take of any scene. The old-fashioned *number slate* is being replaced gradually by an internal numbering mechanism.

ELECTRIC FREEHEAD

When camera motors first were introduced, some cameramen were so short-sighted as to predict that the end had arrived, that with an electrically driven camera there would be no need for a man to operate it, because the director could do it himself. Time has proved these prophets wrong. Today the director of photography has operators, assistants, technicians, and loaders to help him.

All this is mentioned as preface to another improvement which I am about to suggest, an improvement as revolutionary as the camera motor was in its time. Many of us who were so fortunate as to be able to help save democracy have seen the automatic machine gun tiltheads installed in planes. During the great blitzes the casualty rate of machine gunners was very high. Something had to be done about it, and something was done. This new tilthead was invented, and no longer did the machine gunner have to stick out his head. Instead of operating the gun and aiming it, he looked through the *finder*. When he moved the finder, tilted, or panned, the machine guns turned and converged automatically with it, aiming at the target with the greatest accuracy.

If this instrument was so useful, why couldn't it be utilized successfully for production of motion pictures? It would make an ideal *automatic tripod freehead*. Tripods have improved somewhat since the original tripod head was loosened and with the aid of a club was used as the first freehead. The converted machine gun head would be quite an improvement over the present wheel-driven one. Just imagine the operator looking through a finder, and as he turns it by the slightest touch simultaneously tilting and panning the camera, getting exactly and accurately the same field of composition seen in the finder. It would be a definite step forward in methods of motion picture production.

REFLECTORS

Because some of the old lighting units used metal reflectors with an arc or an incandescent lamp, *reflector* has remained the Hollywood term for a lighting unit. Just as painters use different brushes for different results, so does a director of photography utilize various types of reflectors for the variety of light effects which he may have in mind. We try to imitate light effects that we know exist in nature. In outdoor scenes they are either sunlight for day scenes or moonlight for night. Inside they are sunlight for daylight and incandescent or any other artificial light for night.

GRIP EQUIPMENT

The tendency in motion picture illumination seems to be toward the realistic, which

means shadows—lots of them. To create these shadows, to beautify, to keep light off the lens, to operate the dolly or crane, and for a thousand other missions, the grip and his tool kit come in very handy.

Wherever the cameraman goes he is followed by the grip and his trunkful of magic gadgets. Many of these tricks have no names, but all have their special purposes, and are used at some time or other during the production of a picture. Many of them are described in what follows.

TRIPOD TRIANGLES

For silent shots the old Mitchell type NC camera is taken out of the blimp to facilitate moving around, and is placed on a tripod. On stone floors, or where the tripod points would puncture, scratch, or do other harm, we use a *triangle* under it. There are three kinds: the star, the folding type, and a solid triangle; all are made of wood. On hard floors, a triangle keeps a camera from slipping.

TURNBUCKLE

When we shoot a plate for process, or any other scene where a steady camera is absolutely essential, we *tie* it down. This is done with a heavy metal chain, turnbuckle, and stage screw. This method is used also when shooting on a moving train, car, truck, or on the deck of a moving ship at sea.

CAMERA DOLLY

To be able to move around with the camera, we have taken it off the traditional tripod and put it on a dolly, where it stays most of the time during the shooting of a picture. The dolly is a four-wheeled vehicle pushed by the grip's assistant. It holds the blimp of the old type camera, and the camera within the blimp. The camera can be changed quickly from a position little above floor level to a position six feet above the floor (Figs. 4, 5).

Dollies have hard rubber wheels, and passage over a nail or the slightest obstruction would cause a jump on the screen. To avoid this, the dolly is moved on metal or wooden tracks that come in sections of four, six, and ten feet. A rug is placed under the entire length of the tracks to absorb floor squeaks and to silence the steps of the assistant grip who pushes the dolly.

Fig. 4 *Camera Dolly with Blimp in High Position*

Fig. 5 *Camera Dolly with Blimp in Low Position*

ADJUSTABLE CAMERA PLATFORM

If the setup is higher than the dolly arm can reach, we use a *platform*. Platforms are made of wood, and are adjustable from two to six feet; for a twelve-foot platform, one of the six-footers is placed on top of another, and they are braced heavily to avoid acci-

Fig. 6 *Steel Tubular Parallel*

dents. Platforms are used also to place high lamps or sun reflectors. The new type steel tubular parallel rises from five feet to twenty feet (Fig. 6). There is also a folding adjustable parallel which is available in heights of four and six feet (Figs 7, 8).

CAMERA CRANE OR BOOM

To be able to move from a low setup to a high one, or vice versa, and from a close-up to a full long shot of a set, the dolly is inadequate. For this purpose we use the *crane* or *boom*. The small baby boom is used for small sets (Fig. 9), and the big boom is used for sets in which greater height is required.

7

Fig. 7   *Adjustable Platform. Low Position*

Fig. 8   *Adjustable Platform. High Position*

Even though a crane has rubber-tired wheels, tracks are used in some studios where the floor is not entirely level. These tracks are made of wooden boards of different lengths.

THE RECEDING TRACK

The moving of the camera, or *trucking* as it is often called, is done either by crane or dolly. This is all very simple, but if the director wants to make a shot that starts with an

8

insert of a ball on top of a table (Fig. 10, position *A*) and pull back to a long shot of the entire set (position *B*) he may run into difficulties with fixed tracks. As the camera

Fig. 9   *Small Camera Crane*

recedes, the end of the dolly track gets into the picture (Fig. 11).

This problem has been partially solved by having an extra grip pull up sections of the track as we truck back. However, this is dangerous, for the view finder on the camera does not indicate what goes on underneath

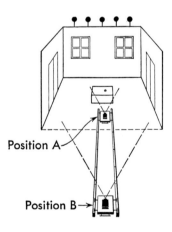

Position A

Position B

Fig. 10

the camera, and it is only after having seen the rushes that we know whether the grip's high hat did or did not get into the picture. The tracks now in use are made up of sections that join straight on; therefore it is difficult to detach one section from another.

Besides, if we wanted to dolly back to our original position *A* it would not be possible to join the sections in time. With the new type of track shown in the diagram these

Fig. 11

Fig. 12

problems are practically eliminated. Figure 12 illustrates a section of the track. End *A* of the section hooks on to end *B* of the preceding section. The ends are not cut straight, but diagonally, thus making it possible to pull sections back, also eliminating the bump as the dolly wheel crosses from one section to another (Fig. 13).

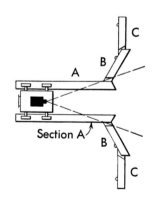

Fig. 13

To facilitate transportation the track is made up of several sections of standard design but of different lengths; it can be made up of sections of any size depending upon how much has to be pulled back to clear the foreground line. The new track is inexpensive to manufacture; in fact the track now in use

may easily be converted into the new type. Considering the time that is lost with the old tracks and also the possible retakes, the new tracks would soon pay for themselves.

THE DESTYCRANE

Wherever we happen to look, the postwar tendency seems to be toward speed and more speed. In order to hold the movie-goer's attention, future films will have to move as fast if not faster than life itself. No matter how modern the camera dolly or how streamlined the boom may be, they are both becoming a bit too slow. In some studios where stages were not built for this extra weight, tracks have to be laid. Floors are uneven and bumpy, and it takes entirely too many rehearsals to make a good shot.

The solution for constant, smooth, and fast camera movement is use of the *destycrane*. It is called that because its arm, like that

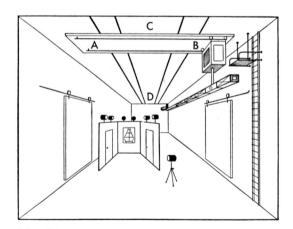

Fig. 14

of destiny, reaches everywhere. Its design and operation are very simple (Fig. 14). There are four parallel rails running in one direction, built on the ceiling of the stage. On these rails a platform runs between points *C* and *D*. Underneath the platform there are two more rails and on these the carriage holding the crane arm runs between the points *A* and *B*. During the rehearsal of the scene the cameraman gives all necessary instructions to the boom operator in the cabin, who carries them out in the take. It is all done electrically. The assistant cameraman is also in the cabin and follows focus by remote control.

There is a phone connection between cameraman and boom operator. The camera has a horizontal pan of 360 degrees and vertical tilt of 180 degrees. In other words the desty-crane enables the camera to move in any direction at any time and any speed desired. It can go from an insert of a book on a shelf to an extreme long shot holding almost the entire stage.

The construction and installation of the destycrane may be a bit costly, but considering the saving of time and improvement of the motion picture technique, it will more than pay for itself the first year. Besides it will open new horizons to the imaginative cinematographer, writer, and director. The wildest of T-Men-ish ideas can be realized at short notice and with little or no difficulty. The free movement of destycrane allows us to shoot entire scenes without as much as one cut. Destycrane is definitely a step forward in streamlining the studio, and no modern motion picture stage can well afford to be without it.

SET JACK

The *set jack* is a device used to move a wild wall around quickly and with as little help as possible. It is employed also for transporting sections of a set from the carpenter shop to the stage where the set is assembled (Fig. 15).

GOBO

Goboes are wooden screens made in various sizes and used primarily to cut light from reaching the lens. There are other purposes for which this photographic tool is used. In night shots where the background is jet black, we place a platform with a lamp on it right in the picture, and cover up with a black gobo; it is a perfect black camouflage. If a light happens to hit the finder from behind the camera, it obstructs the vision of the camera operative; a gobo may be used to remedy this too. To absorb light, goboes are painted black (Fig. 16). A double gobo which can be raised to a height of ten feet is known as a *folding slider*. It also is made of wood and is painted black.

Fig. 15   *Set Jack*

Fig. 16   *Goboes*

FLAG

When there is no room for large goboes for cutting off light, a *flag* is used. This is really a miniature gobo, named because of its shape when mounted on a stand. It may be of plywood, but is much lighter if made of black cloth with a metal frame. A wooden flag is painted black to absorb light. Flags come in different sizes: 6 by 36 inches, 8 by 20 inches, 9 by 30 inches (Figs. 17, 18).

OVERHEAD SOLID TEASER

These are oversized flags used to cut the backlight from the lens. They are made of black cloth or of wood painted black. Their size permits cutting off the light of a row of backlight reflectors. They usually are mounted on overhead stands (Fig. 19), or sometimes are suspended in the air from catwalks.

Fig. 18 *Flag*

Fig. 17 *Flag*

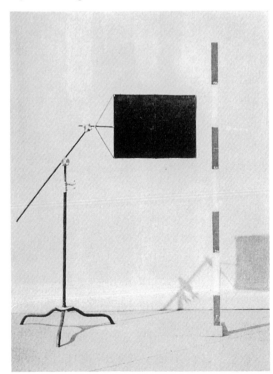

Fig. 19 *Overhead Solid Teaser*

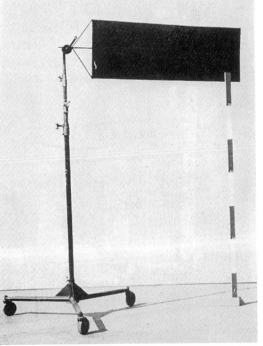

Fig. 20   *Dot*

TARGET

For smaller shadows, or where there is no room for a flag, we use a *target*. A target three inches in diameter is called a *dot* (Fig. 20); larger targets are six inches and nine inches in diameter. Targets also come in halves, called half-targets (Fig. 21). Targets may be made of opaque black cloth on metal frames, or of wood painted black. There are also scrim targets in different sizes and in single, double, and triple layers (Fig. 22).

SCRIM

A flag made of a translucent material like gauze or net is called *scrim*. It is used for beautifying purposes of diffusing, softening, or cutting off light. If it has no frame, and one end is open, it is called *open end scrim*. Scrims come in different densities, single, double, and triple (Figs. 23, 24). The *chin scrim* is a U-shaped scrim in single, double,

Fig. 21   *Half-Target*

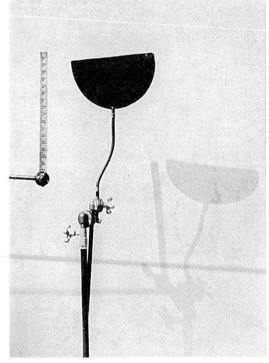

Fig. 22   *Targets*

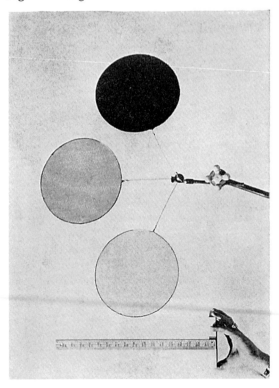

or triple layers, used to cut the light off hot white collars worn with black dinner jackets (Fig. 25).

BLADE

Blades are small flags used for cutting off light, or when only a thin shadow is required, as in light surgery. They come in solids, or in single, double, or triple scrim (Figs. 26, 27).

CLIP

The *clip* is a tiny flag that can be clamped on the reflector, camera, matte box, or the like (Fig. 28).

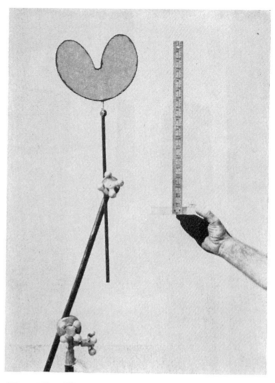

Fig. 25   *Chin Scrim*

Fig. 26   *Blade*

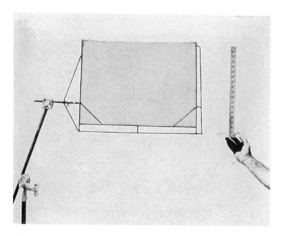

Fig. 23   *Scrim*

Fig. 24   *Scrim*

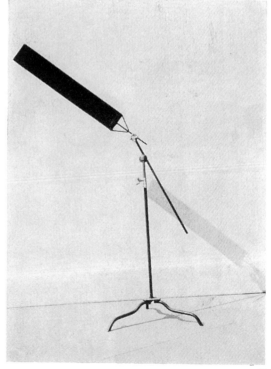

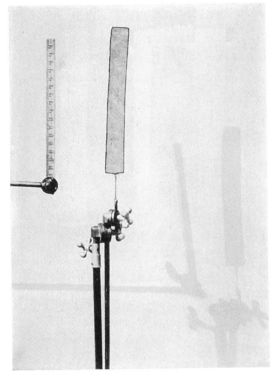

Fig. 27 *Blade*

Fig. 28 *Clip*

COOKIE

When a surface is too hot (too much light) and we want to throw a shadow on it to break up the light, the shadow of a gobo or even of scrim would be too much; therefore we use what is called a *cookie*. Cookies are really flags with different designs cut out of them. The designs sometimes resemble natural ones like that of a tree branch with leaves, a dead branch without leaves, a bouquet of flowers, etc., or the familiar patterns of architectural designs. They come in solid wood which throws opaque shadows, or for softer transparent shadows are cut also from celo (celloglass), a transparent glass-like material. Sizes vary from that of a flag to that of a target (Figs. 29, 30, 31).

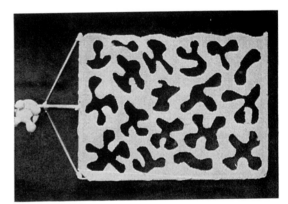

Fig. 29 *Cookie*

Fig. 30 *Cookies*

Fig. 31   *Cookie*

Fig. 32   *Window Frame*

Fig. 33   *Ear*

WINDOW FRAME

Window frames made of plywood in many designs are used to project the effect of a window on a wall (Fig. 32).

EAR

When the broad (soft, shadowless lamp) is fresh and sends light in all directions into either the eye of the cameraman or into the lens, an *ear* is placed on it. This is really a flag with a hole in it (Fig. 33).

STANDS

Various kinds and sizes of stands are used to hold flags, scrims, targets, and other similar devices. The *gooseneck* is part of a gooseneck lamp, without the lamp, of course; the gadgets are soldered, clamped, or screwed to the end. *Century stands* are tripods used to hold flags and other heavier gadgets. One stand is 44 inches high, and the heavy *overhead stand* rises from 6 feet to 25 feet. To hold a tree branch, a *tree branch adapter* is fastened to a heavy Century stand; this can be used inside or outside with sunlight (Fig. 34). To hold gags together and to clamp them, an *Adapter clamp* is used.

Fig. 34   *Century Stand with Tree Branch Adapter*

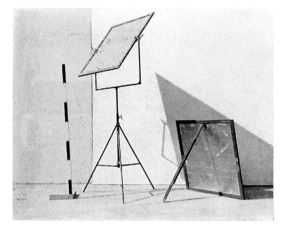

Fig. 35 *Sun Reflector*

Fig. 36 *Mirror*

Fig. 37 *Butterfly, Black Drop, Furniture Dolly, and Dolly Track Rug*

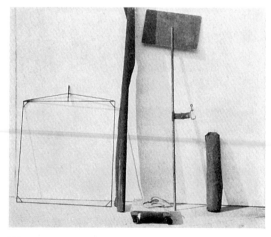

MISCELLANEOUS EQUIPMENT

Various handy devices are used for raising props, cameramen, or actors to different heights above the stage. These include:

Pullman or *one-step*

Three-step, often used by cameramen for the higher setups

Apple box, similar to the one-step

Furniture blocks, which are small three-steps made of 2-inch by 4-inch joist, to provide heights of 2, 4, and 6 inches

Cupblocks, which are similar to furniture blocks but with hollow sides for legs of chairs, for greater safety

Risers, little platforms, 2, 4, and 6 inches in height

The grip transports his equipment in a large *grip's truck*, a *grip box*, and a *grip kit*. The *grip's personal tool kit* is a belt containing simple tools and rolls of tape used to cover up high spots, blemishes, or defects on sets. *Stepladders* of various heights are part of the grip equipment.

If the grip wants to get the next picture, he must see to it that the cameraman is comfortable at all times. For this purpose he carries what is known as the *red apple stool*.

GRIP TOOLS FOR EXTERIORS

SUN REFLECTOR

This is made of wood, coated on one side with gold leaf and on the other with silver. It is mounted on a portable and demountable stand that rises from 6 feet to 12 feet (Fig. 35).

MIRROR

This is a glass mirror in a wooden frame that is used to light up green trees, bushes, etc., and other dark spots where the other reflectors fail (Fig. 36).

TIN

The tin is somewhat weaker than the mirror, but hotter than the gold or silver reflectors.

BUTTERFLY

This is a scrim used to cut and soften the harsh sunlight. It comes in different sizes, with metal or wood frames on which the scrim net is stretched. There are small butterflies in round and square shapes, medium-sized ones 4 feet by 4 feet (Fig. 37), and a large one 12 feet by 20 feet for shading larger areas.

UMBRELLA

This is a regular beach umbrella used on exteriors to shade the camera from the

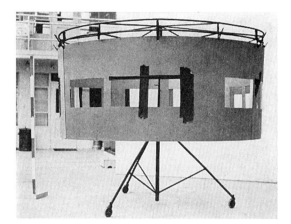

Fig. 39 *Cyclodrum*

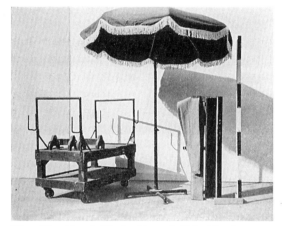

Fig. 38 *Beach Umbrella and Grip Truck*

Fig. 40

sun and to protect against rain or snow (Fig. 38).

CYCLODRUM

This is a device used to project light effects and also shadows on the process stage. It consists of a hollow cylinder with room enough inside for an arc lamp; it is mounted on a large stand and may be rotated in either direction and at various speeds. Shadows may be painted on the surface, or little cutouts may be made for train window effects (Fig. 39). The drum can be demounted, and tree branches, cookies, or other objects mounted to its frame for different types of shadow effects (Fig. 40).

CHAPTER 2 _____

MOTION PICTURE ILLUMINATION

The motion picture screen play is divided into *sequences,* each of which is made up of a number of scenes. From the point of view of illumination, a scene consists of *sets, props,* and *people.*

The Set

In the early days of the motion picture, films were made out in the open, on their natural locations. As the industry grew and prospered, when stories were laid in foreign countries, and in difficult terrain to which it was impossible to take the entire production staff, location sets were built, illuminated by natural sunlight. This practice was later improved by placing the set on a revolving platform which turned with the sun, thus taking advantage of the direct sun rays all day long. As the stories grew in scope, sets became larger and more expensive. Privacy was needed, so the industry moved inside, into barns which have gradually developed into the huge modern sound stages of today.

Exact replicas of faraway locations, such as the desert of Africa, the jungles of South America, or the streets of Vienna, are still built on the back lot, or on private ranches specially reserved for shooting purposes.

Reproductions of original exterior or interior locations are called *sets.* When built inside on a sound stage, the sets are divided into two classes: *interior-interiors,* such as the inside of a home, a department store, an office building lobby, a church, a railroad station, a jail, etc.; and *interior-exteriors,* such as a street, the façade of any building, a patio, a garden, a forest or other landscape.

To facilitate lighting, sets must be built with as many *breaks* as possible, and not made up of flat walls. The more doors, windows, heavy moldings, or other breaks, the better. A staircase, columns, and other foreground pieces all add to the beauty of the set. All woodwork should have a shine, just as in real life.

Of utmost importance is the color of the set. In black-and-white photography most colors photograph well. However, one warm color easily blends into another. In order to separate faces from the background, cold colors are usually recommended for the painting of sets. For pictorial effect several shades of blue are used. Cold colors are easier and faster to light, and the results are much better. Warm-colored sets may have a pleasant psychological effect upon the artists, the crew, and visiting executives, but do not justify the poor photography which results when combined with warm-colored faces.

Props

All articles that are used to decorate the set, be they furniture, glassware, flowers, or silk curtains, are called *props.*

While on the subject of props, we may as well mention that in the early days of motion picture photography shiny props were said to photograph badly. As a matter of fact, some cameramen have new automobiles milked (sprayed with a chalk and water solution or water paint) even today, to eliminate any possible specular reflection. Highlights, the life of photography, were puttied down; no wonder some of the pictures were so flat. Today we know that with the new antihalo film, the more shiny props we have on the set, the better. Without the sparkling highlights of glazed china, silverware, plate-glass mirrors, copper dishes, and other highly reflective objects, a set would photograph very dull indeed.

People

When the preliminary set lighting is completed, the director of the picture rehearses the scene with the principal artists while the stand-ins stand by and watch. When the rehearsal is over, stand-ins and extras step in for the final lighting, while principals retire to continue rehearsing lines, change wardrobes, or have the final touches of make-up and hairdress checked.

Rigging for Illumination

The preparatory work of placing the reflectors in their respective positions is called *rigging* the set. The average height of a set is about ten feet, although higher sets are often built in various dimensions for particular scenes. Sets usually have three walls, with one wall *wild*, that is, movable on roller jacks. This wild wall may be entirely eliminated if it happens to be in the way for certain setups. Adjoining the top of the set, suspended on chains from the stage ceiling, are the platforms for the reflectors (Figs. 41, 42). In most studios these platforms consist of 2-inch by 4-inch joists, joined together into units, leaving enough room behind the reflectors for the electricians to walk by, with a railing completely around for the safety of the operators. The platforms are divided into *bays*. Each bay generally holds three reflectors, and has one operator assigned to it.

Ceilinged-in sets are lit entirely from the floor. Experiments are now being made with the object in mind of eliminating all over-

Fig. 41

Fig. 42

head construction. When successful, production cost will be reduced considerably.

Lighting Equipment

Inside the dark barns, sunshine was no longer available, so a new source of illumination had to be found (Fig. 43). First it was necessary to illuminate the sets, props, and people to a degree permitting them to register properly on the film; second, to reproduce the different light effects of life. Theatrical lights were brought out from Broadway. The first lamps used for illumination were mercury-vapor lights. They were followed by theatrical arcs and spots. Later on came the incandescent lamps, or *inkies*, which we now use in combination with arc lamps. The following

19

Fig. 43

are the reflectors generally used today in motion picture illumination.

ARC LIGHTS

In black-and-white motion picture photography, whenever we want a sunlight, moonlight, or other sharp shadow effect, we use arc lights.

The *Brute* (Fig. 44) is a 225-ampere arc lamp for sunlight and moonlight effects.

The *Molarc* (150-ampere model) (Fig. 45), also known as the *170*, supplies both spot beams as narrow as 8 degrees and flood beams as wide as 48 degrees. The special *Morinc* lens is corrected for spherical aberration, and the brightness of the illuminated area is therefore greatest at the center, tapering off at the edges. In this way dark centers and ghost patterns are eliminated. Although this lamp is designed primarily to furnish light of constant spectral quality for color photography, it finds extensive use wherever illumination of high uniform intensity is required.

The *Molarc* (120-ampere model), also known as the *90*, provides illumination of medium intensity. Because it may be adjusted to give any beam divergence between 8 and 44 degrees, it is suitable for all types of light-

Fig. 45   *150-Ampere Molarc*

Fig. 46   *Duarc*

Fig. 44   *Brute*

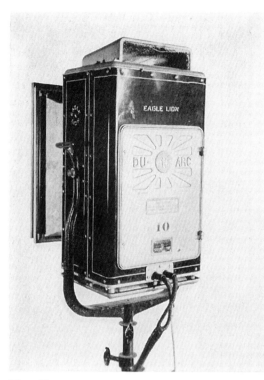

ing requirements. The beams from several lamps can be overlapped without building up spots of high intensity.

The *Duarc* (Figs. 46, 47, 48, 49) is a 40-ampere twin arc lamp, producing illumination considered equivalent to daylight. It may be tilted for either floor illumination or overhead lighting. The lamp is supplied with a sandblasted diffuser in three sheets, which prevents radiation of injurious ultraviolet rays; clear glass also can be supplied if required. The diffuser frames are of a design which prevents escape of leak light, and permits demounting the glass for changing or cleaning.

The *overhead scoop* is a twin arc lamp, used suspended, for illumination of backdrops where a Duarc would be too heavy.

Still in use, but gradually disappearing, are the *65* (Fig. 50), a smaller arc spotlight, and the small *35* (Fig. 51) spotlight.

Fig. 47

Fig. 48

Fig. 49

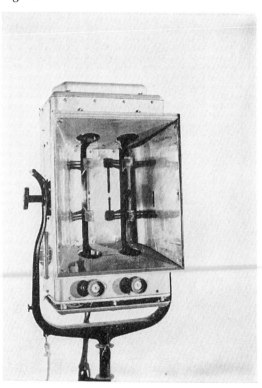

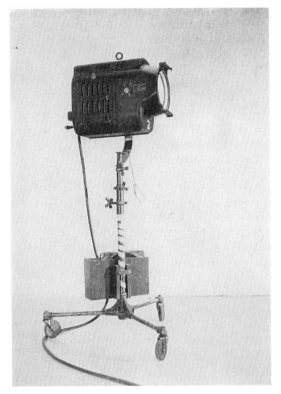

Fig. 50 *The "65" Arc*

Fig. 51 *35-Ampere Arc*

INCANDESCENT LIGHTS

The *Senior Solarspot* and the *Senior Spot* (Fig. 52) are the most powerful of the incandescent lamps. Each is equipped with Fresnel lens and means for adjusting the beam from a narrow spot to a flood.

The *Junior Solarspot* (Fig. 53) and the *Junior Spot* are used with either 1000-watt or 2000-watt bulbs. They are used when the greater illuminating power of the Senior lamps is not required. Their equipment is similar to that of the larger lamps.

The *Baby Solarspot* and the *Baby Keg-Lite* (Fig. 54) are the next smaller lamps, using either 500-watt or 750-watt bulbs as required. An accessory called the *Foco Spot* (Fig. 55) is available for the Baby Keg-Lite, permitting projection of backgrounds of various shapes. The attachment includes a condensing lens, a disk in which are cut apertures of various shapes, and an objective lens.

Fig. 52 *Senior Spotlite*

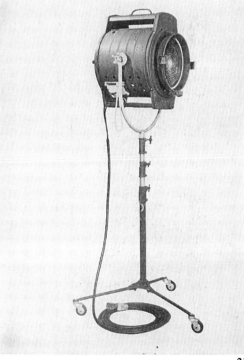

Fig. 53   *Junior Solarspot*

Fig. 54   *Baby Keg-Lite*

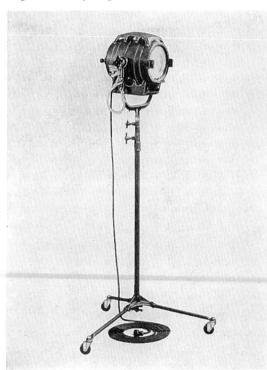

Fig. 55   *Foco-Spot*

Fig. 56   *Midget*

The *Midget* (Fig. 56) takes a 200-watt bulb.

The *Dinky-Inkie* (Figs. 57, 58, 59) is the smallest of the incandescent spotlights, and uses either a 100-watt or a 150-watt bulb.

The *single broad* (Figs. 60, 61) uses a 500-watt or a 750-watt bulb in a sheet metal reflector; it is provided with a diffuser.

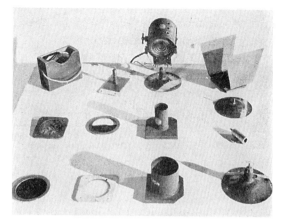

Fig. 59 *Dinky-Inkie and Its Equipment*

Fig. 57 *Dinky-Inkie*

Fig. 58

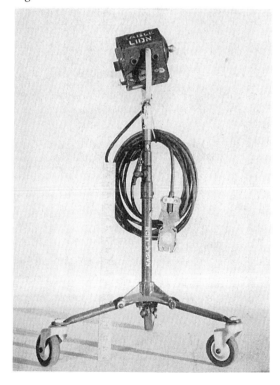

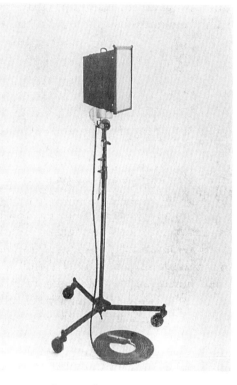

Fig. 60 *Single Broad*

The *double broad* (Fig. 62) contains two 1000-watt bulbs.

The *Cinelite* (Fig. 63) is a lightweight piece of equipment especially designed for portability. It uses a 500-watt or a 1000-watt bulb in a domed reflector, and provides a soft light. A diffuser may also be held before the bulb in a diffuser frame.

25

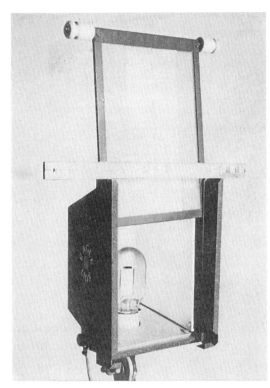

Fig. 61   *Single Broad*

Fig. 62   *Double Broad*

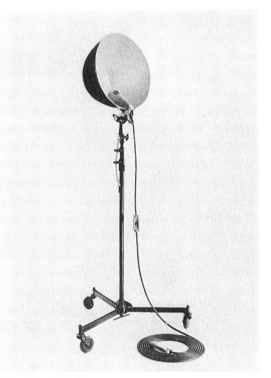

Fig. 63   *Cinelite*

Fig. 64   *Swinging Keylight*

The *swinging keylight* (Fig. 64) is a lamp designed to cast moving shadows. It is fastened to a swinging arm, and is moved slowly up, down, right, and left, as the effect requires. If we were to photograph the real interior of a rocking airplane or ship with a motion picture camera, we would notice that the shadows do not remain still, but move up or down according to the movement of the plane or ship. Most sets are stationary and cannot be rocked, and the effect of a stationary keylight is accordingly a steady shadow. To achieve the illusion that the plane or ship is rocking, the shadows must move; the swinging keylight was designed for this purpose.

The *boomlight* (Fig. 65) consists of a Baby Keg-Lite mounted on a small boom, similar to the one used for the sound mike, but smaller in size and lighter in weight. It is so adjusted that the lamp maintains a constant angle of adjustment up to 45 degrees from horizontal. The boomlight is also called the *menace* because of its bad habit of falling over if not carefully balanced.

The *Streamlight* is a step forward in motion picture illumination (by the author). Visiting tourists and front office executives often ask why it takes so long to light a set—why this expensive, complicated system of illumination—why all the men and reflectors—when in real life the weirdest light effects can be obtained merely by lighting a match, a tiny candle, or by turning an electric switch. The answer is that it is not that simple. Lighting for motion pictures is a different problem from that of illuminating for the supersensitive human eye.

These often repeated questions made me think, nevertheless. We must admit that rigging and lighting have not changed much, if at all, in the past few years. We had a very good excuse in the war. But with the fighting over, and with television, radar, and use of atomic energy now realities, it is about time to start looking for improvements.

Take, for instance, a simple scene in a small hotel room. The script calls for Mr. X to enter the dark room and turn the light switch which lights a single suspended electric lamp bulb. Now for this insignificant scene we have two crews—a rigging crew to set the reflectors, dimmers, etc., for the light effect the script calls for, and the regular working crew to light the set. Once the gaffer and his men have roughed

Fig. 65 *Boomlight*

it in, the director of photography enters and makes certain artistic changes. All this, of course, takes time. The scene is now ready to be shot. But it seldom works in the first take. Either the turning of the switch is late, or the lights come on in several installments for a single bulb. So another take, and another, until one is printed. On the screen it still looks unreal, something is strange about it.

After having experimented with several ideas to simplify set illumination, I have worked out an invention as a suggestion for improvement. It is a new reflector called the *Streamlight,* and is a combination of three kinds of lamps, senior, junior, and broad (Fig. 66). The streamlight is suspended from the ceiling in the middle of the set. It has an arm around it so as to enable us to angle it. It includes one senior in the center, pointing straight down, illuminating the floor, furniture, props, and the people directly below it. Around the senior, six juniors are built at an angle of about 30 degrees; these light the

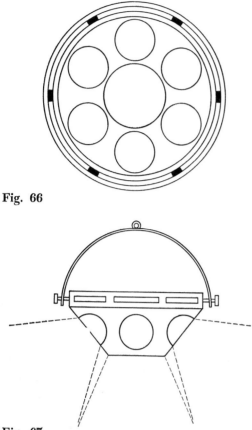

Fig. 66

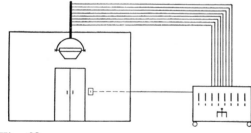

Fig. 67

people, and also the walls all around, up to a certain height. Above the juniors, around the entire circumference of the lamp, is a strip of lamps for filler light. This can be made up either of tubes or bulbs. This light overlaps on the walls from where the juniors left off (Fig. 67). The Streamlight is controlled entirely by its own dimmer box (Fig. 68). The lamps can be turned on, off, or dimmed, either separately or simultaneously. The practical light switch on the set is connected to the dimmer, and when the actor turns it, the light comes on instantly, illuminating the set with a natural effect (Fig. 69).

Figure 70 shows how the different parts of the set are lighted by the different parts of the lamp. Figure 71 shows the Streamlight as seen from above, and how each junior covers a different section of the set. Figure 72 shows a set rigged the old-fashioned way, with all the reflectors necessary to light a relatively small set. The Streamlight is primarily designed for smaller sets, but a battery of

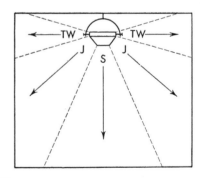

Fig. 70

Fig. 68

Fig. 71

Fig. 69

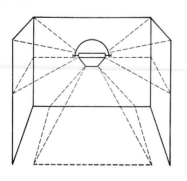

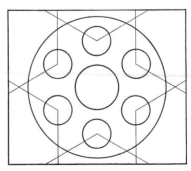

Streamlights can take care of larger sets also. Its real value will be discovered once it is put to work. It is economical, quick, and simple in operation.

Pans (Fig. 73) are used for illumination of the background or backings, either suspended up high, or on the floor. This lamp is just a plain pan containing a powerful bulb. It throws a general light in all directions in front of it. Pans are also used suspended, for overhead lighting of big sets.

A *Gimmik* is used where there is little or no space to hide a bigger reflector. This is a small but powerful globe, which, because of its small size, can be hidden in a confined area.

Photofloods are used to accentuate the practical lamps and brackets in interiors.

Overhead banks, or *houselights* are strips of several lamps arrayed in a bank (Fig. 74).

The *work light* is a plain lamp on a stand, with a bulb of about 100 or 200 watts, used for what its name implies, work, rehearsals, and during set construction. It is killed when shooting a scene.

DESIGNATIONS OF DIFFERENT TYPES OF LIGHTS

Keylight, or principal light, is used to light either individuals or groups.

Clotheslight is used to build up the light on dark clothes.

Frontlight is the one that comes from the direction of the camera.

Crosslight can come from either the right or left, up or down, but always *cross*.

Toplight comes directly from above.

Cross backlight or *kicker* comes from the rear, either from up high, or from the floor.

Backlight originates directly from behind, mostly from high, but can also come from the floor.

Eyelight is used to brighten up the eyes of individuals. It has hardly any exposure value and reflects only from the shiny surfaces of the eyeballs. It is usually placed at the height

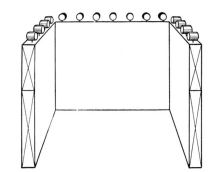

Fig. 72

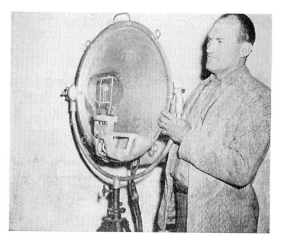

Fig. 73   *Pan*

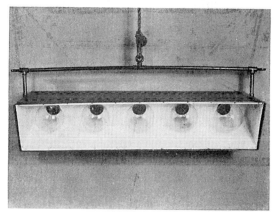

Fig. 74   *Overhead Bank*

of the eyes, and is extremely helpful in close-ups for improving photographic quality.

Fill and *filler light* is a shadowless soft light, used to fill in when the keylight is too strong and the shadows are too deep.

29

The Theory of Illumination

Ever since primitive man rose and retired with the sun, daylight illumination has been known to exist. The world has progressed, but in interior photography, lighting still imitates the principal light, or sunlight, and the secondary and tertiary lights, the reflected light from the clouds and the surrounding landscape.

When in nature a tree is illuminated by a single light source, the sun, an impression of roundness is given. This is so for a number of reasons: first, the variation of reflective qualities of different points of the tree's circumference; and second, the sensitivity of the human eye to the different light densities. In photography it is different. In interior light-

ing, if we use one light source, even a round object photographs flat (Fig. 75). We correct this by adding to our keylight a filler, kicker, and backlight (Fig. 76).

Before proceeding further into the complicated subject of lighting, let us briefly review the fundamentals of elementary illumination.

ELEMENTARY ILLUMINATION, ANGLES

Because the screen in the motion picture theatre is a one-dimensional flat surface, it is imperative that we photograph everything from an *angle* from which most surfaces of the subject are visible to the camera.

To simplify matters we select a plain little square wooden block with which to illustrate the theory. If we understand the photography of a square block, we can photograph properly a single piece of furniture, a window, a vase of flowers, a lamp, or a set filled with people, which is a combination of all these

Fig. 77

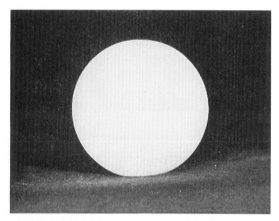

Fig. 75

Fig. 76

30

constituents. *The more surfaces of an object that are visible, the better will be the picture.*

Figure 77 shows a small block. We know it has six surfaces, but facing it straight on, all we can see is one. As we move the camera to one side we discover a better angle, from which we see two surfaces (Fig. 78). When the camera is raised a trifle, we see three out of six surfaces (Fig. 79). After we move the camera more, we soon find out that *no matter where we place it, we cannot get a better picture of the block.* Under the circumstances this is the best we can do, so this is our best *angle,* and it is from this position that the picture should be photographed.

LIGHTING

The next step in photographing an object is to light it. No matter how elementary the object, the approach to its illumination is about the same.

We determine our light source, which may be either natural or artificial. The principal natural light sources are sunlight, moonlight, skyshine, and the northern lights. Some artificial light sources are street lights, auto headlights, lighthouses, the stage spotlight, flashlight, lantern, candlelight, oil burner, a match, torch, fireplace, campfire, phosphorescence, and all the variety of electric and other lights of the modern household.

Suppose, for instance, that the light source is a reading lamp. By use of a small *testlight* we determine the position from which the light will properly illuminate the scene, and yet will appear as if coming from the reading lamp. This position will be that of the principal or key light.

By use of an exposure meter, the key and the over-all illumination on the set are measured, keeping in mind the light balance necessary to give whatever feeling or mood may be required for the scene. If additional light is needed, a broad may be placed on each side of the camera to insure that no part of the set will be underilluminated.

Fig. 78

Fig. 79

Fig. 80 *Wrong*

Fig. 81 *Right*

Fig. 82

In order to avoid confusion resulting from multiple shadows, a filler light may be required, which is usually placed as near to the camera as possible.

Unless the entire picture to be photographed is one flat surface, such as a plain wall, it usually has a foreground and a background. The illusion of depth can be enhanced by separation of the two; that is, if the foreground is dark, the background should be light, or vice versa (Figs. 80, 81).

Mirrors will also enhance the illusion of depth by reflecting the well-lit opposite side of a room. Flat monotone walls can be broken up by casting shadows upon them (Fig. 82).

The combination of a foreground, having visible as many surfaces of the object as possible, each surface having a different brightness, and a background of a different tone, makes a perfect picture.

THE PURPOSE OF ILLUMINATION

The purpose of illumination is twofold, that is, for quantity and for quality.

In lighting for *quantity* we light for exposure, to make certain that a sufficient amount of light reaches every corner of the set, and that it is properly balanced, in order that no part of the film shall be underexposed or overexposed.

In lighting for *quality,* we strive to bring out the following values:

1. Orientation—to enable the audience to see where the story is taking place
2. Mood or feeling (season of year and time of day)
3. Pictorial beauty, aesthetic pleasure
4. Depth, perspective, third-dimensional illusion

ORIENTATION

When reading a book one's imagination travels without geographical or other limitation, wherever the story takes it, sometimes even beyond. In viewing a stage play, the field is somewhat more limited. Here the eye can travel only from the full-length view of the stage to a closer picture of the actor's physiognomy, with the aid of opera glasses, depending upon the distance one happens to be from the footlights. It is almost impossible for a member of an audience in the gallery to appreciate facial expression even with opera glasses; in spite of the broad gestures of stage technique, to a great portion of the theatre audience the finesse of the play is often completely lost.

In the motion picture theatre, this deficiency has been greatly overcome. The screen offers the advantage of an ability (although we do not always utilize it) to photograph the story from the position from which the director thinks the audience would like to see it. The success of any particular film depends a great deal upon the ability of the director to anticipate the desires of the audience in this respect.

The camera is the eye of the audience. When it moves closer, the audience moves with it. When it concentrates on a particular item, the audience concentration is devoted to that item alone. The increasing tendency in modern screen technique is to move the camera. With the camera mounted on a dolly or crane, several angles can be taken in one single trucking or crane shot without a cut. Too much camera movement is just as bad as none, like catsup on bad food. It is used to cover up.

MOOD

Every member of a production staff reading a final shooting script visualizes the story from a different point of view. The producer sees the story as a whole, the public's reaction to it, casting problems, business and financial details. The director sees it as a picture, divided into sequences and scenes, creating in his mind the characters and the dialogue, and worrying about music, sound, and editing. The actors live their parts, learn their lines,

and consider their wardrobe and make-up, while the prop man thinks of his props, tricks, inserts, etc. The director of photography visualizes the picture purely from a photographic point of view, as determined by lights and the moods of individual sequences and scenes. In other words, how to use angles, set-ups, lights, and camera as means to tell the story.

PICTORIAL BEAUTY

Extreme long shots, although not used as profusely as in the films of yesteryear, add to the production value of the picture. Musical comedies with their gorgeous settings, outdoor pictures with their magic spell of natural beauty, take the audience into a dream world. Long shots are also handy in showing unusual, out-of-the-ordinary places. Although short scenes in the amphitheatre of a hospital, the research laboratory of a chemist, the interior of a cathedral, a motion picture studio, and other places the average man may never see in a lifetime cannot save a bad picture, they are always of great interest.

DEPTH

The illusion of three dimensions—photographic depth—is created by a geometric design of placing people and props, breaking up the set into several planes, and the proper distribution of lights and shadows.

At night when we look into an illuminated room from the dark outside, we can see inside but cannot be seen ourselves. A similar situation exists in the motion picture theatre during a performance. We sit in the dark looking at a light screen; this gives a definite feeling of depth. In order to continue this depth on the screen, the progression from dark to light must be followed up. The spot which should appear to be the most distant should be the lightest, and vice versa; the illusion is carried out by employing a full scale of shades from black to white. Figure 83 and Figure 84 are both flat surfaces, yet one gives a sensation of depth and the other does not.

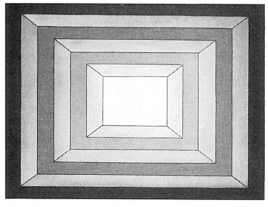

Fig. 83

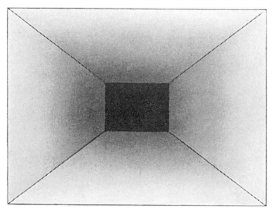

Fig. 84

If possible, backdrops which are only partially visible should be of an off-white color. These can be used for both day and night scenes and are speedy to work with. Enlarged translucent photographs are also used as backings. These usually represent some well-known building, bridge, or other landmark we try to feature. These backings are known as *translites,* and are illuminated from the rear. The lighting of the other type of backings is done with Pans or Scoops suspended in the air from high, or hidden behind the set on the floor. This light is supplemented with broads or Duarcs from the floor.

KEY OF THE PICTURE

The *key* of the picture (not to be confused with keylight) depends upon the category of the screen play. From the point of view of illumination there are three main categories: comedy (further subdivided into musical comedy and slapstick comedy), drama, and mystery. The illumination of each of these types of screen play requires a different approach. Once the key of the picture is decided upon, the script is broken down into its constituents; the sequences and scenes and the mood of the lighting of each one are worked out separately.

Musical comedies are lit high and brilliant with a stylized, dreamlike light. For this type of photography, light sources and logic in lighting mean nothing. A feeling of gaiety should prevail throughout the entire picture from beginning to end, and the sets must be lit accordingly.

One of the really difficult tasks in motion picture creation is to make people laugh. Photography, like music, has its psychological effect upon people. If we wanted to make someone laugh, we would hardly think of playing him a sad 'cello solo. In comedy photography, any lighting which might keep the audience from laughing must be avoided. A low-key scene might be upsetting and spoil the comedy effect. The lighting of a slapstick comedy scene should be gay—absolutely light-hearted—and in as high a key as our present photographic and laboratory facilities will allow without going into a senseless flat lighting. This gaiety of mood may be carried out throughout the entire picture, in long shots as well as in close-ups.

ROUGHING IN

For the purpose of demonstration, let us take an average living room set with three walls, a door from the outside, a window next to it, and in the background a dining room. The camera is set up for a long shot taking in the entire set, and as the action about to be photographed takes place in the daytime, our light source will apparently be the sun sending a stream of light through the window.

First of all we must light the background and that part of the set in which the actors will not walk around. This is known as *roughing it in*.

Next we light the interior living room. Sunlight always brings gaiety to a house. If the window happens to have white lace curtains it will not stand excessive backlight without burning, and for monochrome film light blue or green curtains will suit the purpose better to maintain the impression of white on the screen.

For photographing through the window, two crisscross arcs are used, one from each side. The bluish light from the ordinary arc is very deceiving; it looks bright to the eye, but in reality is insufficient for the camera. To correct this we mix in some inkies and add some seniors to the already strong sunlight. A yellow gelatin called the *Y-1.*, when placed in front of an arc will correct the light from blue to reddish-yellow (the characteristic color of incandescent lights), so that all of the light is of the same color temperature.

In shooting a long shot of a three-wall set, we see two side walls and one back wall. The best way to light the side walls is to back crosslight them, the left wall from up high right, and the right one from up high left (Fig. 85). This type of lighting will not only

adequately light, but will bring out the values of the set—accentuate them. If shiny objects happen to be along the path of the light they will reflect it and give the set life, pep, and brilliancy. Side walls should be lit darker in the foreground and lighter in the background, using strong crosslights on the back wall. If you cannot use crosslight, toplight may be used. If that too is impossible, employ frontlight, but never from the exact camera height; frontlights should be placed either higher or lower than the camera, and the light should be broken up with shadows.

When the walls are illuminated, the furniture in the room should be cross backlit with a light that is not so strong that it can burn out the design of sunlight on the floor.

For fillerlight a Duarc is placed on each side of the camera. The set is now roughly lit and ready for rehearsal.

REHEARSAL

In comedies, more than in any other kind of a screen play, action comes first, last, and always. The action must be well lit so that it can be seen all the time; but in close shots the actors' faces should be the lightest spots on the screen.

The set described above might have the following action. A bell rings, a man from the inside opens the door, and a couple walks in. They stop, talk, then all three walk over to the couch and sit down. As they walked across the set, it was apparent that the general light was inadequate; the faces were underlit and consequently went muddy. When the rehearsal is completed, the stand-ins step in and we light the faces. Individual keylights are added and balanced with kicker lights. One more walk-through, and we are ready for the take.

THE TAKE

With the rehearsals over, the photographic worries really begin. During the shooting of the scene we must make sure that (1) all

Fig. 85

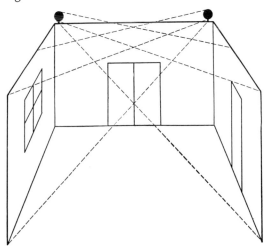

lights are on; (2) no light moves; (3) dimmers are correct; (4) there is no voltage drop; (5) actors return to their designated positions (marks) exactly as in rehearsals; (6) one actor does not shade the face of another too extensively; (7) make-up was not damaged.

TRUCKING SHOTS

Some people have the mistaken idea that a trucking or dolly shot is faster to light than a stationary one. Nothing could be further from the truth; not only would haste sacrifice photographic beauty, but it takes time to hang the many lights necessary.

If the script calls for a trucking shot—with dolly or crane—from a long shot to a medium shot or even a close-up, then the long shot lighting must be combined with lighting for the closer shot. This is not exactly an ideal condition for lighting. In the long shot, the camera takes in the entire set, so there can be no lights on the floor; but for the closer shot they are absolutely essential. High reflectors cause deep shadows, exaggerate cheekbones, make deep-set eyes, none of which are favorable to feminine faces. Consequently we must strike a happy medium, not using reflectors from up high, but suspended on ropes and brought down almost to the upper camera line. Reflectors equipped with dimmers can be installed on the dolly or crane, and faded in as the camera moves in on the close-up.

ADVANCED LIGHTING —THE POETIC APPROACH

All throughout a dramatic picture the lighting fluctuates. We retain our gay sequences, which are lit brightly, gaily. Sad scenes are lit in a lower key. The mood of tragedy is enhanced by a strong contrast of deep blacks and glaring whites—shadows and highlights. In drama we light for mood, we paint poems. Lighting with its ups and downs becomes a symphonic construction, paralleling the dramatic situations. Here the purpose of a long

36

shot is not only geographical, but also to establish the mood of the scene, to help tell the story. With the aid of this visual concert we actually hypnotize the audience, taking them out of their everyday, nervous world and into the realm of a fictitious, but more pleasant one.

If a scene calls for daylight, the director of photography asks: "What part of the day is it? Is it out in the country or in the city? Is it dawn, breakfast time, or teatime? Is it winter with its soft daylight pouring in through the bay window—light in that part of the room only, leaving the rest in semidarkness? Or is it summer, with strong sunshine illuminating the entire set? Does the scene take place in the north or in the tropics where the sunlight is so strong that interiors seem dark even in the daytime?" All these factors and many others must be considered in lighting for drama.

People, especially those living in the country, have a fair idea of different atmospheric changes that indicate coming weather. A pure white sky would perhaps add to the depth of a picture, but it would never be accepted as indicating or even suggesting the approach of a snowstorm. To know dramatic lighting the photographer must familiarize himself with *light in life*—the different light effects as they really exist. Figures 86, 87, 88, and 89 illustrate the types of natural lighting charac-

Fig. 86 *Sunrise on the Golden Horn*

teristic of sunrise, noon, sunset, and evening, respectively.

To illustrate the changes of lighting that occur in nature, we shall return to our familiar living room set. Let us assume that it is part of a home somewhere out in the country. Suppose it were possible for us to watch the constant changes of light in chronological order during the short space of twenty-four hours. We would witness the following:

DAWN

The room is dark. Furniture and other objects are hardly discernible. Little by little, our eyes become accustomed to this strange luminosity, this *light in the dark,* and we begin to see. This experiment reminds us of the development of a photographic plate. First the sky outside appears, then the highlights all around become visible. Dew drops on the trees sparkle like jewels as the exterior slowly takes shape. The dark trees stand out against the early haze. It is dawn.

SUNRISE

After the dark of the night, sunshine is always welcome. As the sun rises, light begins to pour in. This arrival of another sunrise—a new day, a clean page—is cheerful, high in spirit. The effect of the first rays of the rising sun becomes visible in a design on the ceiling above the window, producing long shadows. We can hear the birds chirping. It is daybreak.

Gradually the atmosphere changes; it is getting lighter. The flowers, trees, the entire garden take their early morning sun bath. The picture which only such a short while ago looked so gloomy, so mysterious, now takes on an optimistic look. It is morning. The horizontal sunrays illuminate the wall, making it sparkle. The shadows are more transparent. This scene is familiar to all. We have seen it time and again. It is breakfast time.

As the sun rises, the shadows fall. . . . It is high noon. Outside there is still sunshine,

Fig. 87   *Solitude*

Fig. 88   *Sunset in Santos*

Fig. 89   *Istanbul*

but inside we see a strong but diffused light coming from all directions. It is not as beautiful as the light play of the early morning.

It is late afternoon. The sunlight is romantic but sad, lovely, but sorrowful. The knowledge that the sunshine is leaving us, even though only for the night, instinctively influences the sensitive human soul.

SUNSET

The scene shifts. The orange-colored rays of the setting sun return inside once more as though to bid farewell. This is a spiritual beauty of short duration. The shadows stretch, the diffused light, reflected by the sky, weakens. The foreground is already silhouetted, the shadows disappear, the room is dark. Outside, it is twilight; inside, the last vestige of light on the ceiling leaves, and the entire picture plunges into total darkness. Evening is here, night has fallen.

EVENING

The room is softly lit. The hottest spot is the table with its white linen table cloth and the silver candelabra.

The family is seated around the table. Dinner is served. The main light source (the chandelier) is suspended directly above the table, seconded by the candles on the table, reflected in the shining eyes of the well-rounded, happy faces. Occasionally the kitchen door opens and sends in a burst of white light, illuminating the back wall. The clock ticks on. A transformation of scene has taken place—the dining room is now dark, with a design of the window produced by the moon visible on the wall, and showing the shadow of the curtains blowing in the gentle evening breeze. In the living room the lights are still on. The different lamps projecting a variety of shadows make an interesting pattern. The ceiling reflects the light, giving the room a peaceful atmosphere.

Then the lights are turned out, leaving us in the dark once more.

MOONLIGHT

The moon emerges from behind the clouds and sends a beam of bluish, silvery light into the garden. This creates a ghostly effect, with its sharp highlights and opaque shadows. There is suspense in the air. The atmosphere is tense; anything is likely to happen at any moment.

As the light travels, the environment takes on a new outlook. The moonlight hits the lace curtain directly, lending it a soft glow, a romantic feeling, not unlike the shimmer it produces on the ocean surface. The light from the curtain fades and becomes translucent. The room is semidark, bathed by the reflected light from the garden.

It is incredible how a new and different light can change not only the mood, but also the setting. Outside daylight is appearing in the distance. We have come to the end of our experimental journey.

These poetic feelings are of utmost importance to the student of advanced photography. Unless he understands them, he can never hope to be able to convey them to others through the medium of pictures, and all illumination becomes just so much light.

ACTUAL ILLUMINATION

Our living room is once again a set on the stage. We reconstruct the different lightings witnessed over the period of a day and night.

DAWN

At this time of the day our only light source is the glow on a distant sky. This we imitate, reconstruct, with Pans from the floor. The general light is soft, diffused. This effect we attain by setting up diffused broads or Duarcs in several places, but always hidden from the point of view of the camera (Fig. 90).

INTERIOR INTERIOR

The only light at dawn is coming in through the window. Although it is not a strong, pro-

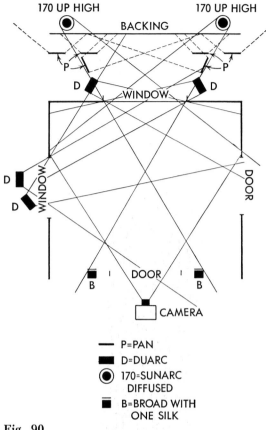

170 UP HIGH   170 UP HIGH

BACKING

P   P

D   WINDOW   D

D

D

WINDOW   DOOR

DOOR

B   B

CAMERA

— P=PAN
■ D=DUARC
◉ 170=SUNARC
    DIFFUSED
▬ B=BROAD WITH
    ONE SILK

Fig. 90

nounced light, nevertheless, photographically it is our only light source, and is going to be the hottest spot in the picture. In lighting a dawn scene we cannot use an arc for our main light source unless it is diffused, as the arc light throws definite sharp shadows. Several well-diffused reflectors must be used, criss-crossed from different directions, to establish an immediately recognized, definitely outside, dawn light source.

There is quite a resemblance between the light of dusk before dawn, and the twilight after sunset. Neither light has sufficient strength to penetrate deep into the room; it creates a feeling of light around the window, and gradually darkens away from it.

LIGHTING A SUNRISE

Take the light prepared for a dawn effect, build up the outside with a few additional Duarcs, build up the interior lighting from up high and also with frontlight, take the diffusers off the arcs shining in through the window, and you have the light ready for a sunrise scene.

BREAKFAST TIME

An overexposed negative will not give you a picture of daylight. All negatives must be normally exposed. It is not the quantity but the quality that establishes a mood, which determines the theme, the message of the picture.

The light that establishes breakfast time is very similar to that of the sunrise. It is now, however, later in the day, the sun has risen above the horizon, so we change the shadows on the wall. We raise the density of the key-light; also we add more frontlight by either adding more lamps or reducing the diffusion somewhat. Outside it is daylight. The sky is lit, the trees are well modeled, with strong highlights. For this effect we employ several arcs from one light source as high up as possible.

LIGHTING A SUNSET

If east has not been established on the set by using the window for sunrise, then we can use it for sunset. However, we cannot use the same window for both unless we change the direction of the light, as everyone knows that the sun rises on one side of the house and sets on the other.

LIGHTING AN EVENING DINING ROOM

Unless the design of the chandelier is such that we can hide some high-intensity photo-flood globes inside it, its effect is carried out —imitated—entirely from above the set (Fig. 91).

Suppose we are shooting from one end of the table. First we keylight the actors on the left side of the table from up high right, and those on the right side from up high left. This will not only key the people around the

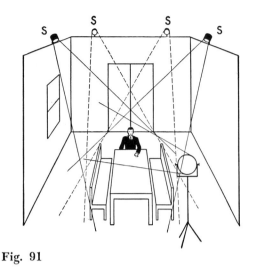

Fig. 91

table and model the opposite side, but will establish the mood, light the lower part of the walls, and throw a design of a spotlight on the floor. Now we add a back-kicker on the people, hotter than the keylight. On the persons sitting at the far end of the table we add another front key. To those in mid-distance we add more front light and leave those closest to the camera in semi-silhouette. This will build up depth. The general appearance from the distance must indicate that the light emanates from the chandelier above. Servants in the background are not lit, so as they step into the foreground they come into the light, giving the effect a natural lighting.

WINDOW SHOTS

There is something appealing about a window that gives a romantic mood to a picture. It makes an excellent frame. It is through the window that our wishes, hopes, and dreams exit; we expect them to return through the door in the form of good fortune.

The illumination of window shots is quite perplexing. Take, for instance, a picture where a person is standing against the sunlit curtain of a window. The old-fashioned way of lighting this was to light the window from the outside, and the person, in flat key from the inside. This two-way light produced a contra-

dictory, confusing feeling. The average layman may not understand lighting, but every child can tell sunlight when he sees it. The new school of photography allows us to light realistically. Subdued, low-key faces with strong cross and backlights, are nowadays accepted without any comment, even in daylight shots.

The correct way to light such a picture is with an arc from the outside. If possible, mix in some inkie light coming from the same direction. This will take care of the curtain and the incoming sunlight. It will also outline the contours of the person's face and figure. If possible, use a light blue curtain. This will allow the use of a stronger light from outside than will a white one. Inside, we add a crosslight of less intensity than the arc outside. On the side of this crosslight, next to the camera, we add a broad diffused with several silks. The feeling of this picture will be that of outside sunlight, provided the backing is lit in a high key. For that uniform lighting, we use a Duarc or two (Fig. 92).

Fig. 92 *Marsha Hunt*

MOONLIGHT AND WINDOWS

The lighting scheme for moonlight scenes at the window is about the same as it is for a daylight scene, except that we eliminate the light on the backing, and also the front filler.

TWO-SHOT AGAINST A WINDOW

Where the picture is that of two profiles against the curtained window, we use two backlight arcs, one from the right and the

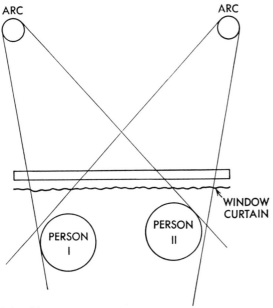

Fig. 93

other from the left. This will light the profiles of both persons. The balance of the lighting is like that for a single person (Fig. 93).

SHOOTING IN FROM OUTSIDE

There are times when we must improve upon nature's lighting. Such a shot is one through the window from the outside, of a person inside (Fig. 94). If we simply imitate natural sunlight, the wall outside and the window will burn up.

This we can improve by shading the sun-

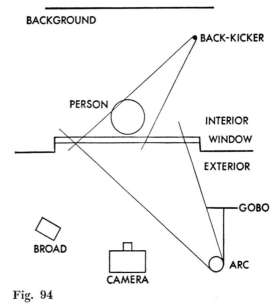

Fig. 94

light off the wall and window, either with gauze, a tree branch, or both. The arc is placed on one side of the camera, usually from a high position, so that it does not reflect in the window glass. On the soft side of the camera we place a broad, shielding the glass panes from it also. If this high key leaves heavy shadows, then we fill in with a low-positioned baby on the key side. This light with the tree shadows will give a natural daylight effect. To round out the face we add a kicker from the inside. Backlight would not look natural; therefore we eliminate it. To separate the head from the background, we light up the latter. Otherwise the background is usually left dark, or with a shadow design of another window on the wall without any filler light.

INTERIOR EXTERIOR

In lighting exteriors inside, we must imitate nature as closely to the traditional pattern as possible. People have positive pictures (mental images) of the appearance of exteriors. Establish your light sources and light accordingly.

41

WRITING FOR LIGHTING

The time will come when light will be given its proper place in screen play writing technique. Instead of machine-gunning the audience with earsplitting, harsh dialogue, motion pictures will use more music, both audible and visual. People will leave the theatre, not with a headache as they now so often do, but with a relaxed feeling of having seen and heard a beautiful concert.

Fig. 95

CHAPTER 3

MYSTERY LIGHTING

Where there is no light, one cannot see; and when one cannot see, his imagination starts to run wild. He begins to suspect that something is about to happen. *In the dark there is mystery.*

Mystery in lighting is not a Hollywood in-

vention; it is as old as man himself. There is an age-old saying that all evil happens at night; that, while sunlight is beneficial to mankind, the cold blue rays of the moon are supposed to produce the opposite effect.

According to an old oriental legend, ghosts

Fig. 96 *Seance*

do exist, but only in the absolute darkness of the night. For an individual to travel alone in the dark is considered dangerous. In the slightest light, be it that made by a person carrying a lantern or a group of people making up an "energy," what we might call today a live battery, the evil spirits lose their destructive power. In the dimmest of lights, the ghosts disperse. We are not concerned here with ghost stories, but it is interesting to learn that the power of light in the dark was known to man long before we began to employ it in mystery lighting for motion picture photography (Fig. 96).

Fire

There were fires before there were fire departments, hence we have no official record of what the first light was. We assume, however, that the moon must have been the first light man saw in the dark of the night.

Then came the lightning which brought with it fire. Because of its sudden and, to primitive man, mysterious appearance, and the death and destruction it brought in its wake, it has certain unhappy associations in the mind of man. It creates fear in some people who, at the approach of an electric storm, still draw all the shades, or, if they happen to be in bed, pull the blankets and pillows over their heads.

Man soon discovered how to make his own fire, and since most animals were afraid of it, he used it as a protective measure at the entrance of his cave. This flame must have been the first visual music. Flames have a certain magic appeal, and we still use them on our dinner table in the form of candles.

The primitive fire developed into the campfire; and soon man learned to harness this phenomenon and put it to practical use. As he moved inside he took the fire with him, and he still has it in the fireplace. As the world got colder this served not only as a stove to cook with, but also as a heating device.

Then he began to use the flame as an illuminant. He liked to see the play of light and huge shadows. First the torch, which he carried along with him into the night; then the oil lamp, the candle, the match, the petroleum lamp, gaslight—until we arrived at today's illuminant, the electric light, when Edison placed the filament in an airtight enclosure and gave us the electric lamp.

People are getting tired of the chocolate-coated photography of yesterday. They have had enough of it. In the latest films there seems to be a tendency to go realistic. This trend will no doubt have its influence upon amateur, still, and movie photography.

There is no better opportunity for such realistic lighting than in mystery illumination (Fig. 97).

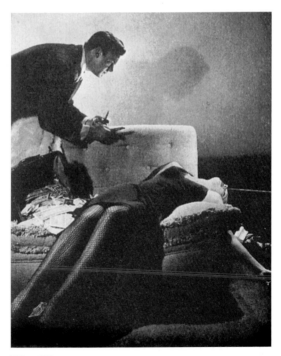

Fig. 97

MYSTERY LIGHTS; FIRE EFFECTS

The light of some real fires, such as that of a forest fire, is strong enough to register on our present-day sensitive film. The fire itself

Fig. 98   *Paul Henreid*

is usually the light source, but if there is any foreground action, the light on the people must be built up to required strength.

THE EFFECT OF LIGHTING A CIGARETTE

In our daily life, we are accustomed to see a face lit by the sun, moon, or some normal artificial light source. When a man lights a cigarette in the dark of night, the lighter or match creates an unusual light effect on his face. The flame itself picks up, but the effect on the face is much too weak photographically.

A satisfactory imitation can be created artificially by using especially made-up strong matches, or two tiny arcs held in the palm of the hand. These arcs are of course connected to an electric outlet. We time the light of the arcs with that of the match or lighter,

and as soon as the cigarette is lit, kill them (Fig. 98).

The fire of a burning cigarette can be registered on film without additional artificial light if the person smoking the cigarette is silhouetted in the foreground. Focus in this case must be on the cigarette fire, otherwise it washes out. If the face is fully lit, or even lit in a low key, the effect on the face itself must be built up. This is done with a baby on a dimmer (Fig. 99).

The following light effects can be used to great advantage to heighten the mystery of a scene:

Ship-wrecked figures on a raft, in complete darkness, with only the phosphorescence of the ocean waves breaking the ink-black of the pictures; in the distance, the fluctuating light of a lighthouse

The effect of passing auto headlights on the ceiling of a dark interior

Fluctuating neon or other electric signs

Fig. 99

BABY ON DIMMER

Fig. 100

The light of a passing streetcar on an otherwise dark street

The hanging light on the ceiling of a cheap gambling joint (Fig. 100).

Searchlights of prisons or concentration camps

Flashes of guns in absolute darkness

The opening and closing of a refrigerator that has a light inside, in a dark kitchen

The well-known street lamp (Fig. 101)

The hanging lamp swinging on a warehouse wall, on a stormy night

The revolving light of a lighthouse

Very effective is the light effect where, during a fight, the only visible light is on the blades of the knives.

Fig. 101

Fig. 102

Sets and Mystery

Surroundings can help a great deal in establishing a mood of mystery. Slums, bars, gambling joints, where the filament of a lamp is the only bright spot, and other dimly lit places are good (Fig. 102). For illumination of these places, a few photoflood bulbs strategically placed are sufficient (Figs. 103, 104). When shooting neon or other electric lights, wet the pavement to get reflections of the light sources in the picture.

THE POOR MAN'S MYSTERY

If there are no lights available for night shots, even though they be of mysterious nature, they can be made with filters on sunlit exteriors (Fig. 105). A combination of Wratten filters No. 23 and No. 56 can be used.

Fig. 104

Fig. 103

Fig. 105

We must be sure, however, that the picture has the feeling of night. Practicals and head-lights of automobiles should be turned on; they help establish night. A white sky should be avoided. When buildings are white, we stop down a bit more than the exposure meter reads. There are pictures which, no matter how far one stops down, never make good night scenes (Fig. 106). Photofloods will help the situation; they can be cut in on the city light mains or run off a battery.

Fig. 106

Lighting for Lightning

Lightning in motion pictures is employed for the same effect it is known to have in real life—to create fear, to enhance drama with its blinding flash of white light and huge, moving, mysterious shadows.

To imitate lightning in motion picture photography we use a lightning machine. There are three kinds in general use:

1. The old barrel of salt water which acts as a resistance, and uses a bundle of carbons tied together; touching the two poles together creates a huge flash of glaring light, the duration of which can be controlled

2. The bank of inkie bulbs, which gives out a brief flash of light for a short distance only (Fig. 107)

Fig. 107 *Lightning Machine*

3. A bank of inkies, but with the projecting type of globes, which emits a lightning flash that carries a longer distance

Although the effect of a lightning machine is strong enough to register in a fully lit room, it is mostly used with action taking place in sets lit in a low key.

When lightning is used as a light source, it should definitely not come from in front. This powerful light would burn out all faces and other details in the picture. We place it at the

50

rear, properly shaded from the lens and the eyes of the cameramen; or have its effect come through the window or door (Fig. 108). In other words, we use lightning as a backlight or crosslight only.

Lighting a Campfire Scene

Whether the campfire is outside in a natural setting, on a stage with a painted backdrop, or on the process stage, its illumination is about the same. The light source must appear to be the fire itself (Fig. 109). Strong backlights are used. People usually sit around the fire, forming a circle. Inside this circle, behind the people, frontlight reflectors are hidden. This carries out the fire feeling on the faces in the background. Outside the circle, strong crosslight reflectors are placed, covering the entire group. Hardly any frontlight is used on the people in the foreground. If the background happens to be a painted backdrop, we light the lower part of the backing, giving a "rising sun in the distance" feeling. This also may indicate the last rays of the setting sun. For this, Pans or Broads are used from the floor, hidden by the set itself. The center of interest, the hottest part of the picture, is the circle of faces of the people around the fire; we light accordingly.

How to Illuminate a Fireplace Scene

Various light effects can be produced on sets which have the fireplace as the light source. High flames throwing strong dancing shadows on the walls spell mystery. A fire with only a glow, a dormant fire, symbolizes an emotional fluctuation in the participants of the scene around the fire (Fig. 110). In such pictures there is romance. The diagram (Fig. 111) shows the distribution of reflectors for the illumination of fireplace scenes.

Before going into the lighting of such a set, we find out if the fireplace itself is in the picture, and if it is wild (movable). If not, its back is taken off and four small arcs (35

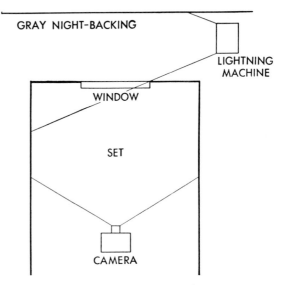

Fig. 108

Fig. 109

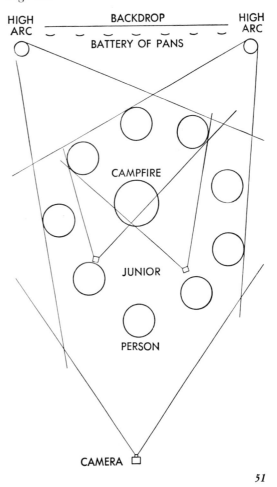

Fig. 110

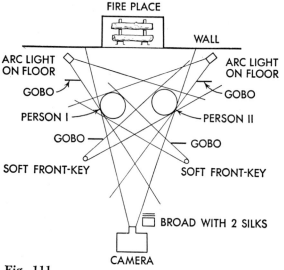

FIRE PLACE

WALL

ARC LIGHT ON FLOOR

ARC LIGHT ON FLOOR

GOBO

GOBO

PERSON I

PERSON II

GOBO

GOBO

SOFT FRONT-KEY

SOFT FRONT-KEY

BROAD WITH 2 SILKS

CAMERA

Fig. 111

ampere) are placed on the floor behind it. We arrange two low ones on the floor, pointing towards the ceiling, and two higher ones covering the floor of the room. The four reflectors should cover the field for the light effect. Use the flame of the real fire for the shadow effect.

If the fireplace happens to be in the picture and we would see the arcs, another setup of lights must be improvised, in which the angle of our light source might be a bit different from that of the actual fireplace, but hardly noticeable on the screen. Instead of using the

flame of the fireplace for the effect, we place a burning oil-soaked rag in front of the arc light, and those flames produce the necessary shadows.

For close-ups of fireplace scenes, we soften the effect. Expression on masculine faces can be accentuated by using the arc itself as the key light.

The Candle Flame

As a rule, candles suggest gay scenes, weddings in the church, dinner parties in dimly lit night clubs (Fig. 112). They are popular with the young because they are romantic, and with the old because they bring back memories. They also make good light sources for mystery lighting. For instance, take the scene of a person walking down the staircase of a dark room with but a lighted candle in his hand.

There are several ways of lighting for a candlelight shot. The most effective is where the candle itself is actually the illuminant. This is done in the following manner: A hollow white artificial candle is built. One side of the candle is carved out, and in this space are placed two tiny arcs, the same as those used for the match effect. If no arcs are at hand, a tiny tubular projection-type bulb can be placed inside it. On top of this artificial candle, is added a piece of a real candle of the same size and white color. It must fit perfectly and look like one piece. The batteries necessary for the current of the bulb are carried carefully concealed by the actor. The wires are hidden in the sleeves. Besides, it is so dark that they will never pick up even if they are left hanging outside. With the open side of the candle held toward the face of the person carrying it, it is not seen from the camera angle, and lights the face and body as though it were a real candle. The real candle on top is lit, of course. The shadows cast by this light are real, and follow the person around. On a

Fig. 112   *Joan Bennett*

Fig. 113

highly lit set, any real candle will do, for it is not used as a light source.

On a set that has many candles, those in the background need not be real ones. They are too far from the camera for the audience to recognize them. Electric imitation candles are used. This saves the time and trouble of lighting and matching them for every scene and take.

Doubles and Their Illumination

In scenes where the Actors' Guild requires the employment of acrobatic doubles, they are kept in a very low key and lit mostly in direct backlight in order that their faces shall not be recognized when they come close to the camera.

Criminal Lighting

Years ago, when in pictures we showed Jimmy Valentine cracking a safe, he usually carried the typical flashlight in one hand, while with the other he worked on the safe combination. In some scenes the flashlight was placed beside him on the floor. In either case the light source was established as a low one. To create an authentic effect, the cameraman lit the character from a low light which illuminated the face from an unusual angle. It distorted the countenance, threw shadows seldom seen in everyday life across the face. This light, which exaggerates features, became so popular that even in our films of today, when we want to call the attention of the audience to a criminal character, we use

Fig. 114 *Dennis O'Keefe and Wallace Ford*

this type of illumination. This is illustrated in Figures 113 and 114.

PRISON SCENES

There is nothing romantic about the drab, gray prison scene. The prison mood can best be presented with display of lights and deep shadows. Black iron bars are the traditional symbol of captivity. It is sufficient to show the black shadows of bars on a wall to indicate that the scene is laid in a prison (Fig. 115). Interiors of a prison should never be bright, even in daylight scenes. For prisoners the sun never rises. There is a constant pressure overhead. Life in captivity is dark. Although modern prisons are well lit in the daytime, the light source for daylight scenes remains

Fig. 115

the traditional prison cell window, high up on the wall. Through this window comes a shaft of sunlight to remind one of the precious freedom that exists outside, in contrast to the gloomy interior. The stronger the light outside, the gloomier is the inside. If the backing is a painted drop, Duarcs are used to brighten up. For a feeling of inpouring sunlight, arc lights are used. This is the light responsible for the shadows of bars on the prison wall. For winter interiors we use the shadowless Duarcs instead of the concentrated arc. These send in a quantity of light, but not direct sunlight. For night interiors of a prison cell, we use the lamp in the corridor as light source. When the lights are out, the moon makes a strong but sad blue light.

LIGHT IS LIBERTY
AND LIBERTY IS LIFE

Where there is light, there is hope. When one is lost in the dark of the night, and suddenly discovers a ray of light in the far-off distance, he begins to feel more at ease. In motion picture photography the turning on of a light, the lighting of a lamp, the arrival of someone with a lantern, or the sudden appearance of any light is used to enhance drama. "Clear as daylight," goes the old saying. Daylight brings relief.

In contrast to captivity there is no greater joy than to be free, to go wherever and whenever one pleases and do whatever one desires. This can best be depicted with gay light. To show the liberation of a prisoner by bringing him out of the gray prison into the glaring sunlight, city traffic, clouds, wind, children playing, birds singing and chirping, is showing the symphony of life itself.

The Radio Dial as a Light Source

The light of a radio dial seems insignificant. Yet, put the light of the room out, and it becomes the light source. If you have observed, you must have noticed that when we turn the radio on, it flashes a bright light on the wall behind it. This lasts but a second and fades out. The light of a radio dial mixed with the light of the dying embers of a fireplace can be used for mystery pictures. A person in this room can see outside in the dark.

The Power of Light

To realize the power of light and what it can do to the mind of an audience, visualize the following little scene:

The room is dark. A strong streak of light sneaks in from the hall under the door. The sound of steps is heard. The shadows of two feet divide the light streak. A brief silence follows. There is suspense in the air. Who is it? What is going to happen? Is he going to ring the bell? Or just insert a key and try to come in? Another heavier shadow appears, and blocks the light entirely. A slight hissing sound is heard, and as the shadow leaves, we see in the dim light a paper slip onto the carpet. The steps are heard again. This time they leave. The strong light appears once again and illuminates the note on the floor. We read it as the steps fade out in the distance:

"It is 10 o'clock. Please turn off your radio. The Manager."

———————————————————————

CHAPTER 4

SPECIAL ILLUMINATION

It would be a risky and costly undertaking to send out an entire crew to photograph a real snow, rain, or dust storm, to wait around on the beach for the real fog to roll in. In Hollywood we prefer to build sets for such scenes, and shoot them inside the huge sound stages free from any outside interference. The illumination of such sets being of a special kind comes under the heading of *special illumination.*

There seems to be an old theory (even some professional photographers adhere to it) that an underlit negative spells night. This has proved to be wrong. All negatives depicting either day or night must be fully exposed. The difference between one and the other is the feeling which the audience immediately recognizes and accepts as day or night. *There is no such thing in motion pictures as a completely blacked-out screen. The audience will not accept it. Always have some kind of light.* Black screens have been tried by some audacious vanguard directors, but without success.

The human eye is so sensitive in the dark to the slightest of lights, that the smallest brightness appears like a strong light; consequently there is a tendency to underlight night exteriors, be they on the stage or outside. It is advisable to be doubly cautious and measure lights with great care to assure proper exposure.

Lighting the Street

Once the light source is determined and the mood established, the illumination proceeds in about the same manner as it would on any other set. Just as the light source of an interior scene is a window in the daytime or a lamp at night, a street has its light sources, which must be considered when establishing the lighting scheme. Another important factor that influences the lighting of a street is the season of the year.

Although the well-known *Main Street* of the small town so familiar to all is fast disappearing from the scene, in pictures it still exists and will for some time continue to do so. To understand the lighting of streets we must first know the existing light sources. As the clock advances, so changes the light and with it the mood of the scene.

The first lights to go on are the store lights followed by the city lights, the street lamps on the corner. Then come the lights of private residence windows, apartment house entrances, bars, cafes, neon and other advertising signs, automobile headlights, the streetcars, light effects of matches, the cop's flashlight, and others. Add to this the fires of old boxes on the sidewalks and you have the neighborhood street of the metropolis.

Later on the stores go dark, the neon signs go out, people retire for the night, and only the bars remain alive, showing an occasional splash of light as doors open. Streetlights are still on, and when those too go out only the moonlight remains, to be replaced soon by the first inkling of daylight.

The light on residential streets is different from that of the business section. Here we

Fig. 116 *Paris*

often see the light in front of the home, a lantern in the garden, or a ray of light escaping through the curtains from the living room.

SLUMS AND WATER FRONTS

These places are usually poorly lit and ideally suited for criminal pictures. Occasionally a truck passes by with its glaring headlights. A bar with its electric sign, a cheap hotel with its fluctuating sign, and the night watchman passing with his flashlight, checking on door entrances, all contribute to the lighting of a street scene. When all lights go out here too, nature's own huge light, the moon, illuminates the scene.

In the distance a ferryboat is crossing, and we see the reflected lights of a passing ship on the oily waters of the bay. All this is accompanied by the noise of a juke box, called music.

FOREIGN STREETS

Figures 116, 117, 118, 119, 120, and 121 show various foreign streets in daylight. Some

Fig. 117 *Old Jerusalem*

Fig. 118 *Yesterday*

Fig. 119   *São Paulo, Brazil*

Fig. 120   *Old Turkey*

Fig. 121   *Rio*

of the big cities in foreign countries still light their streets with gaslight. But many streets are still in ruins, a reminder of World War II, and only the bleak moonlit stones are visible, with occasionally a mysterious shadow passing by.

In the small towns of Europe when the peasant has done his day's work and had his dinner, he goes outside on the street to smoke his pipe. There in front of his little but clean house sits the entire family, discussing the topics of the day, until the last vestiges of daylight disappear. The only artificial light that follows on these streets is that of the village inn where celebration goes on as usual.

Rain

"I just love to drive in the rain," one hears so often. What could be the reason for one to "love to drive" on a dangerously slippery, oily street in the rain? One answer is *light-play*—reflections on the shiny, wet surface of the street. They are music.

For motion pictures rain must be produced artificially. The most common method is the use of rain pipes, which are rigged over the entire set about to be photographed under rain (Fig. 122). In addition to this, another spray of water is used from a fire hose in the foreground directly in front of the camera. For those who wish to economize, the poor man's rain effect can be produced with just the water in front of the lens covering the entire picture, and in the background some people walking around with shiny umbrellas. This will give a perfect illusion of rain on the set.

Many a cameraman after having looked at

59

Fig. 122

the rushes of the first rain assignment in his photographic career has left the projection room with a puzzled, surprised look on his face. Somehow or other the rain just did not pick up. It could not be the laboratory. No, that excuse is old-fashioned. There is no developer that can eliminate rain drops from a picture. The only explanation is that it was not illuminated right.

In order to make rain register on the screen it must be lighted in a special way—backlighted. This light is reflected by the millions of the rain drops, and we have a curtain of rain. Frontlight goes right through it. If possible, we shoot rain scenes against a black background.

As there is usually no moon out when it rains at night it would be a mistake to have a keylight or any shadows at all unless caused by other light sources, such as a street lamp, a store, a window, etc. Some cameramen have tried to shoot real rain, but only for reasons of economy. In some instances these scenes turned out to be impressively realistic.

In reality the set should be dark, but for purposes of photography we need some kind of a light, even if its source is invisible. This is accomplished by diffusing all concentrated lights, or using only light reflected by white screens, which gives us the *no principal light* feeling of rainy nights.

When it rains the pavement is wet and reflects all existing light sources. We must be careful with strong backlights—they pick up. For interiors a rain-spattered window is sufficient to establish the weather outside. This is economical and very effective.

After the rain the atmosphere is usually clear. This mood can be used to symbolize a dramatic situation, as for instance, to parallel a scene of clarification of a psychological problem.

Summer Moonlight

In real life when we see two people walk on a moonlit street they are usually backlit, silhouetted against the haze or lighter walls. As we come closer to them, in the same light we begin to discern faces and other details. In photography it is different. The lens of the camera has no automatically changing iris, nor has it an imagination. It sees only what there actually is. Its iris cannot close at will. This lack has to be corrected with the aid of light and scissors (cutting).

In long shots where the general atmosphere is important it does not matter whether we see faces or not. It is the picture as a whole that counts. But as we approach the dark figures, the audience anticipates seeing details. They were trained for that. They want to see facial expression that helps tell the story. So we build up the front light in medium shots and cut to close-ups for facial expressions, always retaining the moonish, mysterious feeling established in the long shot.

For moonlight effect use a single light

source. Shadows should be opaque. Arc lights are ideal for this purpose. For light that comes out of stores inkies can be added to the lights already in use, in order to retain the yellowish tinge. Moonlight should come from one direction, although this need not be followed out in different setups.

Autumn Fog

The feeling of fog scenes is by no means a gay one. The tendency of nature is to use fog to cover up. In motion pictures it is most used in dramatic scenes (Fig. 123). Its illumination should parallel this feeling, and should be in a low key.

Like rain, fog also must be produced artificially for interior motion picture photography. In order to understand the intricate illumination of fog we need to know something of how fog is produced artificially. There are several known ways of making fog; we may use atomized Nujol, steam, dry ice, smoke from burned magnesium, a plain smoke bomb that fills the stage, or fog filters. Although the special effects department of each studio has developed its secret fog formula, atomized Nujol is the most universally used. When Nujol is sprayed by the fog machine, its millions of translucent particles fill the atmosphere, remaining there just long enough for the scene to be photographed. This cloud of oil vapor can be moved by means of a blower to imitate a rolling fog. The oily particles of atomized Nujol settle on the faces of actors, creating a sheen of reflective quality that picks up all incident light. This property gives it a realistic feeling.

Magnesium produces a fog at lower cost, but one that is less effective than vaporized Nujol. Good enough results have been obtained with it as the poor man's fog. A handful of magnesium is placed on a tin pan and lit. This causes an explosion which fills the atmosphere with smoke particles that photograph like fog. They settle rapidly, so a new explosion is required for almost every take.

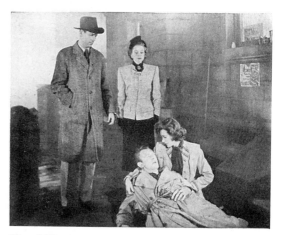

Fig. 123

If neither Nujol nor magnesium is available, or if the space is too big to be filled with either, fog filters can be used. The effect of filters is entirely different from that of any vapor. It is more like an evenly distributed, heavy diffusion with no feeling of depth at all. Its only good feature is that it throws circles around lamps which actually resemble those of real fog. Fog filters are usually made of glass, and come in different densities. There is, however, an old-fashioned fog filter little known any more. It is made of a white, gauzelike material, and is placed in front of the lens and backlit.

FOG ILLUMINATION

Whenever a scene is going to be photographed through the heavy, pea soup-like artificial fog, it needs a special lighting treatment. Fog has a tendency to flatten out the light, to reduce highlights. It also absorbs a considerable part of the light. It takes the actinic value out of it, making it a red light without any guts. Exposure must be calculated accordingly. We light on a higher key and with greater contrast than we would under normal conditions and measure the light through the fog. A strong frontlight has a tendency to thin out the fog. This helps in lighting a close-up, making it stand out while in the background the fog continues to roll heavy. To get depth we use a wide-angle lens; out-of-focus fog is very unpleasant to look at.

Fog photographs lighter than it looks to the eye. Actors are dressed in dark wardrobe so that they stand out against the back haze. In the foreground where the action takes place the fog should be thinner. This makes the figures stand out with a remarkable third-dimensional feeling.

Fog is particularly suitable for outstanding light effects in the form of shafts of light. Backlight should be carefully employed, because the rays of lamps pick up easily. If possible the entire field of vision should be covered with backlight instead of just an arc ray here and there.

Practical lights should be on all the time, whether fog is used in day or night scenes.

Dust storms, Turkish baths, tear gas, and other smoke bomb effects behave like fog under artificial light. Their illumination is like that of fog (Fig. 124).

Fig. 124

Wintertime

With winter comes dances, with dances come dresses. For dresses we need to have make-up, and for make-up, mirrors. People like to look into mirrors. Perhaps this is because the light reflected from their shiny surfaces causes a pleasant sensation—a psycho-physiological pleasure. When looking into a mirror, the eye cannot focus on both the surface and the image reflected in it; it splits its focus. This creates a pleasant, soft-focus effect. It is readily apparent that split focus is not a Hollywood invention; it existed when the surfaces of lakes or of highly polished copper plates were the mirrors, long before pictures were made in Hollywood.

MIRROR ILLUMINATION

There is hardly a film nowadays in which one is not confronted by the problem of lighting a mirror scene. By softening the vision and so taking off the harsh lines, mirrors diffuse the picture to such a degree that it appears beautiful, pleasant to look at.

Cheap glass mirrors should be avoided because they have a tendency to distort faces. This is not discernible with the eye, but definitely shows in the picture when it is too late to correct; select a good mirror. All mirrors absorb light, but cheap glass is green, and absorbs more than does a white plate glass.

The lighting of a mirror scene presents quite a problem, especially if the mirror is up against a wall. Shooting straight at the mirror would reflect the camera, the crew, and all the lights, so we shoot at an angle. Figures 125 and 126 show how a scene of a person sitting in front of a huge mirror while making up should be illuminated.

The keylight is placed near the camera, high enough so that its image cannot appear in the mirror (A). Intensity of the keylight should be read from its reflection, for accuracy. The reflection of the reflector illuminates the person sitting before the mirror, and therefore becomes the actual keylight (B). The reflector itself acts as a backlight. For filler light, eyelight, and clotheslight, both the person and his reflection are illuminated.

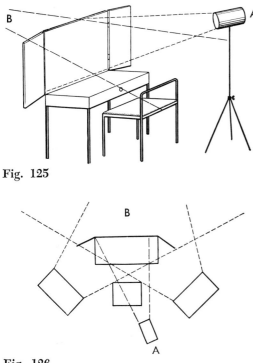

Fig. 125

Fig. 126

A hanger on the wall may help place some of these lights. To create an illusion of depth, walls reflected in the mirror should be dressed, cleared, and lit more strongly than the wall around the mirror.

ICE

If ice were used in motion pictures only in the ice revues, its illumination would belong with that of musical comedies. As used in other types of screen plays, however, the nature of its illumination is different. In motion pictures certain surfaces do not look real at all when photographed as they are; ice is one of them. Normally lit natural white ice photographs as dirty, and if slightly overlit it burns

up. To improve its pictorial quality, the temperamental ice had to be made up. Experiments were made with painting the surface of ice used in the scene of a picture. After a few spills by the skaters, and consequent slightly bruised legs and sprained ankles, this system was abandoned. The experiments with ice make-up continued. Good results were attained by painting the ice, and when the paint was dry, adding a coating or two of transparent ice on top of it. The question of color came up. Several tints were tried until finally we arrived at blue as being the best of all.

ICE ILLUMINATION

With strong illumination, blue ice can be photographed light, but with the light kept off, it photographs dark. Against this dark shade of blue the flesh color of girls' legs stands out in desired contrast to please all. Blue ice is also ideal if the ice happens to be the surface of a lake. It looks as though it reflected the blue of the sky.

The illumination of people on ice is similar to that of any other musical comedy or drama, depending on what the scene may be.

Ice photographs best when its surface is wet. This makes it look like a huge horizontal mirror, and its illumination is not unlike that of any other reflective surface. It reflects the set behind it and the people with their attractive costumes. Before the scene is taken the surface of the ice is first scraped clean, absolutely smooth. Then it is sprayed with a thin layer of fresh water, just sufficient to shine, but not enough to ripple when skaters pass over it. The water should cover up all the skate marks on the ice. Once the top transparent surface becomes worn off, it is dangerous to skate over it. Again it is scraped, but usually after the day's work is done, and fresh water is frozen on top of it overnight.

Up to not so long ago sets in Hollywood studios were made up of walls alone without any ceiling. On top of the walls were the platforms holding the reflectors used to illuminate the set. The lamps were there and it was easy to have them turned on. That explains why so many of our pictures were much overlit. In illuminating ice, backlight is too much abused for good photography of a picture. From certain high setups the reflections of backlight pick up on the wet surface of the ice. Experiments and experience have taught us that omitting most of the backlight not only eliminates unwanted reflections of reflectors (and is an economical measure), but definitely improves the photography of the picture because it looks more natural. In the past when wooden ceilings reflected in the ice they were painted black. This involved work, time, and expense. Today we concentrate our lights on sets and people and leave everything else on the stage dipped in black light, in absolute darkness. Only in scenes when reflections of reflectors are desirable should we use backlight from above. Sometimes the reflection of a single arc can be used for the moon, and quite effectively.

BLACK ICE

Although blue photographs dark, if you want absolutely black ice, black is still the best color to use. Against this brilliant black ice people should wear light or shiny metal costumes. Sets should be painted in ivory color. This gives a perfect reflection. Backlight has a tendency to *milk*—fog—the black ice. It should be kept off.

Photographing ice surfaces offers an opportunity for many tricks. By spraying the ice lightly the surface ice becomes rippled and destroys the image of reflection. As the spraying stops and the water surface settles again, the image once more becomes visible, clear. The picture reveals itself, it *fades in*. For fade-outs the procedure is reversed. As the water on the ice absorbs quite a lot of the light, the reflection of the keylight must be measured. We overlight the people.

POLISHED SURFACES

All polished surfaces with a luster, wet surfaces, polished floors of dancing places or of night clubs, shiny furniture, oil-painted walls, objects of art, tea sets, silver of any kind, etc., should be lit indirectly. Leave the direct light off them and let them reflect the surrounding, well-lit images. For example, a dark piano photographs better by leaving all direct light off. We just let it reflect a nearby lamp, or for day scenes a sunlit window. If we light shiny objects directly they may pick up the filament of the light source and cause a glare.

ARTIFICIAL SNOW

Several forms of artificial snow have been tried in shooting snow scenes. Entire crews, lights and all, were taken to frigid air chambers and there scraped ice was used. This was also tried on the set at the studio. Then bleached corn flakes were tried and were found to be the most economical, retaining their great resemblance to real snow. Individual flakes float like real snow flakes through the air currents created by wind machines. For snow on the ground gypsum powder can be used. A sprinkle of mica dust gives it the Christmas-tree sparkle.

For imitation snow on evergreens, first wet the trees. Then place heavy pieces of absorbent cotton on the branches. When this is done, wet the cotton and pour corn flakes on it. To make it glamorous sprinkle it with mica dust. With an occasional handful of corn flakes thrown in the machine-made wind we get a nice snow scene (Fig. 127).

Whereas rain drops have to be lit from the rear, snow flakes must be lit from the front, or they just don't pick up. If the background is dark it helps bring out the white snow. The illumination of artificial snow is as complicated as is the lighting of real snow. The presence of two light sources, the original

Fig. 127 *Snow Machine*

(the reflector) and the reflected (the snow) puzzles the beginner.

If the scene happens to represent a street scene, we imitate natural illumination and follow out the patterns made by well-known traditional light sources, the moon, the light of store windows, street lamps, torches, and the like. If the scene is of a musical comedy, it belongs in the category of dreamlike lighting.

Dream Lighting

It is one thing to give a musical comedy a dreamlike lighting, and another to illuminate a scene depicting a dream. There is no limit in lighting scenes of this nature. One really can go from the sublime to the ridiculous and get away with it. The more original the lighting of a dream and the more imagination used, the more effective it can be. For such scenes it helps to design illogical sets sprinkled with odd shadows (Figs. 128, 129).

Train Light Effects

Overlighting black objects was one of the serious mistakes of the old school of motion picture photography. To get good results, we light a railroad station normally, following the patterns of existing light sources. These can be the light from the station, outside lamps, or, on a dark, deserted station, the light emanating from the train itself.

Fig. 128

The light effect on a figure illuminated by light from a moving train can be simulated in various ways. One is to use a revolving cylinder with pieces of mirror mounted on it, similar to those used in dance halls, but in cylindrical form. A strong, concentrated light is projected into this, which in turn throws a moving light on the person, giving the illusion of light coming from the windows of a moving train. The apparent speed of the train is controlled by the speed of rotation of the cylinder. Another system is the revolving cyclodrum used on the process stage for the purpose of making shadows, etc. A strong arc light in the center of the drum throws a fluctuating light through the moving windows suggesting the passing of a train.

Long shots of a Pullman interior after the beds are made can be dark, with an occasional shaft of light coming from one or two sections. A nice light effect is created when the conductor passes with his lantern.

Flares lit as emergency lights behind trains

Fig. 129 *Lynn Bari and Donald Curtis*

make interesting lightings. If intense enough no artificial lighting is necessary.

Some studios have their own little railroad stations; they have no train problems. It is the smaller companies that have the headaches when it comes to train scenes. They learned from the old saying, "necessity is the mother of invention." Because they cannot afford to build a real moving train, they build an imitation, and instead of moving the train they move the camera (but in the opposite direction), and get the same or at least similar results. This is done by putting the camera on a dolly on tracks. To this dolly another is attached. On the second dolly there are trunks and other props found on a railroad station platform, people waving their hand-

kerchiefs, and the station master with the customary bell, etc. We move the camera in the opposite direction to that in which we want the train to move. The result on the screen is a moving train (try it sometime). Steam blown past the windows adds to the realism.

It may seem strange, but the interior of a train compartment is lit lighter for night shots than it is for day scenes. This is because in the daytime the light comes in from the outside leaving the inside dim, while at night it is lighted artificially from the inside.

Most Hollywood pictures show night train interiors with beautiful romantic cloudy backgrounds shot in the daytime with night filters. This of course is not true to life. They fit some of the chocolate-coated films, but if you want realism you must light realistically. When the lights are on inside a train compartment, there is very little to be seen of the outside. The modern train is well illuminated inside; this kills all outside lights. Only if the train passes a highly lit railroad station, another train with lighted interiors, auto headlights, or street lights and lighted advertising of towns in the dark of night, can we see the background.

If we turn the lights out, the outside becomes clearly visible. For such scenes and for day interiors of a train, a background process or transparency screen is necessary.

Everybody knows how a train looks inside. Therefore the illumination of such sets should be as realistic and true to life as possible. Lamps inside the train are high, so keylights are placed high. Inside made-up berths when reading lights are on, the light can come from the side of the lamp.

An interesting light effect for a night interior of a train compartment is achieved by showing the reflection of a man (Fig. 130) on the glass pane of the window.

We separate the platform of lights from the set, so that when the train is shaken the lights won't shake with it. We shake only when outside of the train; once inside, riding is pretty soft, and no shaking is necessary. Foreign trains may be shaken both inside and outside—it will never even approach realism. They are pretty rough riding.

Fig. 130   *Alfred Ryder*

Interior of a Plane

The interior of a plane is similar to that of a train. The lights of towns directly below or approaching lights on the flying fields are sometimes visible. The interior illumination is like that of a train compartment. For key-light we use the swinging key.

Steamship Interiors

The modern ship is built in such a way that the ocean is not always visible from inside. Windows in the dining room, bar, etc., are "blind." Lighting inside is indirect. Especially in the bar, everybody—I mean everything—is lit from the inside. The illumination of these sets falls into the category of normal set lighting.

Tents

For day interiors of a tent, we have the walls backlit, with shadows of tree branches or of people walking by projected on them. For night shots we place the light source inside, or when in total darkness, use the moon, lighting the tent walls from outside as in day scenes. A scene showing rows of tents in a camp, where all lights are extinguished as taps is blown, makes an impressive picture.

Gags and Tricks

Many a scene with gags requires the use of wires. For this purpose we use the thinnest of piano wire; it is usually dull, but can be shiny if the situation requires. Lines of shadows on the background of the picture directly behind the scene help to disguise the wires. We keep light off the wires, and in night scenes if possible have a little object like a hot lamp right in the foreground to distract the attention of the audience from the wire.

Transparency or Process Photography

One of the least publicized departments of motion picture photography is the *background process department*, better known as the *process department*. It is well that imaginative writers create the most fantastic scenes taking place in the remote corners of the world under all climates and conditions. But they must be put on the screen, and it is up to the transparency department to put them there.

COMBINED PHOTOGRAPHY

In the old European armies, when a soldier was discharged he received a diploma-like, engraved discharge paper. On it were his name, record, and in the middle a headless soldier standing near a table and dressed in the uniform of his regiment, holding his cap in his right hand. With this diploma, he went to a near-by photographer who made a picture of his head and printed it into the empty space, completing the picture of the soldier. As the soldier's cap was printed on the paper as being held in his hand, he was photographed without his cap on. Sometimes in the great rush this was overlooked and the soldier forgot to take his cap off. The final picture showed the soldier with two caps, one on his head and one in his hand! As far as I can remember, these were the first combined photographs.

BACKDROPS

Later on came the backdrops representing different exteriors. A person was photographed against one of these drops as though he were standing in the garden, in the mountains, or on the beach. These backings are still in use in photo studios of amusement parks. This was the beginning of background photography. Experiments continued, and enlarged photographs of authentic backgrounds replaced the painted drops. They are still in use in motion picture photography, especially in the latest rear-illuminated translite forms (Fig. 131). The enlarged photograph was replaced by the transparent screen where

Hedy Lamarr

background action scenes could be combined with foreground action. This phase of combining pictures is called the *background process* or *transparency photography.* Figure 132 shows a scene with plain background, and Figure 133 shows a similar scene with process background.

During the war, millions of soldiers were sent to various locations to shoot, but not motion pictures. These men know a real London fog, were disappointed in the women of the jungle, and recognize Rio, Budapest, or Cairo when they see them on the screen. No more will they buy Hollywood-made Africa. Backgrounds now have to be authentic.

Long before a film goes into production, the process department, like all others, receives a shooting script. It is studied carefully, and from this it is decided how many scenes will be shot with process photography, and how many plates and stereos will be needed. If the process library does not happen to have the necessary plates, a *second unit* is dispatched to shoot them. Sometimes they take along the wardrobe of principal players and use doubles. Stolen shots are made of passers-by, sometimes with the camera hidden from view in order not to attract attention.

Fig. 131

Fig. 132

MINIATURES

Process photography is used also to provide such background action as fires, explosions, and mountain landslides. *Miniatures* of the desired scenes are built and photographed in the studio; the speed of the camera is set to match the scale of the miniature model. The reflectors used for illumination of miniatures are smaller in size than those used in ordinary set illumination. Although miniatures are handled by a separate department, their illumination must be supervised by the director of photography. The process of lighting miniatures is slow, and requires patience; it is an art by itself.

Fig. 133

69

Fig. 134 *Ted Weisbarth Photo*

THE KEY

When the background is developed and printed it is called the *key*. (Sometimes I wonder whether there are not more keys than directors in the movie industry. We have the key grip, low key, high key, keylight, the key of the picture, key technicians. The inventor must have been a locksmith.) There are two kinds of keys, one with life action, called a *plate,* and another without motion, called a *stereo.*

The word *plate* in motion picture background photography refers to a strip of film, not a glass plate such as those sometimes used in still cameras instead of films. The plate should be made about 200 feet long in order to avoid the necessity for repeated re-

winds for additional takes. The plate is photographed with a regular 35 mm motion picture camera, but the frame aperture is opened to the so-called *full aperture* in order to utilize that part of the film ordinarily reserved for the sound track, and thus to obtain as large a picture as possible. When the camera is not to be moved or panned, it must be anchored securely to insure steadiness. This is done with a pair of small camera jacks or by tying a heavy weight under the tripod.

A special fine-grain film is used, and it is specially developed and printed to make it suitable for rephotographing. The old theory that a plate must be "washed out" is now obsolete; a good plate more than any other scene needs a range of densities from deep black to hot white; the greater the range, the better is the reproduction.

It is advisable to have at least two prints of the plate on hand, one dark and one lighter. Besides, if one gets worn out from rehearsals or gets scratched, the second one is needed. Old plates with shrunk sprocket holes usually are destroyed.

To the amateur photographer, a *stereo* means a stereoscopic pair of pictures which, viewed in a stereoscope, give a third-dimensional effect. In motion picture process photography, however, a stereo is a transparent glass plate positive, which may be a contact print from a 4 by 5 inch negative, or one produced by reduction from an 8 by 10 inch negative. The negative for the stereo is made in either a 4 by 5 inch Speed Graphic or an 8 by 10 inch view camera. The stereo is projected on the transparency screen in the same manner as is the plate. Stereos are more convenient to use than are plates because they need no rewinding for successive takes. They are good indefinitely because they do not shrink. Figures 134, 135, and 136 show typical stereos without any background action.

PROCESS TOOLS

The following are the special tools used in process photography:

1. Background projector (Figs. 137 and 138)
2. Transparency screen

Fig. 135 *Ted Weisbarth Photo*

Fig. 136 *Ted Weisbarth Photo*

3. Standard 35 mm camera with interlock motor
4. Communication system from camera to projector
5. Motor-driven cyclodrum
6. Wind machine (Fig. 139)
7. Silent electric fan (Fig. 140)
8. Cobweb machine (Fig. 141)

The screen for process photography is made of a translucent cellulose material; it has a smooth side on which the picture is projected, and a rough side facing the camera. When the scene is being photographed, the camera and projector are interlocked, and the two scenes, foreground and background, are combined. For pan shots more than one screen can be used. Spaces between screens must be covered by part of the set, or carefully concealed by shrubbery, trees, or similar objects.

Fig. 137 *Teague Process Machine*

Fig. 138

Fig. 140   *Silent Electric Fan*

Fig. 139   *Wind Machine*

Fig. 141   *Cobweb Machine*

PROCESS ILLUMINATION

Although in general, rigging and lighting for process photography differ little from the procedure for an ordinary scene, there are some special tricks. No stray light must be allowed to reach the screen because it would spoil the quality of the plate. For that reason, very little front light is used, and any filler light must come from up high. Keylights are usually cross, or if a front keylight must be used, superfluous light is goboed off the screen. If the person being photographed is above floor level, a low filler light also can be used.

The plate is run first, and the light source is decided upon. Then the foreground, scenery, and people are lit. The light must be so balanced that foreground and background appear to merge. A tree, a bench, water, or a shadow or two can help blend together the parts of the picture where the set ends and the screen begins. Care must be taken to light the set so that sunlight or moonlight in both foreground and background appears to come from the same direction. Any mistakes in this respect make the picture look fakey, and the audience will recognize it immediately.

AUTOMOBILE INTERIORS

Interiors of automobiles showing passengers (Fig. 142) are not shot on actual location; it is simpler, much faster, and more economical to shoot them on the process stage.

For this purpose a mock-up is used. Formerly it was part of an old wrecked automobile, but now specially constructed mock-ups are made for the purpose (Fig. 143). They can look like new cars and also can be taken apart (Figs. 144, 145, 146). An actor sitting at the steering wheel cannot see the screen behind him, and therefore does not know when the car is supposed to be turning; it looks fakey on the screen when the road turns and the steering wheel remains still. To remedy this, a special effects man on the floor watches the screen, and by moving the arm shown at the lower right of Figure 147, turns the wheel when the car is supposed to turn. To give the effect of a moving vehicle, moving shadows are projected on the people seated in it. The

Fig. 142 *Marsha Hunt and Dennis O'Keefe*

Fig. 143

Fig. 144

Fig. 145

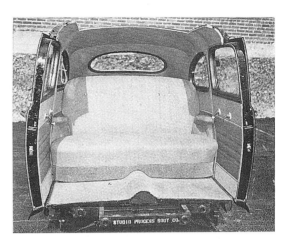

Fig. 146

Fig. 147

greater the speed of the shadows the faster the car seems to go, and when motion of the shadow stops, the car appears to have stopped also.

What do we see of an automobile at night? The headlights. Why, then, go to the trouble and expense of shooting plates? Use the poor man's process. Get two flashlights and mount them on a tripod; then have someone move them around on a dark stage behind your car so that they will be visible through the rear window. It is economical and the result will be novel and extremely interesting.

TRAIN SHOTS BY PROCESS

Reasons of economy often require that train shots be made on the process stage. For realistic lighting the light source may be a flat light from the front, or a beautiful backlight through a window; in the latter case the faces are silhouetted. To get a feeling of motion the train set is shaken a bit; moving the camera back and forth also helps.

THE MERRY GO BACKGROUND

This is a huge disk that revolves like a phonograph record. If you put trees on it and revolve it, it has the appearance of the countryside seen from a moving train. It can be used to shoot miniature plates just by changing the scenery.

TOMORROW'S PROCESS

Modern camera technique calls for a free, flexible camera, yet when we want to shoot up or down against a transparency screen we are told that it is impossible. The picture diagrams (Figs. 148, 149, 150), offer a constructive improvement designed to solve this prob-lem of process flexibility. Figure 148 shows the mechanism in normal position:

A. The projector
B. Stationary screen in frame
C. Camera
D. The floor, which is made up of sections. No matter what the position of mechanism, these sections remain level.
E. One axis on which floor mechanism rests
F. Base of the entire mechanism
G. Floor of pit
H. Side walls of pit
I. Safety railing at edge of pit
J. Center of mechanism
K. Connecting rod of floor sections
L. Subframe of transparency screen (not visible in Fig. 148)
M. Detachable safety railing for crew (can be inserted in any section)
N. Auxiliary ladder leading down to bottom of pit

Figure 149 shows the mechanism in position with the camera shooting up, and with the screen parallel between camera and projector. The cast remains level all the time. This low position enables one to shoot at high buildings, up at the clouds, airplanes, mountains, etc.

Figure 150 shows the mechanism in a position where the camera is shooting down. Again the screen is parallel with the camera.

Fig. 148

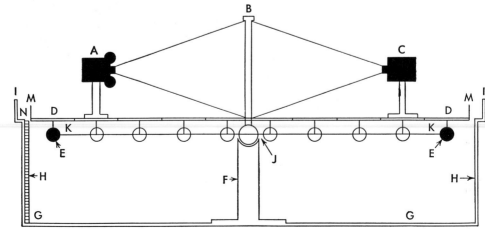

This position is ideal for shots down into the valley from an airplane, down a city street from a skyscraper, and a great variety of down shots used in today's modern camera setups.

The mechanism is so built that the weight of people or props can be balanced from the other side. Both the director of photography and the director of process are on the camera side. It is from this side that the entire operation is directed (at last, something is directed). Here is the intercommunication system, also a warning signal which sounds as the mechanism descends or rises. This helps to avoid accidents. There is also an auxiliary ladder, so that if someone wants to get off the platform, he can do so without moving the mechanism. Scenes can be shot while the mechanism is standing still, or in motion to give the effect of camera movement. At the pressing of a button, the mechanism goes into operation, and all movements are synchronized. With this new improvement, it is up to all the three directors, and, of course, the imaginative writer, to go ahead and try something new.

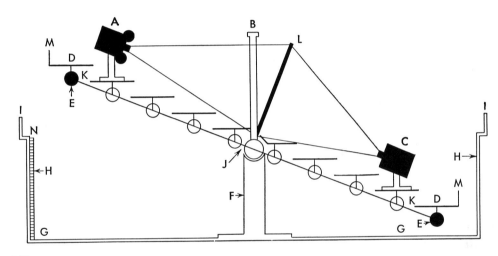

Fig. 149

Fig. 150

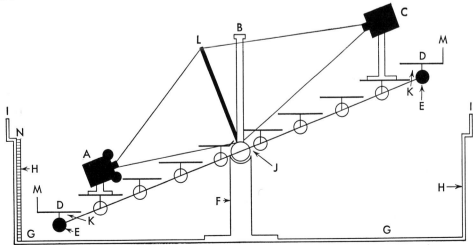

THE TURNTABLE

"Process shooting is slow" goes the old saying, which is absolutely wrong. Process shooting can be as fast, if not faster than the regular procedure. Only the process stage needs improvements. One thing that would speed up process shooting is the *turntable*. Let me explain it.

When we shoot a scene on the process stage, usually several angles of the same scene are necessary for cutting purposes. If we want another angle, the entire set has to be changed, turned around. Suppose we are shooting the interior of an auto. First, we shoot the straight-on angle. When that is in the box, the director wants another, perhaps a three-quarter angle. The car has to be moved around. The motor is running, and the stage is filled with poisonous carbon monoxide gas. The cast and crew complain of headaches, everybody is sleepy, and there is a general slowdown in production speed. Nobody even suspects the real trouble. The car is finally put in place for the next angle. The scene is rehearsed, the lamps which had to be removed are reset, the set is relit, and the scene

is retaken. All of this takes time, and if we want a reverse angle on top of it, it will take more time, which in production lingo means money. An auto is easily moved around, but suppose we have a more complicated set, such as a South Sea island, palm trees, huts, fishing nets, etc., or any other complicated type of construction. Suppose it is a Pullman car. What then? Either the director is discouraged from taking the necessary angles, and the picture quality suffers, or it means a complete re-dress, relight, re-everything, and everybody suffers. We send for more men to move the scenery. So we wait and wait, while the entire crew is sitting around and chewing the fat.

For years, I have been endeavoring to replace this rather primitive and expensive system with a faster, more economical, but at the same time, practical one. The answer is a *built-in turntable* on the process stage, in front of the transparency screen. Its installation might be a bit costly, but considering its advantages, it would more than pay for itself. Figures 151 and 152 show the turntable in a side and top view.

Fig. 151

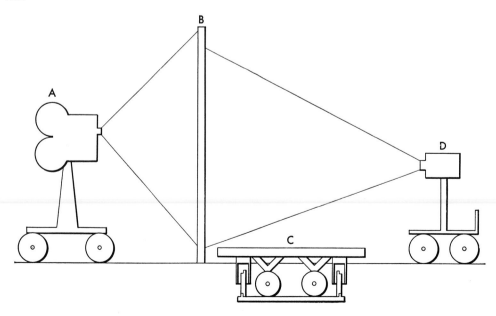

A is the background projector.
B is the transparency screen.
C is the turntable.
D is the camera.

Vehicles are placed and sets are built right on top of the turntable. As the lights are not going to be removed, they too can be left there. When we want to change the angle, all we have to do is press a button, watch the set turn, and stop it at the exact spot we would like to shoot.

Anyone with a little imagination can immediately grasp the unlimited possibilities which open up with the use of this new, perhaps radical device. Reforms of any kind are never unanimously welcomed. Remember, this is offered as an idea only, subject to improvements, as sometimes one idea starts an avalanche of others. It is now up to the inventive genius of writers, directors, and cinematographers to take advantage of it and improve our present day pictures.

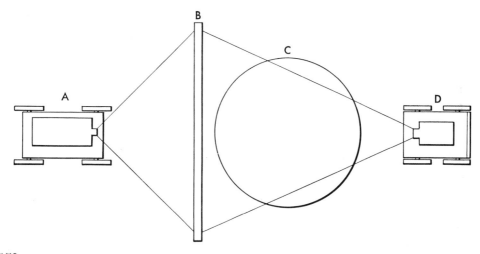

Fig. 152

THE HOLLYWOOD CLOSE–UP

Starlight

The old like to look young, the young younger. We have all heard people say they could not have their pictures taken because they were not *photogenic*. This silly obsession has proved to be a fallacy. Just look at the gorgeous close-ups of the stars in Hollywood films. True, most of the stars are really beautiful; but those who are not are made so with the aid of an artistic hairdo, a touch of magic make-up, and the unquestionably hypnotic power of carefully distributed lights and shadows. Not all of us are born beautiful. Good photography can supply what nature has sometimes failed to give us, beauty, charm, good posture.

It is much more difficult to light for movies than for still photography. Therefore, we shall use the former for the purpose of illustration. Movie lighting technique can be applied to any kind of photography. If you can light for movies, you can light, period.

The Close-up Is Born

Ages ago, the cave-scratchers made portraits of their favorites. The Egyptians carved them on stone walls. Silhouette invented the making of a likeness that was named after him. Stieglitz, the great American photographic artist, made outstanding portraits long ago; but it took the film industry a long time to invent the motion picture close-up.

For years, action films were photographed from a distance. All you could see on the screen were clouds of dust. While screening such a film, some people suddenly felt that there was something wrong. They wanted to see more of the actors' faces. They ordered retakes with more light poured on them. The result was burned-up, overlit faces, but they were still too far away for facial expression to be appreciated.

It took cinematographers years of heated discussion to prove a simple truth: that in order to make faces distinguishable, it is a mistake to overlight long shots. In life when we want to speak to a person, we approach him. Why not do the same in motion pictures? Seats in theatres are fastened down. When the audience feels the desire to see more of an actor, it cannot possibly move closer to the screen. It is far easier to bring the actor closer to the audience by cutting or dollying to a closer view of him, featuring the face only, where a twitch of a muscle or a wink of an eye can sometimes tell the story. On the legitimate stage, an electromagnetic contact is established between the actor and audience. This cannot be done in motion picture theatres. The best we can do is a one-way transmission of energy from the screen to the audience. Hence the importance of close-ups.

Rules for Close-up Illumination

As far as I know, there are no rules or laws for the creation of close-ups or portraits. It takes time, patience, good taste, and a sense of balance. However, if we closely analyze

Fig. 153 *Mary Meade*

Fig. 154

pictures of great masters of light, we find that to illuminate a beautiful close-up, we must observe the following:

1. Angles
2. Size
3. Composition—foreground and background
4. Theme—emphasis on center of interest

ANGLES

Setups in long shots are varied to tell the story from the proper angle. In close-ups, the reasons for changing angles are manifold. In feminine close-ups, the most important is to beautify the star, to correct and to symmetrize. If you study faces, you will find that

some people have impossible profiles, while others look better in profile than in full face. Some look their best from a three-quarter angle. You will also notice that, in most faces, one half of the face is different from the other. Very few people have symmetrical faces, with both halves equal. Search for the best angle, and when found, use it.

SIZE

Why do we make close-ups? To see the face. That being the case, let us see the face only and leave out everything secondary, or at least keep it subdued in tone. Limit the size of the portrait or close-up to whatever you are trying to feature.

COMPOSITION OF CLOSE–UPS

When we look into a mirror, we look at our eyes. When we look at a picture of any kind, we instinctively look at the upper part of it. This is because the eyes are in the upper part of the face. If we haven't found in the picture what we are looking for, our eyes start to travel. Therefore, whenever possible, place features of interest in the upper part of the picture, or, as we call it in pictures, above the *half-line* (Fig. 153).

FOREGROUND IN CLOSE–UPS

Foreground pieces should be employed with great care in composing close-ups or portraits. They can easily distract. Never use a lighted lamp, over-exposed curtains, or any other hot object in the foreground, because light catches the eye; they should be in the background. By the time the eye accustoms itself to the bright light, either the scene is over, or the iris of the eye is so closed down that the face featured in this instance appears entirely too dark. If they have to be used, inasmuch as they are already established, then dim them down considerably. In two-shots, have the lamp in the center (Fig. 154), in single close-ups, ahead of the face, never behind. Especially are hot spots unpleasant to look at when they are out of focus. If you have to have a foreground piece, keep it dark. Venetian blinds make excellent foreground pieces.

The old-fashioned idea that, in making a close-up in motion picture photography, the head of the person had to be in the exact center of the picture is now taboo. A head can be in a corner or on the side of the picture. Combined with some objet d'art or some decorative theme, it can make a perfectly balanced and acceptable composition (Fig. 155). The frame and part of a painting showing an exterior make an excellent combination with a head close-up.

Eyes usually should be in the upper part

Fig. 155

Fig. 156

of the picture. Figure 156 shows how a picture looks when the eyes are placed in the lower half. No matter how beautiful a hat may be, cut it in half if it stops you from putting the wearer's eyes in the upper part of the picture. When a person looks up, place him in the lower part of the composition;

83

when he looks down, put him in the upper part (Fig. 157). Figure 158 shows how mistaken you can be in placing them in the wrong part. Generally, leave more room at the side of the picture toward which the subject is looking. This allows the imagination to travel. Behind the head is yesterday, uninteresting. We cannot change it. Ahead of it is tomorrow, full of expectations. We can still mold it (Fig. 159). A head can be against the side line of the picture when, for example, there is the suggestion of fear or menace behind (Figs. 160, 161).

COMPOSING FOREGROUND AND BACKGROUND

When composing a picture, keep an eye open for the background. Have no lights or other objects growing out of the head (Fig. 162). A lamp shade may look like a hat or crown if left directly behind the head in the background. The foreground can be blended into the background with, for instance, the frame of a picture. Drawings or any other design on the wall also make a good background (Fig. 163). Rembrandt knew the secret of leaving the background dark and lighting only what he wished to feature.

THEME

In motion pictures, a close-up is usually part of a group or two-shot, but there are also single close-ups. Whichever class it belongs to, a picture needs a theme. In films there is no time to waste. By merely looking at the picture, the audience should know or re-

Fig. 157 *Mary Meade and Wallace Ford*

Fig. 158 *Wallace Ford*

ceive an impression of what it is all about. The thought must be put over in the shortest length of time. In portraits the same rule applies. Your picture should convey an idea, a message. To accomplish this, have the person do something—read, hold a book, play the piano or other musical instrument, paint, or whatever action may suit your picture.

If we wish to feature a necktie, a jewel, a medal, or part of a dress or uniform, etc., the face can be subdued. Always light what you try to feature.

Tools Used for Making Close-ups

LENSES

Close-ups can be, and sometimes are, photographed with any of the lenses in gen-

eral use. Most good lenses, however, have a tendency to sharpen the image, to reveal and even exaggerate hidden blemishes, wrinkles, etc., much to the disadvantage of the person photographed. Close-ups of Hollywood stars are known the world over for their exquisite beauty. They are the export of the American film industry, and should be photographed with lenses especially designed for the purpose of beautifying. The portrait lenses used in the making of the famous glamorous Hollywood close-ups are usually of 75–80 or 100 millimeters focal length.

In the past, especially on lower budget pictures, in order to save precious time it was customary to take advantage of the existing long shot illumination, and use it for

Fig. 159 *"On Duty"*

Fig. 160 *Mary Meade*

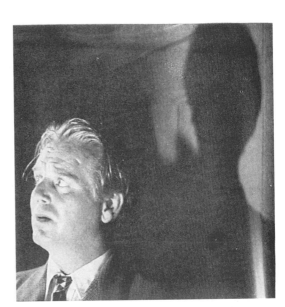

Fig. 161

Fig. 162 *Marsha Hunt*

shooting close-ups. When a long shot was made, instead of moving in on a close-up and relighting they merely switched lenses. The result was a flat, overlit, and usually disastrous close-up. This can easily be explained. In a long shot the face of an actor may be only a small part of the picture. Sometimes, to suit the balance of the lighting scheme, the scene is overlit. When we change lenses, we eliminate everything but the face, and all we get is a flat white surface. Fortunately, this practice is slowly becoming outmoded. *To get quality, every close-up or portrait should be lit separately and balanced individually.*

There is an old belief that cameras don't lie. This is true to a certain extent only. To suit our convenience, for the purpose of beautifying, the camera can be made to lie. Such lies, by means of which a person can be made to look much prettier and younger than she really is, are not only permissible, but altogether desirable.

Fig. 163 *Spanish Beauty, Mary Inclan*

In real life, when we look at a person we like, but who is not as beautiful as we would like her to be, we automatically and unconsciously half close our eyes, diffuse, soften our vision to make her appear more beautiful. We close our eyelashes and actually hypnotize ourselves into a state of admiration. By doing this we eliminate harsh lines. By placing this imaginary rose-colored glass in front of our eyes, everything appears just like a dream, so romantic, so beautiful.

Photographic cameras are cold, heartless instruments. They do not possess the automatic diffusion of the human eye. The picture has to be softened artificially. This process of making the camera lie is called *diffusion*.

LENS DIFFUSION

While diffusion of the sight has been known to exist since Adam laid eyes on Eve, lens diffusion in motion pictures is a typical Hollywood invention. Each master of lights has developed his own secret formula. Generally, there are two kinds of lens diffusers used in motion picture photography: a silk-like gauze, usually homemade, and the standard manufactured glass diffusion disk, a flat glass with slightly raised concentric rings pressed on to it. In some instances a combination of both silk and glass is used. Manufactured glass disks come in round and square shapes, and with varied degrees of diffusion. In addition there is the variable-diffusion glass. This is a long piece of optical glass, clear on one end and soft on the other. It is used on traveling shots, from extreme long shots where diffusion is superfluous, to a big-head close-up where it is absolutely essential. This glass is slid by hand through a frame in front of the lens, gradually, as the camera advances or recedes. The diffusing glass or gauze is placed in front of the lens in a holder or frame. By varying the distance of the diffuser from the lens we also vary the degree of softness. The further away the diffuser is from the lens, the softer is the image. The selection of the degree of diffusion depends entirely upon the effect we are after. Softer lenses require less diffusion than do sharp lenses. While glass diffusion has practically no light absorption factor, gauze diffusion reduces the light considerably. In calculating exposures for close-ups, allow for this absorption—open the diaphragm or add to the strength of the key-light. To determine the exact amount of light absorption, hold the gauze diffuser in front of the exposure meter. Some lenses of still cameras come with built-in diffusion; this can be modified to different degrees by the mere turning of a handle.

In motion picture photography, diffusion of close-ups should be gradual. In order to avoid brusque, heavily diffused close-ups which disturb the audience, diffuse scenes before and after each close-up. In close-ups with lamps, candles, or any other flames, gauze diffusion is preferred. It adds sparkle to the eyes, throws a pictorial halo around the flame, and does not produce multiple images as does its glass equivalent. Gauze diffusion gives the skin a velvety texture seen only in the better class of pictures.

The usual rules for diffusion are: generally no diffusion on long shots or distant views; light diffusion on medium shots; heavy diffusion on close-ups, especially feminine portraits. The best way to learn how to use diffusion successfully is by experimenting—make mistakes and correct them. In the hands of inexperienced photographers the use of gauze diffusers can result in gray, muddy photography.

Diffusion also is used to blend harsh, pronounced highlights and shadows in landscapes. It is recommended especially for love scenes or for any kind of romantic outdoor photography (Figs. 164, 165).

Anyone who has a little patience and who is fortunate enough to find in the attic an old-fashioned dress of chiffon or fine net, such as great-grandma used to wear, can make his own lens diffuser. Narrow frames about two or

Fig. 164   *New Orleans*

three inches square (Fig. 166) are cut from plastic, sheet fiber, or other suitable material, and placed on a drawing board. A somewhat larger piece of the dress material is placed over each frame and fastened to the drawing board with thumbtacks. Shellac, glue, or other cementing material is applied carefully to the dress material where it covers the frame only (Fig. 167). When the cementing material is thoroughly dry, the excess cloth is cut off even with the edges of the frame, and any excess cement is scraped from the frame (Fig. 168).

Fig. 165

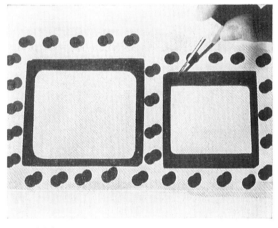

Fig. 167

Fig. 166

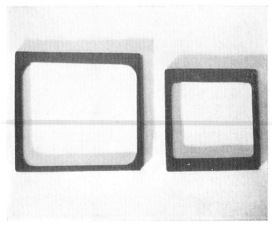

Fig. 168

LAMP DIFFUSION

Diffusion of a light source with a silk or other translucent material disperses the light into a million little lights, which serve to fill in unwanted shadows, grooves, and wrinkles. Lamp diffusion also is used when the light is too strong and there is no dimmer available to cut it down (Fig. 169). Diffusers for broads are made of white silk fastened to wooden frames; they come in single, double, and triple layers (Fig. 170). Diffusers for the other reflectors are made of heavy gauze fastened to wire frames; they come in single and double layers. They also come in halves which can be turned around in any direction, cutting out only one-half the light. Silk and other translucent materials are used also on juniors and babies when employed as key-lights.

Fig. 169

LAMP ACCESSORIES

Arc lamps produce a bluish light, and inkies produce a yellowish light. To correct an arc to a yellow light we use a yellow gelatin before it; to correct an inkie to blue, we place a blue gelatin before it. These gelatins are mounted on frames or rings similar to those of the light diffuser gauzes. Gelatins are used also before eyelights to add color to under-pigmented blue eyes.

As the name implies, *barn doors* are door-like contraptions. They are made of metal and are placed before the reflector to cut the light down, up, or sideways. They can be turned around so as to cut diagonal shadows. Barn doors come in different sizes to suit the reflector used—large ones for juniors, smaller ones for babies, and tiny ones for dinkies (Figs. 171 and 172).

Funnels and snoots are metal tubes of various sizes which, when placed before reflectors, cut down the size of the field of light. The large ones are called *funnels.* The smaller ones, called *snoots,* are used on dinkies for eyelights and the like (Fig. 173).

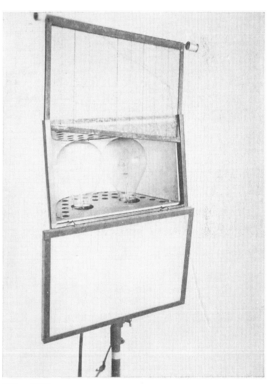

Fig. 170

Side arms or brackets can be attached to a lamp stand at any height; they are used mostly for supporting eyelights.

When a light is too strong, as when an actor gets into a hot light by moving forward during a scene, we reduce the light by means of a *dimmer.* Dimmers come in singles and in a

Fig. 171

Fig. 172

Fig. 173

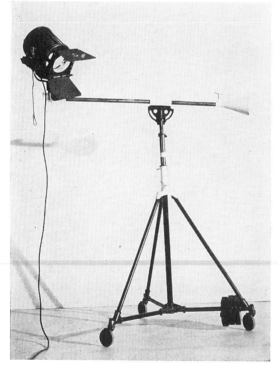

Fig. 174 *The "Bardwell" dimmer*

combination of units of different values, called a *dimmer bank* (Fig. 174). An inkie should not be dimmed down too far because it goes into the red and loses its actinic value. Duarcs can be dimmed on inkie dimmers. For dimming other arc lamps, we use *shutters*. A shutter is similar to a metal Venetian blind, and is placed before the arc light; the intensity of the light can be controlled by pressing a single lever (Fig. 175).

SILENT ELECTRIC FANS

Silent electric fans are used for creating a silent breeze which blows hair gently without making trouble for the sound crew.

Fig. 175

The Clock System of Placing Reflectors

In setting up the lighting scheme for a close-up there are literally thousands of positions where the reflectors could be placed to get good results; the stage could be filled with them. It is not essential for the student of photography to know them all. A few of those most frequently used in motion picture illumination will suffice.

For the purpose of illustration and to provide a better understanding of the positions of the different reflectors, we herewith introduce the *clock system*, similar to that employed in gunnery practice by the Armed Forces during Act II of the great show of World Wars. The space covered by this system has the shape of a truncated cone, with its smallest section at the camera, and with circumference increasing as it includes the actors to be photographed, and ending on the background behind them. In this cone there may be assumed to be as many imaginary circular planes as required, each with a design similar to the face of a clock, but without hands.

To simplify matters we shall demonstrate three circles only, A, B, and C (Fig. 176). Circle A is at the camera; circle B surrounds the actor to be photographed; circle C is at the far end of the cone. All circles are viewed from the camera position, and have the hours clearly marked on them. A reflector at 3 o'clock means that the lamp is placed in a position corresponding to that of 3 o'clock on the face of a clock.

THE ORANGE RULE

It can hardly be expected that the student of photography who has taken only a few lessons in lighting can step right in and light a close-up or portrait and do a good job of it. Because not every student can afford to hire a living model, we have devised the *orange rule* as a means of economical step-by-step instruction in illumination. As a substitute for the human head, because of its similarity to it, we have selected the simple orange (it can be from Florida or California). The orange is round, has an exaggerated porous skin texture, is of warm color, but has no temperament, is easier to get along with, and is much less expensive to acquire than a living model. If, as in Figure 177, we place the testlight

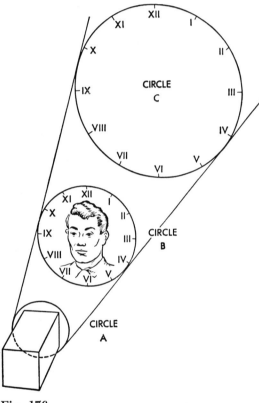

Fig. 176

walks, laughs, and makes faces, retouching is out of the question. Crosslight should be used only for special lighting effects, or as clotheslight.

Now let us take our testlight and place it

Fig. 177

Fig. 178

at 10 or 11 o'clock in circle *A*, we have what is called a *crosslight;* this exaggerates the pores of the skin. Crosslight looks well in old paintings where the artist eliminated at will every effect he thought would detract from the beauty of his picture. Even in portrait photography, where retouching can correct many mistakes and undesired blemishes, crosslight can be used. But in motion pictures, in a close-up of a feminine star where she talks,

94

at 12 o'clock, still in circle *A* (Fig. 178). We immediately notice how the pores of the skin begin to disappear; we are now actually retouching with light. This proves that the flattering key for feminine close-ups is undoubtedly the front key, somewhat above eye height. A front key is not necessarily a flat light. Add a kicker to it at 9 o'clock and a backlight at 12 o'clock, both in circle *C*, and a certain roundness of the face appears; this accentuates beauty (Fig. 179). A true student of photography, if he is at all an artist, does not stop with the placing of the keylight. He continues to add light for modeling, until there remains little room for improvement, always retaining the feeling of a single light source. The keylight may make a picture, but additional lighting is required to make it outstandingly beautiful. In long shots details are important; as a matter of fact we look

Fig. 179

for them. In close-ups we conceal them. A well-lit face should be neither too light nor too dark.

Practicing with the orange will teach the student certain basic facts about illumination. If you can light an orange so that it looks or photographs as smooth and round as a billiard ball, you are ready to light close-ups and portraits of living people.

CREATIVE ILLUMINATION— INSPIRATION IN LIGHTING

In lighting a close-up a technical knowledge of lighting is very important but far from sufficient. In order to light creatively, inspiration is essential. It is most difficult to describe just what inspiration is, and how one is to acquire it. Webster calls it the *awakening or creative impulse*. One way I know of becoming inspired is by listening to good music. Chains of sensations are set in motion. It is my firm belief that sound waves absorbed

in the form of good music become transformed into light waves which through illumination can result in beautiful, artistic pictures that are aesthetic pleasures. Perhaps the sound waves enter the ear and thence a sort of storage battery in the brain, later to emanate as electroencephalic vibrations in the form of ideas for visual art, in this case photography. For good photographic results in motion pictures there is inspiration in good music, in the art director's design of sets, in a well-written script, and in convincing interpretation by the actors. What is inspiration? I don't know. But I do know that it exists, and that it electrifies one.

LIGHT AND THE HUMAN FACE

The first step in illumination is the study of light and the human face. If you watch carefully, under varying circumstances in subways, buses, streetcars, in the open, on beaches, at home, or elsewhere, you will find that faces look absolutely different when silent and expressionless than when they laugh, smile, talk, or cry. Hitherto unsuspected hidden wrinkles and harsh lines suddenly appear on the otherwise beautifully smooth surface. One profile differs from the other; the right half of the face looks different from the left. At certain angles the eyes disappear; at others they look their best. Under favorable lighting the prettiest face can look distorted, ruined. With each change of light on a face, new properties emerge. Light also brings out character never suspected.

In the illumination of a close-up there are two main groups, feminine and masculine.

Feminine faces, both blonde and brunette, may be divided into the following categories; the lighting of each requires a different approach:

Long face with high forehead
Round face with low forehead
Applecheek face
Cheekless face (flat)
Character face

While in feminine close-ups we strive for beauty, in masculine pictures it is the character of the individual that we accentuate. There are exceptions to this rule too. There are, for example, the juvenile of fifty who would like to continue to look young indefinitely, and the young genius who wears a beard to look older than he really is. A masculine face is not unlike a landscape. The nose is the hill (sometimes like a mountain), the eyes are the shiny lakes, the hair is the forest, etc. Such a picture should be a symphony of highlights and shadows. When it comes to shape of masculine faces, they fall into the following classes:

Long face with high, sometimes corrugated forehead
Round flat face
Mongolian face
Face with large protruding ears
Asymmetrical face
Face with large nose
Character face
The out-of-focus face

A close-up is first conceived, then planned, and finally lit. Before the artist lights a close-up he has two images in his mind; one is the person as he sees her, and the other is a gorgeous vision of the same person—an inspired picture—the way he visualizes the star on the screen. He then proceeds with his lighting, carefully watching the face being lit. When it looks the way he visualized it, when the two images coincide, that is the picture. Besides talent it takes time, patience, study, and repeated screen tests to find the proper angle and lighting for a star.

MAKE–UP FOR A CLOSE–UP

For a beautiful close-up, good make-up is absolutely essential (Fig. 180). Perhaps make-up is the wrong expression—*cover-up* would be more appropriate. Whatever its name, it is not new. The ancient Greeks smeared the faces of their actors, and even of the directors, of the legitimate stage. The

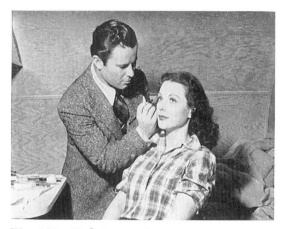

Fig. 180 *Hedy Lamarr being made up by Frank Westmore*

clowns of the circus have painted their faces for ages, so as to make their features lighter and more visible to the audience in the far corners of the tent. Make-up as used for motion picture photography is a Hollywood product. Years ago, when cameramen used orthochromatic film which was not sensitive to red, faces used to photograph spotty. Blemishes and red spots were exaggerated. Roses and oranges photographed black. Something had to be done about it. A grease paint was invented to cover up. When this paste was smeared over the face of the actor, he photographed light. Facial make-up has since become so successful that today it is used not only in photography, but as street make-up, by millions of women, day and night, all over the world. In skillful hands make-up is an art. It can make old people look young and beautiful, and vice versa.

Except for characterizations, with the modern camera technique very little make-up is used today by men. The old idea of powdering has been discarded. Even with grease paint on the face, a natural shine is now demanded by most photographers.

THE NEW DEAL

In motion picture photography, the expression *new deal* has no political significance at all; it simply means what it says, a new deal in lighting.

Before we move in from a long shot to a close-up, all cables, lamps, and other equipment are "wrapped up." The lighting of the close-up requires an entirely new scheme. Sets are lit mostly from up high. Close-ups are illuminated from the floor. Exceptions are crane or dolly shots, where lamps on the floor would get into the picture.

Before going into the interesting but complicated process of close-up illumination, the photographer should know what the person to be photographed is going to do. Is she going to sit still or move around, talk or sing, smile or cry? In which direction is she going to look? How is her facial expression going to change when speaking her lines? Is a kicker going to give her a nose shadow? Will her lips quiver? Is anyone going to shade her? All these and many other factors are of the utmost importance in getting the good results that make Hollywood close-ups world-famous. From this reasoning, we establish a rule: With but few exceptions where the scene calls for a special type of illumination, *feminine close-ups or portraits should always be beautiful.* In films they are the jewels of the picture, in stills, the decorations of the desk or home.

A picture can be beautiful, yet have mood and feeling too. Therefore, even in scenes which call for mood, for special feeling, it is the rendition of feminine beauty we strive for and attain by keeping the key low.

THE TESTLIGHT

The traditional procedure in illumination of close-ups is for the cinematographer to go ahead and light in a leisurely manner. By this method he follows in the footsteps of the old masters, and takes the usual few steps back, squints at his work of art, and if it is not entirely to his liking, issues orders to "dig 'em up" or "wrap 'em up," meaning to take all lamps off the set and start over again from scratch. This procedure is repeated until he finds the light that satisfies his artistic soul. This system of painting was perhaps well suited for the temperament of artists in the days of old, glorious Rome, but definitely is not for the photogratomic age we now live in. It is much too slow, nerve-wracking, and expensive.

With the aid of the *testlight* (Figs. 181, 182), illumination of portraits and close-ups can be improved, modernized, simplified, and speeded up to a great extent. This device, a new combination of existing electric lamp parts, can be assembled by the student at home. It consists of a two-foot aluminum tube at the end of which is an electric socket holding a frosted bulb. Over the bulb is a shade to keep the light out of the photographer's eyes. Through the tubing passes an electric cord long enough to reach the nearest electric outlet, where it is plugged in. As the light of this bulb is very weak, the stage or studio must be darkened for its effect to be appreciated.

The first thing to do is to decide where the light is to come from. For this purpose we hold the testlight in the hand and move it around the face of the person to be photographed. By doing this we create different light effects, moods, and feelings; also we show different angles of the subject, some favorable and others not. When we have found the ideal position for the light, that is, where the keylight is to be placed, the rest of the illumination is merely a question of balancing.

Lighting Procedure

There are two schools of thought concerning the actual illumination of close-ups. One asserts the necessity for securing an overall light first, and only then placing the keylight. This gives a strong negative which can be printed down to a density where blacks are rich and whites remain natural. The other school of thought argues that it is better to

97

Fig. 181 *Joan Bennett and the Author*

Fig. 182

place the key first, and only then, if at all necessary, fill in. The motion picture negative usually is printed in the middle of the scale. It is all right and as a matter of fact desirable to print higher, but never lower, because

then the prints turn gray and lack quality. It is claimed that if the key is flat (front key) little filler is needed, as the key takes care of that. It covers all that the camera can possibly see.

I endorse the first school of thought, especially for beginners. The reason for this is that most laboratories are in business to make money. At times their soup weakens a bit, and on such occasions if you haven't enough filler light, you get a weak negative.

Each scene of a motion picture film may have a different mood. The close-ups of scenes must be illuminated to suit the moods. In portraiture and in home lighting, one good formula for close-up illumination can serve as a base to work from.

LUMINART,
THE EIGHT–LIGHT SYSTEM

The *one-light system* is perfectly satisfactory in portrait photography where we are trying to make a picture of a person; in motion pictures, where realism is an important factor, where people move around and do things, and where we try to make these people appear to be as real as possible, we need more than one light to convince the critical audience.

The *eight-light system* may be made up of eight different lamps from different directions, with various intensities, but the result is that of the one-light system, only more plastic, rounder, and more realistic. Because of the presence of many reflective surfaces in a studio, such as white walls and the like, it is advisable to look at the face being photographed and not at the number of reflectors employed in its illumination. The following eight lights give a basic pattern which is suitable for close-up illumination and which is recommended also for portraiture. When sufficiently experienced, the student can make up his own lighting schemes.

1. Fill light
2. Keylight
3. Filler light
4. Clotheslight
5. Backlight
6. Kicker light
7. Eyelight
8. Background light

The reflectors used for the illumination of close-ups are about the same as those employed for general set illumination, but perhaps smaller in size and in power.

FILL LIGHT

The purpose of *fill light* is to assure us that no surface in the field of view of the lens will remain without any light (be underexposed), that shadows will not be opaque, but transparent, and that a double chin of the person

will not be too pronounced. To secure a general fill light we place a broad on each side of the camera. We put one low on the right side, at about 4 o'clock, and diffuse it with two silks; another on the left side of the

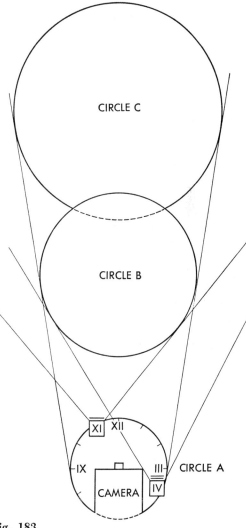

Fig. 183

camera at 11 o'clock, with but one silk before it (Fig. 183). Lights placed at eye height are reflected in the eyes, and thus serve as eyelights also.

KEYLIGHT

We assume that the position for the keylight was chosen with the aid of the testlight.

In motion picture photography the keylight usually is placed on the side toward which the person to be photographed faces. This is, of course, stated with certain reservations, because all faces are different, and some cannot

As we look at the face we are bound to notice that, in spite of the fill, this high keylight casts unwanted shadows on it. To coun-

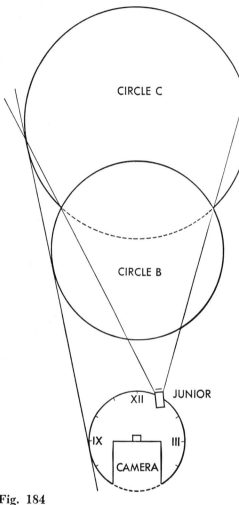

Fig. 184

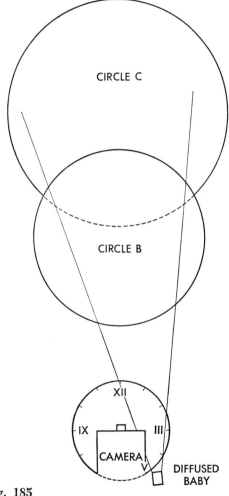

Fig. 185

stand a front keylight. In this case, the position chosen is at 1 o'clock on circle A (Fig. 184). Here we place a junior diffused with one silk, which is essential to soften the light. If a silk is used on the usual baby sometimes used for close-up lighting, the light must be concentrated so that it covers only a small area, because if left open it is weak and not up to required strength. Hence the junior. A diffused senior on a dimmer sometimes is used for a keylight in place of the junior or baby.

terbalance this we place a low baby spotlight, or sometimes a broad, at about 5 o'clock (Fig. 185) directly under the keylight, possibly on a bracket on the same stand. (The less equipment there is around the camera, the more room there is to move around.) This low light fills in the shadows (on top of the fill), and may serve also as an eyelight. *Filler light* must not be confused with fill light. Their mission is entirely different.

In some musical comedies this low reflector

is up to the usual keylight strength, and the keylight is still stronger. In the average type of photoplay, however, it is only a filler diffused down with silks and perhaps a yellow gelatin on top of them, depending upon the desired strength.

CLOTHESLIGHT

A front keylight is definitely flattering for close-up lighting, but in a picture where more than just the face is included, it might burn out the details of the dress texture. This must be avoided. To illustrate, let us assume that the person to be glamorized wears a silver lamé dress. In order to get the necessary illumination on the face, we bring the keylight up to the required strength. The dress being of metallic nature is much overlit because the keylight is too strong for it. Even if the intensity of light were correct, it is too flat and lifeless for the dress. It needs pepping up and correction, so we call on our beautifying assistant, the grip, to bring in the thousand magic gadgets.

The first tool from the box to be used is the open end with single, double, or triple gauze. With this gadget we shade the keylight off the dress up to the neck. We then add a baby or junior spotlight to provide what is known as *clotheslight*, which models the dress, accentuates highlights, and brings out the texture of the material. Clotheslight is a strong crosslight; if possible it should come from the key side to retain the feeling of a single light source. It gives the picture force and strength. As the face is already fully lit, we must be careful that no spill light reaches it; this is accomplished by means of barn doors which are slit down so that the light hits the clothes only. Figure 186 illustrates the use of clotheslight.

This system can be used also if your negative is to be sent to a laboratory where the soup is so contrasty that it burns up the whites and leaves the blacks empty.

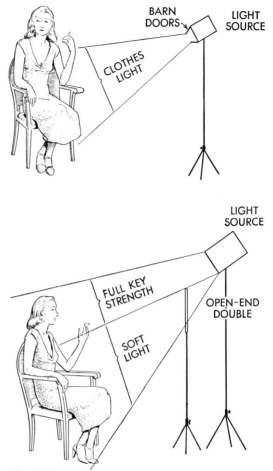

Fig. 186

BACKLIGHT

In the early days of motion pictures, directors were discouraged from playing an important scene against the wall or under the ceiling because the actors could not be backlit. The world is advancing, and so is photography. Close-ups can be shot anywhere, if necessary without any backlight, and with good results.

Backlight originally was designed as a so-called *separation* light, to separate the foreground from a background of the same brightness. In the course of time this light has developed into a multipurpose one. It now is used not only for separation, but also for modeling. It adds brilliance and life to the hair of blondes, and helps the hair of brunettes by preventing it from going abso-

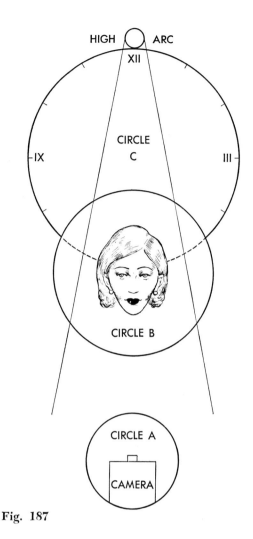

Fig. 187

Fig. 188

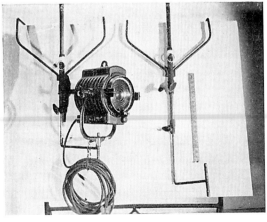

lutely jet black with complete loss of detail. If care is not exercised, backlight can be abused. It must not be too high, because it casts uncomplimentary highlights on the nose and cheekbones of the already well-lit face.

If the person photographed is a brunette, is wearing a white dress, and does not move in the scene, the backlight which is about right for the hair burns the dress up. To remedy this, we shade the light from each shoulder with a single or double open end. If she is a blonde and wears a black dress, to model the shoulders properly would burn the hair up, so we use a solid or gauze target to shade the light from the head.

Any light behind the person can be utilized as backlight provided it is in the correct position (Fig. 187). Arcs are preferred because they seem to give a steel-blue luster to the hair of brunettes, and a silvery touch to gray-white hair. Hangers are used when in close quarters, against walls, inside a closet, etc. (Fig. 188). Plates are nailed to the wall to hold babies. On ceilinged sets where hangers would get into the picture, the boomlight comes in very handy. When very crowded we use a dinkie on a dinkie plate; this lamp is so tiny that it can be hidden behind a telephone, a dictionary, or any other prop. The strength of the reflectors required for the purpose depends considerably upon the characteristics of the developer in which your negative is to be processed. If it is a soft developer, use a strong backlight, and vice versa. When the lighting of the picture is finished, the backlight should be much more pronounced than any other light.

KICKER LIGHT

A close-up lit with a single keylight can be very beautiful. Many photographers use this one-light portrait illumination exclusively. However, there can be no doubt that an additional light on the side of the keylight helps to model and round out the face, thus improving the picture.

In motion picture photography, when a person being photographed turns either right or left profile to the camera and the backlight hits her face, there is no need for the kicker. However, if the backlight happens to be in such a position that regardless of the direction in which the person may look it cannot reach her profile, we add a kicker on either or both sides. If she happens to wear her hair down, the kicker lights and adds luster to it; if her hair is up, the light hits the cheeks and models them.

Some faces are distorted by kickers. In such cases it should be shaded off with a solid flag, eliminating the unwanted portion of the strong light, or sometimes leaving only a ray of it to hit the side of the forehead.

With a kicker on either side and close to the camera sideline, the person can look in either direction, and the profile will be well modeled. Kickers placed at eye height enhance the luminosity of the eyes.

The intensity of the kicker light should be such that, although hotter than the keylight, the total feeling still is that of a single light source. Although its actual exposure meter reading may be lower than that of the main keylight, its light, because of the angle of reflection and the oily texture of the skin, sometimes appears stronger. It must be balanced. The kicker, which usually is a junior or baby on a dimmer, can be placed at any point behind circle B, depending entirely upon the desired effect (Fig. 189).

Fig. 189

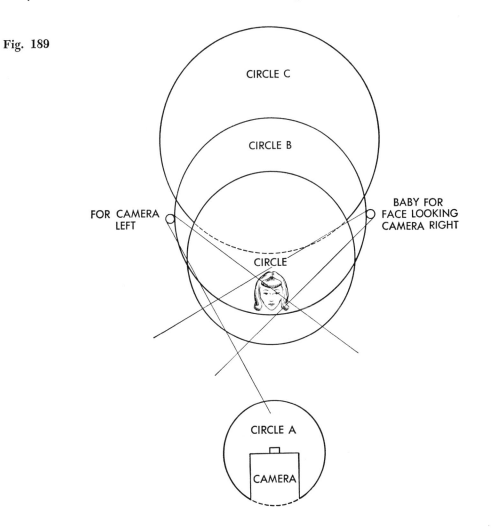

CIRCLE C

CIRCLE B

FOR CAMERA LEFT

BABY FOR FACE LOOKING CAMERA RIGHT

CIRCLE

CIRCLE A

CAMERA

Be it day or night, in real life the human eye always shines, sparkles. This phenomenon is due to the surroundings in our everyday life. There is always a hot spot, an illuminant which, when reflected in the mirrorlike, moist surface of the eyeball, gives it luster, pep, life. A light window, a lamp, the sky, a white wall, a cloud, the sun, the moon, the flame of a candle, all have a tendency to enliven the facial expression through a light in the eye.

On a dark stage where there are no such hot spots, we create one by adding to the lighting scheme a special reflector designed for this purpose. This is called the *eyelight*. There are still some photographers who, once the face is lit, hesitate to add another, even smaller, reflector for fear of overexposure. The result is dull eyes, which look like a dark night, or a shut door. Any low-intensity light which will not add enough light to affect the exposure serves as an eyelight.

If the angle of the keylight is such that it does not reflect in the eye, or in the case of babies or grownups who have sensitive eyes and cannot stand direct light, or people whose eyes just do not pick up any light (deep sockets or slant eyes), the use of an eyelight is absolutely imperative. The reflector used for eyelight can be a junior or baby. It should be heavily diffused, or dimmed to a point where there is hardly any exposure left in it, so that it cannot add to the existing light, thus creating double nose shadows, etc. A dinkie too can be used as an eyelight, although the larger the surface of the light, the larger will be its reflection in the eyes. For under-pigmented blue eyes, add an amber-colored gelatin to the lamp.

If we carefully examine the portrait paintings of the old masters and the still photographs of the new ones, we cannot help noticing the lack of life in some of them. In place of a brilliant eye, there is a dark hole, an empty socket. This gives the person in the

picture the expressionless cold look of a statue. It would have taken the painter only an extra stroke of the brush, or the photographer an added eyelight to correct this deficiency.

BACKGROUND LIGHT

Lighting the person in the foreground of the picture is only part of the illumination of a close-up. The lighting of the background is just as important, and must fit into the general scheme. Backgrounds can be compared to the outdoor sky; there is a barren, desert feeling in a cloudless sky, but as soon as the clouds start to roll in we have a different mood. There is hardly a more beautiful spiritual picture than a sunrise or sunset with its multicolored array of cloud formations (Fig. 190). If we leave the background of a close-up entirely without design, we may get a photograph, but not a beautiful picture. To break up this monotony we project shadows on the background (Fig. 191).

In most profile close-ups, the background behind the person's head should be darker, and the part ahead of it lighter. There are exceptions to this rule, as when a person anticipates something unpleasant, or senses danger from somewhere behind him; or he hears strange noises, the slow, creaky opening of a door, the sound of footsteps, or feels the piercing look of someone present. In such in-

Fig. 190 *"Storm over Jerusalem"*

Fig. 191 *Lynn Bari*

stances, to attract the attention of the audience, we lighten the background behind his head, and darken it ahead of him.

One would think that when we move in from a long shot to a close-up we must match the background lighting. This is not absolutely essential. First of all, as close-ups are photographed with 75 mm or 80 mm lenses, the background usually "falls off." Second, when looking at a close-up the attention should be held on the person, the face in the foreground, and not on the surroundings. The lighting of the background can be stylized to harmonize with the foreground. This liberty of stylizing is very handy, especially on retakes where the original set has already been destroyed, or some of the props returned to rental companies.

Arc lamps are preferred for background lighting for the production of different sharp designs. The 65 is handy for the purpose because it is light in weight and can be moved around easily. For large sky surfaces, where an even white light is essential, Duarcs are used. Reflectors for background lights are usually placed between circles *B* and *C*.

This pattern-of-lighting scheme should serve as a sample. The student can now go ahead, experiment with it, and invent new ones as he goes along.

LIGHT SURGERY

In life, when medicine has failed to cure a patient we resort to surgery. The same is true of photography. When soft lights and heavy diffusion cannot help any more we operate with lights and other instruments. Very few people, even among photographers, know that such operations are possible. Retouching detracts from the character of a portrait. Lights beautify. No school of medicine can give you all the answers; neither can one chapter dealing with light surgery.

In photography, as in medicine, it is the artist who is the most successful; one who can read between the lines. The creative surgeon invents his own tools, sometimes he even manufactures them. So does the real lumin-artist. Not all photographic surgery is done with lights. Some is accomplished by shading.

THE OPERATION

For anesthetic, use good music. It facilitates and guarantees insensibility without after-effects.

Light surgery is good only for still portraits or poses in motion pictures. A person so illuminated should not move. The possibilities of such operations are unlimited. Limited space allows us to mention only a few of the important cases. It is hoped that the serious student of lighting will be awakened to the possibilities of this hitherto little-known branch of photography.

FACES

There are faces which, when lit with one single key, however much beautified, will always be a problem, a headache. No matter at what position of the clock you place the keylight, you may eliminate one trouble, and six others will present themselves instead. On one side, you will correct a broken-nose effect, and on the other, circles under the eyes will appear. With some faces, when lit from high, the nose will appear crooked; and when illuminated from low, the circles under the eyes will be exaggerated.

In such cases use two keys, one high and one low. Cut them in half. On the one from high, shade off the upper part, and on the low one, the lower part. Add a little filler to overlap the dividing line, and we have eliminated the crooked-nose effect, and also ironed out the circles under the eyes (Fig. 192).

As many as four keylights or more can be successfully used on one face alone. Shade the part that does the harm, and use the part of another key that helps.

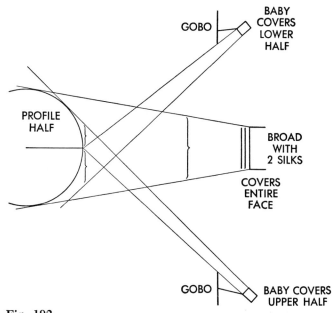

Fig. 192

EARS

Few people have really adorable ears. Even if they happen to be beautiful it is better not to feature them. A gorgeous lighting can sometimes be spoiled by a prominent ear sticking out fully lighted against a dark background. The light should hit the face only. It is not difficult to keep it off the ears. We either move the key around until the light is off the ear closest to the camera, or we shade it off. Use the best suited.

There are some people who have become stars in spite of their outstanding ears. They are the exception to the rule. Persons with large ears are difficult to photograph. Such people when photographed should have their ears pinned back, or be shot from a three-quarter angle.

There are special pictures where the ear is featured. For instance, in a close-up featuring earrings or other jewelry; this picture can be made very effective by keeping the face subdued in tone, and attention focused on the center of attraction, in this case the bejewelled ear.

FOREHEADS

When we look at a portrait, it is the eyes and facial expression we want to see. Unfortunately, the forehead, because of its large, flat surface, reflects more light than some deep-set or sunken eyes. It becomes more prominent. To remedy this, we gauze down the keylight with a single or double open end to the eyebrows. When a person moves, this will cast shadows but in modern lighting, shadows on foreheads are beginning to be accepted (Figs. 193, 194).

Fig. 193

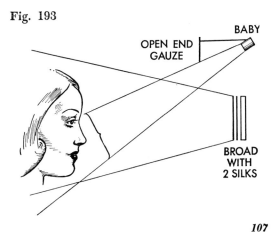

Fig. 194

High foreheads have a tendency to wrinkle. No matter how we try to justify a thinking mood, wrinkles are not beautiful in a masculine portrait or close-up. If shading off does not help, then we add another straight-on light, and fill them in.

EYES

"The eyes are the mirror of the soul," goes the old saying. We have since found out that they are more than that. Not only is the human eye like the lens of a camera, but like that of the television set, works both ways. It receives and broadcasts waves. When we look into someone's eyes, we establish a contact, ready to receive and send messages uninterruptedly. Hence, the importance of eyes in photography. Criminals instinctively avoid looking into one's eyes, hoping to break contact for fear of transmitting secret thoughts. Eyes also have a hypnotic power. If we don't see them, we lose their beauty and their expression—the circuit is broken. It weakens the picture. Two-shots, with two profiles,

108

where the eyes of neither are visible, have no power. Great motion picture directors know this well.

LIPS

Next to the eyes, it is the lips of a person we look at. They too are important and should therefore be made up carefully.

HANDS

Very important and most difficult things to handle in pictures are the hands. Only experienced persons know what to do with them, how to display them to advantage. If you are not sure of yourself, eliminate them from a portrait or close-up. Hands too have a power, a language of their own. Public speakers use them to great advantage. Some masters have painted them by leaving the entire picture subdued, and lighting the hands alone. Such pictures can be works of art and beauty.

NOSEY PEOPLE

Eyes have a tendency to disappear, to hide, but with noses it is just the opposite. No matter what the angle, the nose is always there, and usually appears much more pronounced than its actual size. The oil excretions are much stronger on the nose than on any other part of the face, which makes it shinier, reflecting every reflector in the illumination scheme, adding to its already fabulous prominence. The nose is the part of the face that is closest to the lens, and by picking up all incidental light, it appears as a lighthouse, a beacon. A little extra powder will help subdue it, although only partially, I assure you.

BALD HEADS

Another part of the human anatomy that seems to get undue photographic prominence is a bald head. Its shiny and rounded surface picks up every light in the place, thus creating a comic effect not always desired. To keep backlight off a shiny head top, keep it powdered at all times. Shade the front keylight off with a solid or double open end.

APPLE CHEEKS

Faces with strong, fleshy cheeks are called *apple cheeks.* The illumination of such faces presents quite a problem, especially in motion picture photography where facial muscles move during the acting of a scene. One light might be perfect for one expression and disastrous for another. Big close-ups of such people should be posed, with the least possible movement, dramatic or emotional expression.

To illustrate: A high keylight, let us say at 11 o'clock circle A, might be entirely satisfactory for a person with a serious expression. The minute she smiles, under the same lights, she might look like a different and less beautiful person. The best all-around light for such faces is the "no-key" light. Use a soft front light to replace the harsh key. This consists of two broads, one at 1 o'clock on the right side of the camera, and another still softer at 9 o'clock, both at circle A. These broads, unlike most of them, have to be up to key strength. Under such lights, a person can laugh, smile, sing, talk, or cry. There are no strong crosslights which will distort the face.

When a face is only a small part of a picture, it can afford to be flat; but if it fills the screen alone, it should have highlights and shadows. Use strong backlights and a kicker on the forehead.

CHEEKLESS FACE

Photographically speaking, some faces seem to have no cheeks. Regardless where you place the keylight, the face remains flat, with no roundness to it. To bring out this seemingly nonexistent feature, we add what is called a *cheeklight.* It should be an arc light, but if one is not available, an inkie with a blue gelatin in front of it will do. If the keylight happens to be, let us say, at 2 o'clock on circle A, then add another light directly above it. This will bring out the cheeks. It will lengthen the shadows caused by the keylight, but will add no other shadow.

This added lamp is only for reflection; therefore it can be silked down to a point just before it reaches the red light stage. The skin texture of such people should be shiny, but not oily.

THE ROUND FACE

Round faces are sometimes funny faces, excellent for laughs. Where this is objectionable, it can be remedied with the aid of special lighting. Use a high keylight at about 1 o'clock on circle A. The long shadows will help to lengthen the face. Another way of correcting round faces is by shading off excess light. This is done with the aid of a scissorlike instrument holding a gauze (Fig. 195). With this, we shade the light off the edges of the face or double chin (Fig. 196). The gauze can be of different thicknesses.

For exaggerated comic effects, by eliminating the shadow, the round face can be flattened to a pancake. For this we add two kickers, one at 3 o'clock of circle C, and the other at 9 o'clock of the same circle; then we shade the keylight off the forehead and chin. This will widen the face.

Fig. 195

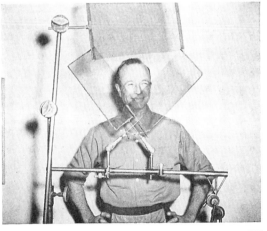

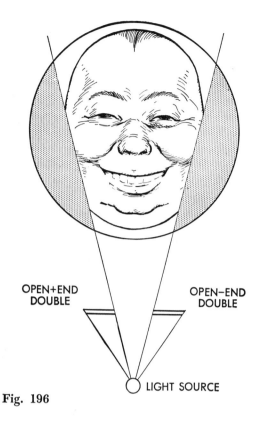

OPEN+END DOUBLE

OPEN—END DOUBLE

○ LIGHT SOURCE

Fig. 196

MIRROR EFFECT

An interesting picture can be made with the aid of a mirror by taking the glass out of the frame, and using that as a silhouette foreground piece. Have the person look directly into the camera. This gives a reflection effect, as though we photographed her reflection in the mirror itself. This lighting should be of a low key. This fits into the boudoir lighting.

SUN–TANNED FACES

We live in a strange world. On a hot, sunny day, when animals usually seek the cool shade of trees, human beings rush to the beach to take sunbaths. Colored girls want to be white, and work for hours to eliminate the kink in their hair, while their white sisters are slaves of the latest tan style, and spend fortunes for permanent waves.

A sun-tanned girl dressed in white looks stunning at a party, but when we try to light

110

her for a portrait it becomes quite a problem. A single keylight will not do justice to both face and dress. If we light for the face and print it down, the dress will be normal, but the face will be more than a pretty tan. Again, if we print it up to suit the face, the dress will be ablaze. This is no problem in real life, for our eyes see only one, either the dress or the face. In a picture they see all, and consequently the technique of shading the keylight off the dress and using a separate clotheslight must be employed.

CLOSE–UPS IN BED

There is hardly a film nowadays without the feminine bedroom, and, of course, the close-up in bed. Because of the nature and the surroundings of close-ups in bed, their lighting requires a different approach.

Close-ups in bed are divided into the following classes:

1. The glamour close-up
2. Moonlight dreams
3. The feverish, ill person
4. The death scene

GLAMOUR, TOUJOURS, GLAMOUR

Unless a person sits up, as in Figure 197, it is most difficult to light a close-up with the bed in a corner, especially against the wall. By pulling it away, it will be easier to light. If the bed head is not in the picture, take it off; that will enable us to use backlight. For the color of the bed clothing an off-white is preferred, and silk or satin photograph better than ordinary linen. If the surroundings are rich, and the bed head shows in the picture, use a bed with silk upholstery. Properly lighted, it sparkles. As the camera points downward, there are only two of the light circles, A and B. Keylight the face from 12 o'clock of circle A. This keylight will burn up the pillow around the face, so we gauze it off with a double that has an open hole in the middle, and a triple around the edges. This

Fig. 197 *Dennis O'Keefe and Marsha Hunt*

gauze leaves the entire strength of the key-light on the face, softens the pillow around it, and tapers off gradually at the edges. Next, we backlight the head from 12 o'clock of circle B. This is really not a backlight, but a top-light, to bring out the cheeks and highlight them. When this is done, we kick the face and pillow from 3 o'clock of circle B. This kicker can be a small arc light. With the pillow ruffled up around the face, this will accentuate face and pillow, giving us sharp highlights. Whether blonde or brunette, the hair against the pillow remains dark. The result of this lighting is a well-lit face with a soft halo around it. As the keylight hits the eyes, eyelight would be superfluous. To soften the picture, heavy lens diffusion can be applied.

MOONLIGHT IN THE BEDROOM

For the close-up of a person asleep, moonlight is the most appropriate. People falling asleep may leave a cigarette burning, but seldom a lamp. Use an arc light from 3 o'clock or the other side, 9 o'clock, of circle B. This will give us a crosslight feeling with little or perhaps no filler light. Apply heavy diffusion. If the person happens to be awake, add an eyelight for the eyes.

CLOSE-UP OF AN ILL PERSON

The light source of such a close-up would usually be a night lamp, a candle, the moon, or perhaps just a "photographic darkness," where features are hardly visible. Whatever the light source, it is always a single light.

111

Fig. 198 *Cathy O'Donnell and Turhan Bey*

If the person is perspiring, the face is shiny, sprinkled with a myriad of tiny pearls of perspiration (Fig. 198). The eyes are shiny; the hair is moist, sticky.

For keylight of this picture, use a 1 o'clock position of circle *B*. Filler is not essential, but permissible. A strong eyelight will bring out the feverish look of the eyes. Heavy lens diffusion helps.

For the lighting of a convalescent person sitting up in bed, use the normal illumination; make it bright, gay.

CLOSE-UP OF A DYING PERSON

The movie illumination of this close-up is similar to that of an ill person. When death takes place, dim the lights, except that of the cross-backlight, which remains full up to out-line the face, down to dark. This light will give the picture a spiritual effect. Keep the background dark.

A close-up of a dead person should be lit with cold moonlight. The mood is that of rest, eternal silence, with the shadows of a breeze-blown lace curtain being the only movement. The keylight is placed outside a window, from either side of the camera, either at 3 or at 9 o'clock; it is a cross backlight. In this exceptional case, bedding can be white, adding to the eeriness of the picture. No filler light is necessary.

CLOSE–UPS INSIDE AN AUTO

These close-ups are usually shot on the process stage. To better understand their lighting, read paragraphs on process lighting.

112

For romantic close-ups, use the moon as a light source. For suspense, mystery, use the dash light, or just an imaginary light.

AGING WITH LIGHT

In motion pictures, sometimes an entire lifetime of a person is filmed in a few weeks' time. Make-up is not always sufficient to make a person look old. We have to supplement lights to the process of aging. Instead of using the glamour keylight we reverse the lighting. Use a high keylight, at approximately 1 o'clock or above. With little or no filler light, the top keylight will exaggerate wrinkles and facial muscles, which will age the person. Have very little or no make-up, use no lip rouge, and leave out the glamorizing back-light on the hair. If possible, the eyes, too, can be left without any sparkling light, making them expressionless. Youthful smiles belie old age; therefore care must be taken with facial expressions also.

MASCULINE FACES

The lines on a man's face are like a soldier's stripes, well earned. They signify character; therefore we must not try to eliminate them, for in masculine close-ups, that is exactly what we are striving for. Corrugated fore-heads should not be mistaken for character; even in masculine close-ups, they should be eliminated as much as possible. Fill in with front light, if high in key. If the key is low, then gauze the light off the forehead.

By lighting a man's face with just a back crosslight on a three-quarter angle, we can get plasticity, an almost third-dimensional illusion. The keylight of such a close-up comes from 2 o'clock of circle *B*. Use little or no filler light, but watch out for noses; they have a tendency to be much too prominent.

MONGOLIAN HIGH CHEEKS

Unlike feminine close-ups, in pictures of men, if we have high cheek bones, we high-light them. They give character. For illumination of this type of close-up or portrait, we use a light at 12 o'clock somewhere between circles *A* and *B*. This light will model the face and highlight the cheeks. To this light we add a little filler from front, and an eyelight. The lighting of the background depends entirely upon the mood desired.

CRIMINAL CLOSE–UPS

These close-ups are lit with the traditional Jimmy Valentine type of so-called criminal lighting. A strong key is placed at 6 o'clock of circle *A* (Figs. 199, 200). A kicker at 3 o'clock of circle *B* will add strength. To this we add an eyelight, but as most of these shots are night scenes, we add no filler light. Back-light is allowable but not absolutely essential.

CLOSE–UPS IN NIGHT EXTERIORS

There are at least two kinds of night close-up lighting. One is a dark silhouette against a lighter background. The other is a light face

Fig. 199

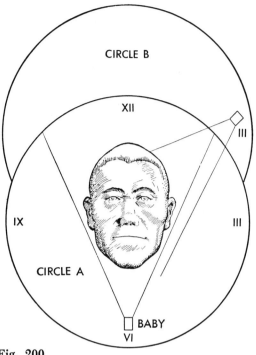

Fig. 200

against a dark background. Silhouette proved to us long ago, with his cutouts named after him, that black against white can make a nice and impressive picture.

CLOSE–UPS OF PEOPLE WEARING GLASSES

For a close-up of a person wearing glasses, we use a high-positioned keylight above 12 o'clock of circle A. This is to avoid glare or reflections of lamps. A nice effect on this type of lighting is a window reflection in the dark glasses. For this, have a prop window or real one placed at such an angle that it reflects in the glasses.

OVER–SHOULDER CLOSE–UPS

Sometimes a close-up is made by shooting over the shoulder of another person in the foreground. In such pictures, the foreground person, who usually is with his back to the camera, should be left dark, almost in silhouette. Just give him a back kicker to sepa-

rate him from the background. The other close-up is lit normally. For composition, the head in the foreground can be cut in any form to suit the picture.

COMEDY CLOSE–UPS

Close-ups of comedy should be lit in a full, high key. By starting with a strong filler light, we are forced to make the keylight still stronger. Keep a gay mood, retain normal skin texture, and do not overlight.

DOLLY AND CRANE CLOSE–UPS

When the camera moves, it is almost impossible to put any reflectors around the person photographed; besides, the lamps may get in the picture. These pictures are usually lit from up high. The reflectors are further away, so larger units are used to get the same intensity of light. For eyelight and filler, we put an inkie and baby on the dolly or crane next to the camera; this travels along with the camera. If the person is too close to a wall, and the baby would throw a spot on it as we move, we use a soft broad instead.

OUT–OF–FOCUS FACES

Scientifically, when a picture is in focus, it is supposed to be sharp. There are, however, faces with rubber-like features (and here I am inviting criticism) which somehow or other never look sharp. No matter how sharp the picture looks around them, their faces always look out of focus. The best we can do (and I am speaking from experience) with these problem faces is to use a strong crosslight. This produces deep shadows, creating somewhat of a contrast.

MENACING CLOSE–UP

No close-up can be more mystifying than one where the features are hidden in the dark, blending into the mysterious background, and only a pair of piercing eyes is visible. The illumination of this picture is very simple.

Use a strong baby, which is up to keylight strength, and light the eyes only. In other words, use a keyed-up eyelight, but slit down so that the face remains dark.

CLOSE–UPS OF COLORED PEOPLE

There is a widespread belief that close-ups of colored people have to be overlit. Nothing

Fig. 201   *Hattie McDaniels*

can be farther from the truth. Although their skin may be darker in texture, they do not require more light than a white person. As a rule, they make very interesting studies for portrait photography. By lighting them normally, we get a bronze-like skin texture, a tint that gives the close-up an unusual pictorial quality (Fig. 201).

CLOSE–UPS ON EXTERIORS

Close-ups lit by direct sunlight are not always beautiful. A face hit by midday sunlight can easily be distorted. The strongly illuminated nose stands out, while the rest of the face is in a deep shadow. Such a picture of a feminine star would hardly make a prize portrait. Most directors of photography prefer to have the close-ups of their stars made inside against artificial backings, stereos, or process plates, where they have full control of their lights. If this is not possible, it is necessary

to throw a tarp around the area photographed, and use booster lights. This is, of course, the expensive way.

The economical way of shooting close-ups outside is to use the sun as backlight. There is more than the required intensity in the daylight filler light. For additional modeling, we add a gold reflector from the side toward which the person is going to look. If the sun

Fig. 202

Fig. 203

115

is too strong and too high to eliminate or use as backlight, then we use a butterfly (Fig. 202). By placing this single or double layer of muslin, silk, or other translucent material over the head of the person photographed we soften the harsh sunlight. When this is done, we use sun reflectors employing the lighting system of interiors. Silver reflectors give a hard, white light. Therefore for face illumination, we use gold reflectors. For eyelight, we use a small-sized gold reflector with a net spread over it. This will allow the person to look directly into it. If the background is not sufficiently lit, or is in the shade, we use silver, tin, or glass mirror reflectors.

Reflectors can be used only on sunny days when there is something to be reflected. If you have to shoot on cloudy days, make silhouette pictures against beautiful cloud formations (Fig. 203).

Humidity shines up the faces, which then reflect light sources. Therefore select their angles.

Until lately, close-ups of skiers and skaters in motion were supposed to be impossible. True, they are difficult to take on the authentic terrain. But why do we have process? Shoot plates of the fast moving background, place your principals going through the movements of a skater or skier, and you have the shot. Everything the mind can conceive, the camera can put on the screen.

In the early days of movies the camera was an instrument to photograph people, sets, action. It was just a necessary mechanism for recording latent images and relaying them to audiences. A film in those days was merely a photographed play—a photoplay.

Then came new ideas. People began to question; why this, and why that? Why the traditional stationary setups always from the same height? Why not move the camera and use it as the eyes of the actors or the audience? Or even go further and use it as the guiding hand of the combination team of director and cameraman, focusing attention wherever desired. The success of the first attempts encouraged others and pictures gradually took on a new outlook.

Today we are once more at a crossroads. Again the audience demands something new, exciting, interesting. We have scarcely begun to realize on the vast potential of photographic possibilities at our command. Anything from the minds and pens of screen-play writers can be filmed realistically, provided, of course, proper use is made of the available materials and techniques.

Fig. 204   *Leslie Brooks*

CHAPTER 6 _____

OUTDOOR PHOTOGRAPHY

When we are outside we see pictures within pictures. We feel their vibrations; some of them bring back memories, others appeal to us because they bear messages. We would like to take some of these pictures and keep them to be able to look at them long after the originals have changed or perhaps entirely disappeared. In the olden days it was the privilege of the few painters who could, to save them by putting them on canvas. Today with the aid of any kind of a camera, it is within the means of all who have appreciation of beauty to safeguard them.

The usual city dweller is so busy doing nothing of importance that he just cannot find time for a good vacation or a short trip to the country. When at last his physician forces him to take one, it is usually too late. The vacation is spent in a hospital, surrounded by the nerve-racking, ear-splitting noises of traffic, steam hammers, and auto horns of the modern metropolis. Fortunately, to the millions who seldom get a chance to go anywhere, motion pictures can bring beauty of the outdoors in the form of entertainment to be viewed in air-conditioned theatres.

Films with Exteriors

It is no doubt the ambition of every producer to make his film outstanding in every way. Yet, strange as it may seem, with but few exceptions relatively little importance is attached to the photography of the picture. While discussing the importance of outdoor photography someone once remarked: "Yes, I can understand, inside on the stage where it is dark, and people, props, and sets have to be illuminated, there is need for an artist—for someone with photographic knowledge. But outside, where God with his powerful reflector, the sun, has illuminated everything, anyone with a Brownie can make beautiful pictures." He has since found out how wrong he was.

It is not absolutely essential to have outstanding photography to make a picture a box-office success. Films have made financial successes without it. However, nobody will question that beautiful exteriors *will help any picture.* People all over the world, especially those who cannot afford to visit far-off lands, love outdoor pictures.

It is as difficult to light good exteriors as it is to light interiors, sometimes even more so. Inside on the stage we have absolute control of lights and light conditions; we can move them around at will. With interior lightings we can use our imagination, we can stylize them. But exterior light effects are too well known to be changed. True, outside, the picture is there, and from the point of view of quantity it is all lit. Nevertheless the theme, the beauty of the picture, must be searched for by expert eyes, and when found sometimes must be corrected with additional reflected sunlight or artificial light. Photographically the sun does not stand still. As it moves the light changes, and so does the picture. One that looks beautiful at ten in the morning looks entirely different at three that same afternoon, and vice versa. The successive positions of the sun provide a variety of lighting conditions.

THE STREET

It is nowadays practically impossible to shoot pictures on a downtown street. Consequently streets have to be built on back lots or ranches where there is less noise interference and more privacy. Before going into the building of such expensive street sets, lighting conditions on the terrain involved should be studied carefully. Remember, the sun rises in the east and sets in the west. It is in the north in summer and south in winter. In California, if shooting toward north, one can be pretty sure that a fair amount of sunlight will hit the location during most hours of the day, even in summer when the sun is up in our hemisphere. The light may be a bit high during noon hours, but long shots, especially in the woods where the light is broken up, can be photographed even though the light does come directly from above.

The old belief that motion pictures can be taken only on a sunny day is passing into oblivion with the horse and buggy of yesteryear. It is now accepted practice to have parts of a street in even deep shadows. Every child knows that a street in the daytime cannot be constantly lit—that its light changes. Does the sun always shine in our lives? Certainly not. Then why should it be so in pictures? A long shot taken on a cloudy day will not have the crisp quality of a picture shot on a sunny day, but it may have a dreamlike mood we have been searching for (Fig. 205).

LOOKING FOR LOCATION

It is uneconomical to take an entire troupe to a distant location and then start to study light conditions and search for setups. Scouts are sent out in advance to gather all possible information about a location long before

Fig. 205 *"The Mosque"*

actual shooting starts. This phase of operation is called *looking for location*.

It happened quite often that business people were sent to distant places to hunt for suitable, beautiful exteriors. When the company finally arrived ready to shoot, they discovered that lighting conditions were deplorable. New locations had to be found in a hurry. This caused confusion and upset the original schedule, resulting in economic catastrophe.

When looking for location it is essential also to have a business man along to take care of the administrative part of the expedition. But ultimately the place will have to be photographed; good light conditions for setups have to be searched for and decided upon. The selection of pictorial beauty should be left to competent artists who know how to find it, and not to people who, no matter what beautiful natural scenery they look at, see only the dollar sign.

Mood in Exteriors

The procedure of establishing mood in exteriors is somewhat different from that followed for interiors. Inside we change our light at will to create a certain mood. This cannot be expected outside where our light source usually is the sun. The mood created by the light outside *is there*. It is up to the photographer to find it. There are different

119

Fig. 206

Fig. 207 *Istanbul, The Sultan's Palace*

Fig. 208

types of daylight, each with a different mood: bright sunlight, hazy sunlight, and skyshine without direct sunlight.

When out in the open we all feel well when the sun shines. This light, be it direct sunlight, or reflected by the countryside, flowers, trees, lakes, meadows, or clouds, has definite psychophysiological effects upon us. A similar effect although on a reduced scale can be created by pictures, reproductions of the original, by reproducing the feeling with the aid of camera films or paper.

Next in power to sunlight are the elements, which also can create mood. Rain, snow, dust storm, cloudiness, and fog, all have their individual moods. Each of the four seasons has its special peculiar feeling or mood. Umbrellas or a turned-up collar can contribute toward establishment of a mood. A sunrise creates a certain encouraging feeling. A sunset symbolizes the close of a cycle. Next to the elements is the setting, which influences mood also. A cemetery, for example, cannot even in the brightest of sunlight look a happy place. When it rains or fog rolls in, it really becomes a gloomy place.

EXTERIORS

Like interiors, exteriors too are divided into various categories:

1. Pictorial view shots, showing the beauty of the countryside (Fig. 206)
2. Geographic long shots, retaining pictorial beauty, but with the purpose of orienting the audience (Fig. 207)
3. Action long shots, where everything else is secondary in importance (Fig. 208)
4. Romantic beauty outdoors, where beauty is a prerequisite (Fig. 209)
5. Mystery scenes. Certain long shots for mystery scenes can be shot in the daytime; some of the night exteriors can be filtered, but as most of the mystery in motion pictures is in night scenes, its illumination falls into the category of mystery lighting (Fig. 210).

Fig. 209 *Prague, Czechoslovakia*

Fig. 210 *"Moonlight Mystery"*

Fig. 211 *"Autumn in Paris"*

Beautiful pictures can be found outside all the year around. Each season has its peculiar beauty appeal to us—different in the city and in the country. Springtime is like a new page in life. Flowers, blooming trees, travel—everything is new. There is hope in the spring atmosphere. Some of us still recall how we used to walk after the water wagon in the summer, with our pants rolled up, barefooted, enjoying the shower of the water. The earth had a peculiar smell, reminiscent of that made by rain after a dry spell. The first drops when falling on the dust rolled like little balls. This picture one cannot easily forget. It is like rain drops beating against one's face. The rusty leaves, the crisp first frost, the overcoat that smells of mothballs, spell autumn. It is the afternoon of the year, the hazy last shine of an Indian summer (Fig. 211). There are two general aspects of winter: the cold, coalless winter, unemployment, smokeless chimneys in factories,

misery, poverty. Life at the winter resort, outdoor sports, skiing, skating, laughter, sunshine even in the wintertime—that is the winter all human beings should have.

Composition

Light alone does not make beautiful pictures. It is essential that we compose our exterior shots. When searching for a setup or angle, don't be contented with the first picture you find. Look around, move up and down and right and left, until you have found the best composition, the ideal spot. Then stay there and observe. If you have the necessary time study your setup under different light conditions.

Fig. 212   *Lynn Bari*

When we photograph a picture the result is one-dimensional. The beauty of the picture can be enhanced by adding a feeling of depth that can be created by use of a foreground piece that fits the decorative scheme of the picture. A foreground piece can be either part of the natural setting existing or growing on the spot—a rock, a tree, a bush, flowers, statues, and the like, or may consist of artificial props placed wherever the camera happens to be set up.

To get the necessary depth, foreground pieces have to be darker than the background; if the sun happens to hit them, keep it off by properly shading them with goboes or flags. There is no prettier picture than the setting sun with a silhouette in the foreground.

As with everything in life, a picture must be balanced. The individual develops this sense best through practice. Sometimes inclusion of a figure or a tree in the foreground will produce a well-balanced composition. If there is nothing growing in the right spot, have someone hold a branch; the result is just as good. It is erroneous to believe, however, that if there is a foreground piece the picture is necessarily well balanced. The lights and shadows too must be properly distributed.

TREES

Like human beings, trees too have their personalities. In photography they help the music of the picture as a whole (Figs. 212, 213, 214). Generally there are two kinds of trees, good and bad. Some good trees bear fruit and are pleasant to look at; they are useful. Some may be sad, others are pictures of gayety. The bad trees are the good-for-nothings. Some have prickly leaves as though to hurt those who come near them. They are a headache for the gardener, bear no fruit, have no flowers, and offer no shade on a sunny day. Like a pretty dog they just give us lots of work. Because of this difference in personalities trees can be used to establish

Fig. 213

Fig. 214 *Santos, Brazil*

certain moods in a picture. Imagine a dead tree fallen by the wayside; a picture of it could be called "Mission Completed" (Fig. 215).

CLOUDS

When shooting exteriors the sky is usually the background of our picture. A sky without

123

Fig. 215 *"Mission Completed"*

Fig. 216 *Old Jerusalem*

clouds is like a wall without any decorations or designs on it; it is a picture of loneliness. Clouds too are of different kinds. There are those which like soldiers parade in front of you (Fig. 216). Some take you into a dreamland, making you forget all your troubles. Then there are the black clouds which bring with them a storm of destruction. There are those which make the farmers happy, bringing rain; the pretty rolling ones which remind you of pretty girls on the beach who never go in swimming. Then there are the clouds we all know which surround the setting sun, inspiring the imagination to travel. And when the sun has set it illuminates these clouds, cre-

ating a beautiful symphony of all colors of the rainbow.

Plain white burning skies can be broken up artificially with skywriting, which turns into fleecy white clouds that stand out against a blue sky. Really beautiful cloud formations cannot be ordered like so many horses; they must be photographed when they are there. As we see, clouds not only prophesy weather, but also help to establish the mood of a picture.

CAMERA ANGLES

To produce a natural effect, the average picture should be shot from eye height. If we want to accentuate the height of a person in the picture, the low setup is ideal (Fig. 217). On the other hand, if we want to minimize it, we raise the camera higher than eye height. When shooting a picture of a crowd, raise the camera high, as otherwise the people in the foreground hide those behind (Fig. 218).

Fig. 217

Fig. 218 *"The Crowd"*

Fig. 220 *The Best Ranch, Colorado*

Fig. 221

Fig. 219

Do not cut the picture into two or more parts. For example, if we have a tree or pole in the foreground and we show neither the top nor the bottom, the picture is cut so that it looks like two pictures (Fig. 219). We can break this cutting line by, for example, tree branches, or someone leaning against the pole (Figs. 220, 221). Foregrounds are used not

Fig. 222 *"Where the Romans Camped"*

Fig. 224 *"Jerusalem"*

Fig. 223

only to give depth, but also to indicate relative size. For instance, if a wall appears alone in a picture, its height is not apparent (Fig. 222), but if we put a person in the foreground, proper perspective is established (Fig. 224).

If we are on the ground and look at someone on a hilltop, we naturally look up at him. If he is in the valley, the opposite is the case—we look down. It is the same in pictures. If we want to give the feeling of someone being up high, we frame her in the upper part of the picture (Fig. 223); if we want to show him as being down we frame him in the bottom (Fig. 224). A person may be on the top of a mountain, but if he is in the lower part of a picture we get the feeling that he is on low ground. An automobile, for example, should be in the lower part of the picture to produce the feeling that it is on the street level. That is the way we are accustomed to seeing a car in real life, on the lower part of our field of vision.

In order that we may understand the mes-

Fig. 225

sage of a picture, it is essential that we lead the eye—we concentrate the attention of the spectator on the most important part of the picture. As the eye is light sensitive, it sees the hottest part of the picture first. We light brightest the part which we wish to emphasize (Fig. 225).

Painting with Sun Reflectors

Sunlight alone, whether direct, reflected by clouds or water, or skyshine, is not always sufficient for our photographic purposes. For instance, sometimes when acting as a backlight it is so strong that the light reflected by the surroundings is too soft for faces. By exposing for one, we lose the other. In such instances sunlight must be supplemented artificially. This may be done either with sun reflectors or with booster lights. In long shots where figures are so small that they are hardly visible and facial expressions can hardly be discerned, where they are just part of the pic-

ture *in toto*, no sun reflectors are necessary. Nature alone takes care of the total light array. However, as we come closer to our subjects the situation changes. To illustrate, consider a close view of a group of people standing in direct sunshine. The faces of one or two may be in direct sunlight, but that of the third is in the shade. If we photograph the picture as is, without aid of additional reflected light, it may not be balanced. The faces of those in the sunlight may be overexposed, while the face of a person in the shade may come in on the under side. This situation prevails where sunlight is especially strong. In order to balance such lighting, we must reduce the sunlight and add reflected light. For this use gold sun reflectors.

The original sun reflectors were large glass mirrors. They were much too heavy to carry around, and reflected light of too high intensity. Tin reflectors were substituted because they are lighter in weight and give a softer light. They were placed on the ground and supported by sticks. As motion picture photography developed into art, the masters discovered that these low reflectors were still not ideal for painting outside pictures. Because of the low light source they distorted the faces of the actors, who in some instances were made to look like screen criminals. As the illumination of motion picture photography gradually improved, these reflectors were replaced by gold ones mounted on lamp stands having wheels. In the slightest wind these reflectors sailed like skaters on a frozen Dutch lake, so the tripods were changed to more substantial, heavy, but demountable iron stands. Gold reflectors with loose gold leaves are still in use for exterior photography. Tin and silver reflectors give a white light, while gold ones reflect a reddish light similar to that of the setting sun.

Contrary to a prevalent misconception, a good photographer, while he may lack experience with sunlight, is just as good on exteriors as he is on interiors.

THE EIGHT-LIGHT SYSTEM
ON EXTERIORS

The formula for exterior reflected lighting, although similar to the inside pattern, is different enough to justify its repetition here.

1. FILL LIGHT

Nature took care of this. As a matter of fact sometimes there is too much of it, so that we must stop down in order not to overexpose our picture.

2. KEYLIGHT

This can be sunlight, either direct or diffused by use of butterflies or other translucent materials. As there is only one sun, if it is used as backlight we must find another light source for the key. In such a case the gold sun reflector is used. This can be used diffused with a net over it to soften the light. Artificial light too can be used for keylight.

3. FILLER LIGHT

There is usually enough fill light to serve as filler also. However, if the keylight is too strong and there is no other means of balancing the light, additional filler is used. For this we can use sun reflectors. For faces the gold side should be used.

4. CLOTHESLIGHT

As this has to be more pronounced than the key or filler, the silver side of the sun reflector is recommended.

5. BACKLIGHT

Because sun reflectors cannot be suspended in open spaces, they can be used as backlight only where they can be hidden behind the people photographed, as on roof tops, trees, etc. The direct sun makes the best backlight. If too strong it can be softened with the aid of the long-necked butterfly.

6. KICKER LIGHT

The best kicker light is the sunlight itself, but if its use is not feasible, sun reflectors will serve. As the reflector must be placed some distance away from the people, the silver side is used because it carries further.

7. EYELIGHT

For eyelight the gold side of the sun reflector can be used, if possible with a net over it. The best is the small gold one made up especially for this purpose. It is small, easy to carry or hold in the hand, and not too difficult to look into directly. This reflects sunlight into the eyes, giving them that necessary sparkle.

8. BACKGROUND LIGHT

Backgrounds are usually lit by nature herself, but if not we "pump" light into them. Glass mirrors are used as reflectors if the background is green, tin if it is dark walls or other dark objects, and gold reflectors if it is white walls, etc.

Even if we don't use boosters, the background can be broken by use of an arc, and shadows can be projected on a monotone wall. *Do not try to illuminate large surfaces with sun reflectors; they never look natural.*

BUTTERFLIES

If the sunlight happens to be too strong to be used even with a reflected filler, or if it is too high to be used at all, then the situation is remedied in the following manner: Place the large butterfly above the heads of the actors. This will soften the sunlight. Different densities of material can be used for this butterfly; with a heavy silk the light can be cut down to a low value. When this is done, the rest of the lighting is carried out as already explained. The back crosslight is also a reflected one with strong white or tin reflectors.

If the reflectors are in such positions that

they cannot be reached by direct sunlight, tnen mirrors or tins are used to reflect sunlight to the gold ones, which in turn illuminate the actors' faces. Strong glary reflectors are difficult to look into. Actors blink their eyes; some can hardly keep them open. This gives them an unnatural aspect, for we never do that in real life unless looking into the sun directly, which is seldom done. Scenes with long dialogue should be lit with soft light so that the actors are not incommoded. In real life few people would stop in glaring sunlight for a long conversation.

Summarizing, reflectors should be used in the following order:

1. Gold reflectors for faces shaded by butterflies over them
2. Silver reflectors for backlight, crosslight, kickers, and dark backgrounds
3. Tins and mirrors for distant dark spots such as green bushes or trees
4. Small reflectors for eyes

When photographing scenes in the shade the effect should be that of shade—*do not overlight.*

Booster Lights

One cannot always guess the weather correctly. Even the weatherman can be wrong with his forecasts. Often when we arrive on location we run into trouble. The sun happens to be in a stubborn mood and refuses to come out from behind heavy clouds. To wait around would mean a loss of precious time. In order to be able to work, we take along an electrical crew and the necessary equipment. This consists of one or more generators and reflectors, usually large units. With this equipment we build up or *boost* the quantity or improve the quality of existing sunlight on location. Hence its name, *booster light.* On some pictures with large budgets, boosters are used even with the sun out. Some of the masters prefer to do their exterior painting with the

softer controllable inkies instead of the fixed one-density, hard, spotty sun reflectors. This is accomplished by *tarping in* a large region (cutting out the sunlight entirely by placing a canvas over it). Carrying boosters involves extra expense, but the manifold advantages more than pay for themselves.

Booster equipment includes a generator with a capacity of 300 amperes or more, and a sufficient number of reflectors. Because even on a cloudy day there is always some light to buck, small reflectors are of no use, and the smallest used is the junior.

THE EIGHT LIGHTS AND BOOSTERS

1. FILL LIGHT

As there usually is enough light even on a cloudy day, nature takes care of this.

2. KEYLIGHT

In boosters the keylight is usually a *170* arc or a senior. Naturally the area to be lighted artificially is limited; large open spaces cannot be lighted with boosters. We can get a fair imitation of sunlight on as much as a city block. Even this is difficult, for multishadows begin to appear where keylights overlap.

3. FILLER LIGHT

There is usually enough light for this too. However, if it is too dark, Duarcs can be used.

4. CLOTHESLIGHT

Small arcs like the *90* can be used for this.

5. BACKLIGHT

Backlight in boosters can be used only if the lamp, an arc or a senior, can be hidden on a roof top or other high place out of the picture. Otherwise we must be satisfied with just kickers.

129

6. KICKER LIGHT

As kickers can be placed beyond the camera sideline, we can use some even in flat country. Arc lights, seniors, or juniors can be used on closer shots.

7. EYELIGHT

For eyelight a junior is used. The units ordinarily used inside would hardly register.

8. BACKGROUND LIGHT

In this case the background light is also the light of the set. If the background is building walls or other close construction, the use of arcs is recommended to light bushes, trees, or other backgrounds. In open country there is no need for background lighting, for there is no artificial light strong enough to light up such an area on a cloudy or dark day.

CLOSE–UPS ON EXTERIORS

Booster lighting outside is not unlike inside illumination, with the difference that even on a cloudy day there is a great quantity of fill light reflected by skyshine. To eliminate this the set must be tarped in. If we use boosters on top of this existing general light, the illumination naturally must be done in a much higher key. The photographer who wants to imitate sunlight must understand it. It is not sufficient to pour a lot of light on walls and people as so often is done. It must resemble the daylight so familiar to everyone.

Painting with Filters

Sometimes when we look at the ground-glass we realize that if we were to shoot the picture "straight" without any artificial correction it would lack something. It would have either too little or too much contrast, etc. In such cases we resort to what is called *painting with filters. In the hands of an artist the filter is just another brush, another in-*

strument used in the painting of pictures. Every photographer has his own ideas of how, which, and what, about filters. It is difficult to tell which is the best filter for the purpose in mind. It is up to the student of photography to go out and experiment with them, and build up his own technique.

When it comes to a Sunday excursion the average person driving a car has no time to study up on the dynamics of the motor, or the scientific explanation of combustion and spark plugs. He wants to get in, step on the starter, and be off. The same applies to the use of filters. The average amateur or professional photographer has not the time or patience to study the scientific properties of glass, colors, and other data on the use of the numerous filters on the market. It is quite confusing, and one cannot be expected to spend the few precious hours of Sunday, which goes quickly as it is, to read mathematical formulas. By use of the filtroscope one can select the filter which he believes best suited to the scene and to existing conditions of light, for the purpose of reproducing in his "light painting" the mood with which the scene has inspired him.

Filters in general use are of either glass or gelatin, and come in squares and circles of various sizes; professional filters are usually either two or three inches square. A glass filter is suitable for use on the outside of the lens; a gelatin filter usually is used inside the camera, between lens and film. We shall not bore the reader with the explanation of each of the filters; there are too many books dealing with that subject exclusively. We shall mention only a few of those most frequently used in everyday photography.

If you like to travel light and want to go out shooting black-and-white pictures with but one filter in your pocket, then take the G of the Wratten series. It is of a yellowish-orange tint that cuts the mist, and on days when the sunlight is soft it builds up contrast, thus deepening shadows. Because of its tint it lightens faces, and brings out clouds without too much overcorrection of skies or darkening of trees. The *G* is definitely the best all-around filter to carry.

The *Aero* comes in a greenish-yellow tint. It is used mainly to brighten greens, trees, and bushes, to which our present black-and-white films are not sensitive enough. Those who do not believe in overcorrection use the *Aero* filter. Also photographers who like to shoot with wide-open apertures use this in combination with a neutral filter, one of the *N* series. Neutral filters are used when the light is too strong and would require stopping down, thereby sharpening a landscape picture too much.

The *56* of the Wratten series is a pure green filter which also is used to brighten greens, or is used as a night filter in combination with another, such as the orange.

A good old faithful orange-colored filter comes in very handy if we have no reflectors to brighten faces when figures are backlit, or against glaring sea or snow. Reds have a tendency to overcorrect and thus dramatize landscapes; some persons like the contrasty clouds and black skies. Both orange and red filters have the effect of darkening blue and green, and lightening yellows and reds.

NIGHT SHOTS MADE IN THE DAYTIME WITH FILTERS

Besides darkening the blues, red filters have a tendency to deepen shadows and build up whites, to overcorrect (Figs. 226, 227). This effect, and limited budgets, have resulted in their use for making night shots in the daytime. These night shots cannot be used for every light condition at night. A filter cannot be used to bring light out of a window, store, apartment house, or restaurant, to simulate light conditions ordinarily prevailing at night. It can, however, imitate a deep moonlight effect. This method is not good for mystery lighting, but can be fair for romantic

Fig. 226

Fig. 227

scenes, chases, or extreme long shot landscape scenes which it would be impossible to illuminate artificially.

The filter factor is calculated, but that allows only for light absorption; in addition, if we want a night feeling, we must stop down another stop or two to weaken the negative and cut out details in the shadows.

The Wratten 72 filter is ideal for night shots; so also is a combination of the 23 and 56, pink and green, respectively. The red filter 29 alone also can be used, but it overcorrects whites. Great care must be taken in making these night shots in the daytime. Make-ups must be corrected, and wardrobe also, because through these filters red photographs light, making lips pale and red objects a light gray or white.

Ocean shots can be made with these filters, to darken the sky and water, and to accentuate the whitecaps, the fluorescent white tops of waves. Use of such filters lightens sand.

NIGHT SHOTS IN THE DAYTIME WITHOUT FILTERS

There are several ways of making night shots in the daytime other than by use of night filters.

Reflection of the sun in the panes of windows can be made into a night shot if sky does not appear in the scene, or if it is darkened to night density.

Another old system is to tie the camera down, shoot the scene in daylight, rewind the film, and when night falls photograph the lights. The camera must be rock-steady, because the slightest movement would throw the lights out of their proper positions and ruin the picture.

If there is to be no sky in the scene, point the camera toward the south in the afternoon. If there are windows, a fair imitation of night can be obtained by placing tracing paper over each window and placing a photoflood bulb behind it. If there is any action in front of the building, use sun reflectors to silhouette the figures; this can be done also with booster lights. In real life a sunset differs from a sunrise, but as photographed they look pretty much alike.

GHOSTS

When a lens is stopped down too far, it begins to photograph its own diaphragm, producing vague spurious images known as *ghosts*. This is especially true of wide-angle lenses such as the 25 mm and 30 mm lenses. Reflection from the glass surfaces of a filter used before the lens may produce additional flare light in the camera; for that reason a

132

gelatin filter should be used inside the camera instead. When there is a glare, as on the ocean or on the sand of a desert, the condition is aggravated. A further precaution is to use a neutral-density filter instead of stopping down the lens; if that does not reduce the light intensity sufficiently, the operator of a professional motion picture camera can cut down the shutter also to obtain a sufficiently short exposure.

DIFFUSION ON EXTERIORS

Because stopping down the lens has a tendency to sharpen the image, more diffusion can be used on exteriors than on interiors.

Fig. 228 *The River Jordan*

Romantic pictures in the woods or scenes including water surfaces look much better when heavily diffused (Fig. 228).

Light Problems

With changes of season or geography the light changes, and problems of lighting arise. The light of Africa differs from that of sunny California, of the mountain tops of Switzerland, or of the pampas of Argentina. When we are tired we are bound to err in judging the light. The intensity of light varies during the day, especially with changes of seasons and geography. *Use your exposure meter.*

IN THE DESERT

In the desert or in any other place where there are no trees, houses, or other objects to break the monotony of large areas, compose your pictures by taking advantage of the long shadows, either early in the morning or late in the afternoon. There are seldom clouds in the desert, but they may be superimposed later on the barren sky by printing in. Heat waves (mirage) throw the picture out of focus, and even filters cannot remedy this condition.

Dust is another of the difficulties to be overcome. Load the camera carefully in order that the fine particles may not enter it; dust is hard to get out later, and may prevent the camera mechanism from functioning properly. If possible, protect the camera from the strong hot sun of the desert by use of a beach umbrella; both camera and film tend to overheat, causing many inconveniences. Ice and a thermometer should be carried for the test box. Remember that you are far from the camera shop, and take proper care of your equipment.

Because the light of the desert is likely to fool you, use two exposure meters for checking, as with snow.

Sunsets in the desert are very pretty; if you are so fortunate as to capture one, you have a picture indeed.

IN THE MOUNTAINS

The prize pictures in the mountains are *early sunrises* and *late sunsets*. The light changes rapidly at high altitudes, so be extra careful about exposure calculations. Winter scenes in the mountains require special treatment.

IN THE JUNGLE

There is not light enough for adequate exposure in the thick of the jungle; neither is there a booster light. In order to get a picture with a still camera it is necessary to make a time exposure. A motion picture camera may be undercranked, watching plants, trees, and animals, the movements of which might be exaggerated by undercranking. Use tropically-packed raw film stock; repack exposed film tightly in cans and shellac them airtight. An icebox or other cooling system is helpful.

Dress and eat lightly; watch your food and drinking water. If you are not well you cannot make good pictures.

Westerns

We could hardly close this chapter on outdoor photography without saying a few words about our eternal Westerns that are so popular the world over. Just as people from Texas like to be called *Texans*, exteriors with cowboys, horses, and beautiful women are not called *outdoor pictures*—they are *Westerns*.

No Western is complete without the final chase. If such action were to be photographed at the normal 24-frame speed, it would be very dull indeed. Everyone is familiar with racing pictures in the newsreels, photographed with a telephoto lens; the horses just never seem to get anywhere. To speed up our horses, we regulate the speed of the camera. The slower the action is taken, the faster will it appear on the screen, where the speed of projection never changes. The chase must increase in tempo. It may start out at normal speed, but by the time it ends, the camera usually is ground at 18 frames per second. The speed may be cut down even to 12 frames per second for exaggerated comic effects. Whenever the camera is slowed down, exposure must be corrected accordingly. To illustrate: For a speed of 12 frames per second, which is one-half the normal 24, a full stop smaller should be used; exposure can be adjusted also by closing the shutter to 90 degrees. Cross-screen action needs not be exaggerated as much (22 frames) as when riders come toward the camera (20 frames). Use of a wide-angle lens increases the apparent speed of riders coming toward the camera, because they appear to cover the ground in less time. A cattle stampede should be photographed at 20 frames per second.

Open country is the best place for long shots or chases. Too many trees hide the riders. Early morning and late afternoon are the best times to shoot such long shots. Start your day with scenes on top of a hill, and leave scenes in a gorge or on a river bottom for later on. For a sunrise or sunset, get a puddle of water, a river, or a lake in the foreground. This will reflect the sun and add to the pictorial beauty of your shot. To symbolize destruction or death, use a barren dead tree in the foreground. If obliged to shoot in a flat light, paint the foreground black; this is not ideal, but it helps.

Clouds indicating arrival of a storm should be undercranked; there is hardly a lower limit to the speed that may be used. It depends entirely upon the effect desired, and also upon the speed at which the clouds actually are traveling. A nice symphonic montage of clouds can be made by having several cuts of clouds, each cranked slower than the preceding one giving the impression of a growing storm.

Clouds of dust help chase scenes, because they pick up from a great distance. To make a real dust cloud, tie brush behind a coach or a horse, and let it drag. (This gag was used as a camouflage in the old frontier days.) Dust is particularly effective if backlit by the late afternoon sunlight. When, on the contrary, we wish to see the details of a scene, dust is distracting. Then a water wagon is used to wet down the road; it may be used also to darken glaring white roads.

For fast, exciting action, pan the riders into the scene; this takes in more territory, and if a 30 mm lens is used, it will be very effective.

Light travels faster than sound. Gunfire battles which are seen first and heard only later should not be shot from too great a distance, or it will be necessary to synchronize them accordingly.

Stunts look much better from a certain dis-

tance. Do not try to insist upon authenticity and shoot them from nearby.

Unfortunately most real Indians were killed in real Westerns, so we cannot always have them. Use Hungarians or Russians, and if they are not dark enough make them up.

Use dark horses for drawing a stagecoach against a white background so that they will not blend into it. Use white horses against a dark background, and for filtered night shots. Horses too can be made up. Of course the weather must be good. Once we painted a horse white; then it started to rain, and before the scene was over, the horse was black again. Horses should be warmed up before a chase to get more speed out of them.

Most Westerns depict the "good old days," when they did not have telephones, telegraph poles, or radio towers, so watch your background. To wipe out automobile tracks from a dirt road, tie a twig to a horse and comb the road.

To indicate transition between seasons, it is nice to use a window snowed in, dissolve into blooming trees, and finally into the falling leaves of autumn.

Different kinds of desert flowers blown by a gentle breeze and silhouetted against the cloudy blue sky make excellent backgrounds for titles.

When on location after a few rainy days, keep your car on the trail or you may get stuck. If stuck in sand or mud, don't try to get out by means of the car's power; you will really dig yourself in. Jack up the car and push, but *hard*.

The New School of Exterior Photography

In exteriors as well as interiors, Hollywood was addicted to the candied (not candid) type of chocolate-coated sweet unreal photography. Then came the war. The enemy was real and could not be present at production meetings. There were no rehearsals on battlefields or during naval or air battles. There was only *one take* of each scene. There were no boosters, no sun reflectors, no butterflies, and no diffusers. The pictures were starkly real. Explosions rocked the cameras, but they also rocked the world, and with it rocked Hollywood out of its old-fashioned ideas about photography. The year 1947 brought a new photographic technique. *Boomerang* and *T-Men*, photographed on original locations, prove that realistic photography is popular, and is accepted by the great majority. Let us have more realism.

CHAPTER 7

SYMPHONY IN SNOW

Fig. 229 *"Ambition"*

I remember as a child, that whenever the first snow fell in the wintertime, we were awakened by whoever discovered it first. We all ran over to the window and just stood there in our long nightshirts gazing and rejoicing at the hypnotizing, wonderful sight, this gift of nature, the first fresh, white snow of the season.

There is something definitely attractive about white. For ages it has been known as the color of innocence. It is pleasing to the eye, and has a calming effect upon us.

Just like human beings, the good earth too likes to change its attire to suit the occasion. For each season it has an appropriate garment. When winter comes, it reaches to

136

Fig. 230 *Aspen, Colorado. (Photo: Tintype.)*

heaven and brings down its royal ermine robe in the form of white snow, with its trillions of flakes of different geometrical designs and all the beautiful colors of the spectrum. Add to this the deep blue sky, the green of the pines, the brown mountains (Fig. 230), pink cheeks, sport costumes, red sweaters, and a healthy bronze tan of the skiers, and you have a picture, a symphony in colors.

On late afternoons the fog starts to roll in, and surrounds the peak of the mountain as though to protect it, reminiscent of someone covering up a bird cage for the night.

On Vacation

Millions of people all over the world live their entire lives without having had the pleasure of seeing snow. Here and there are a few lucky ones who do get away, but most of those are in too great a hurry. After having arrived at a winter resort they continue their city rush. They can't relax and take it easy. Enviously they look at the healthy-looking ski instructors but forget that it took time

and patience to get that bronze tan. They have heard and read about sunshine and vitamins. So as soon as they can they go out and try to get a one-day tan.

Experienced tourists warn the newcomers about the danger of trying to get everything the first day, but human beings remain human beings. They have to learn everything the hard way, by experience. They stay out in the sun all day long. It feels fine. The fresh air is invigorating. It is fun. They don't bother using sun glasses and even expose their civilized milk-white bodies to the penetrating sun rays of the high altitude.

After sunset they return to the hotel. By now they feel somewhat strange. Something *is* wrong. Everything in their rooms looks so reddish. They look into the mirrors and while they see their pinkish complexions, their ears are ringing. They hear the warning voice of the experienced tourist: "Don't try to get it in one day."

The rush continues, but this time it is to the drugstore or the house physician, the bellboy, room clerk, or what have you, only to find out it is too late. The harm is done. They must take the consequences of their carelessness. All kinds of medicines and salves are smeared on the sensitive burned skin, which make them look like Indian warriors. Then they buy sun glasses to protect their temporarily color-blind eyes.

All night long they toss around in bed. They can't sleep. They keep getting up and looking into mirrors to see if there are any possible changes and finally completely exhausted they fall asleep.

Early the next morning they head for a mirror and find their faces puffed, distorted, and wrinkled, and their eyes half blind, sensitive, and irritated, lips cracked, swollen, and stinging. For the rest of the vacation they are confined indoors. Then they rush back to the city, but not without having learned the lesson "what not to do the next time," that is, if there is a next time.

To be in good condition on a snow location one has to feel well. A few words of what to do and what not to do will not harm anyone.

MEDICAL ATTENTION

In addition to the usual medical kit, bring the following essential items:

A reliable sun tan grease or oil

For protection against wind, a camphorated lipstick

Glycerin tablets for a sore throat

A glycerin and lemon juice solution for chapped hands

Once out in the open, you start to burn—sunburn, windburn, and snowburn. On high altitudes you have no city dust, dirt, gases, or smog to protect you. The air is pure, the atmosphere is clear. This is nothing to break the strength of the powerful sun rays. Protect your eyes. Both smoked and amber glasses are good. The disadvantage is that once you get used to black, smoked glasses, you just cannot get along without them for the rest of the vacation. Amber-colored glasses have a different effect. *Consult your physician.*

Do not look out of the window from a dark room at the powerful sunlight reflected a thousand times by the blinding white snow. The sudden light change, injurious to the optic nerve, may produce a severe headache or photopsia. Some day, hotels at winter resorts will have their windows toned down with tinted glass which will reduce the glare of the outside, and make it more pleasant for the tourist. When you leave the hotel for the outside, do it slowly, gradually. There should be chambers of different light intensities for gradual light changes. Don't step outside from the underlit hotel where your eyes are dark-accustomed into the strong sunlight. When you return to the hotel go inside gradually. If possible, and you have the necessary time, the first few days should be spent becoming acclimated to the new and strange surroundings. Do not rush. Remember it took the native population a lifetime to get used to this, and you just arrived.

As a protection against sunlight, cover part of your face with a handkerchief. A few minutes of direct sunlight the first few days is more than enough. You may not get tan in one day, but you will not get burned either. Make sure that your face and other exposed skin surfaces are also protected by sun-tan grease or oil. Rub it in thoroughly. Put lipstick vaseline camphor on your lips. Repeat this several times, for it wears off, especially after meals, drinks, and kisses. Watch the bottom of your nose. That is the place least protected, nevertheless the first place where the snow-reflected light rays burn. This can be very unpleasant.

Sun baths should be taken only during noon hours, and not the first few days, either. Most people think that on a cloudy or foggy day they cannot get burned. More people get burned on these days than on sunny ones when they expect the attack.

WARDROBE

For those who do not ski, knee-high rubber shoes are ideal. Make sure that the snow does not get in your shoes and melt there; it gets cold. Good socks, of camel's hair or pure wool, keep your feet warm.

In the mornings it is usually cold. Dress warmly. Toward noon it gets warmer, and you may take off some of the extra clothing. In the afternoon put your warm clothes on again, before you get chilled. Use warm sport clothes and waterproof ski shoes.

Gloves are not very practical. They stop the blood from circulating freely. Use mittens instead, they are much better. In some of these places there is no laundry service, so bring extra underwear, socks, and shirts with you.

Let us take an expedition to the snow country and bring back pictures of winter to the less fortunate of the cities who, doped by the carbon monoxide gas of the thousands of automobile exhaust pipes, take only one vacation in their lives, and that at the end, and for good.

On Location

For a film expedition to go on a snow location without the *cat* (snow plow) and a sleigh attached to it for the transportation of crew, cast, and equipment, is like going on a fishing trip on the ocean without a boat.

Every professional or amateur photographer who goes up to the snow country takes a camera with him. It is important to have good equipment with it. Remember you are going to sub-zero weather, and a few additional items are needed.

The first days on a snow location should be spent in acclimatization, picking setups, search for compositions, and study of light conditions.

Snow scenes can be very beautiful, but only if well photographed. In order to get good results, the only time to shoot in snow country is early in the morning, even before sunrise, and late in the afternoon, sometimes after sunset. In the time between, the light is flat. Nobody in his right mind would think of taking pictures in similar light inside, so why make the mistake outside?

CAMERAS

Because metal contracts in cold weather, all cameras should have special lubrication or none at all. Batteries are of little use, for it takes double strength to turn over cameras in cold weather, even those with ball bearings. Batteries run down fast. Use the *put-put*, a one-cylinder gasoline motor-generator built especially for this purpose.

Beside the usual equipment necessary for any location, expeditions for snow country need several extra pieces. In some places you will find the snow twenty to thirty feet deep.

Use a triangle under the tripod, otherwise it may sink during the scene.

To keep the cameras warm, use electrically-heated blankets. Have a hand test box handy to develop tests. For background plates have jacks ready. Two good exposure meters should be available. Film is brittle in cold weather, so load carefully. Keep cameras in a cool place, for sudden change of temperature fogs the lenses. Heat your cameras and their motors before shooting. Watch for fluctuating motor speeds and check with a tachometer. For skiers use a hand camera, which is easier to carry to distant places, and easier and faster to handle. Thread carefully, check movements, and watch for scratches. Use watch oil if necessary for lubrication of movements.

THE WEATHER

The weather in high altitudes changes very fast. Don't give up if you go out in the morning and see the sky overcast with heavy clouds. In a few minutes the sun may be out and stay out for the rest of the day. This may, of course, happen the other way too. You are dependent upon atmospheric conditions.

When lighting inside we usually imitate nature. When shooting outside we imitate the inside. Observe your light. When the light looks like one you would not hesitate to use inside, that is the time to shoot. Don't be afraid to shoot especially long shots even in direct backlight. The small-figured skiers on the horizon look very impressive. Watch out for double images; check on the groundglass. Crosslight is ideal, for there is enough fill reflected from mountains, snow banks, clouds, the sky, and the snow on the ground.

The wind, haze, mist, fog, and storm are all elements that make snow scenes beautiful. Those are the colors, the sun is your brush, so go ahead and paint.

The snow that has melted during the warm noon hours begins to freeze again after sunset. It takes on a mirrorlike surface, a gloss,

139

Fig. 231 *"Crisis"*

Fig. 232 *Royal Gorge Bridge, Colorado*

which, although it looks beautiful, is very dangerous to ski on. The top surface breaks through, and the skis get caught. Like all reflecting surfaces, pictorially this mirrorlike surface photographs very nicely, especially if we are fortunate enough to have a wind blow powdery snow dust on top of the frozen surface. Use Pola screens and coated lenses to avoid strong glare. Sometimes slight glares make the shot interesting. Every child knows that when you look into the sun it glares. It is silly to cut out scenes which have a reasonable glare. Panning with skiers one can shoot against the setting sun, if the person we are following covers it up.

Cloudy days are not absolutely wasted. A dark foreground piece against the background of impressively beautiful clouds may make a picture even without sunlight (Fig. 231). Comedy and action scenes may be shot in any light. Make sure that you have a variety of tones, dark figures, trees, buildings, rocks, mountains, etc. (Fig. 232). White snow against a white sky makes a poor picture.

Haze and storm may be taken advantage of for shooting special scenes; for rescue scenes they are ideal.

EXPOSURE

There is an unusual amount of light on snow exteriors; it comes from all directions. If the exposure meter used measures reflected light, its reading under these conditions is likely to be too high. The indicated exposure therefore should be increased, sometimes as much as 100 per cent. Experience is the best teacher. I have found, for example, that exposure indicated by the Weston meter should be doubled. Overexposure I have found to be better than under. Make hand tests if in doubt. Snow looks bad on weak negatives.

SETUPS, ANGLES, COMPOSITIONS

In no branch of photography is composition as important as it is in making snow pictures.

Fig. 233 *Mt. Hayden, Aspen, Colorado. (Fritz Kaeser Photo.)*

If possible, use a foreground piece. Put a tree in the foreground if one does not grow there. If cutting trees is forbidden, take one along, stick it in the snow, and dress it with a handful of snow. Footsteps or ski tracks also will serve to create interest in an unbroken expanse of snow in the foreground (Fig. 233). In order to get tall, impressive figures of people, use low setups. Also, contrast faces against the blue sky. If necessary, dig a hole in the snow and have skiers jump over the camera.

TREES

While trees without snow are just so many black spots against the white snow, they help make good pictures if they are covered with it (Figs. 234, 235). They have something romantic about them. The right time to photograph them is early in the morning. The sun melts the snow off them quickly, especially late in the season. Snow-laden branches (Fig. 236) on these trees look like so many

palms of hands begging for something—more snow? Sometimes they look like outspread white wings, or a lady dressed in a white fur coat.

If you see a small pine tree sticking out of the snow, don't try to pull it out. We did, and when it did not work, tried to dig it out, but that did not work either. There were twenty feet of snow underneath and the tree was a big one.

After frost a tree is left white with no snow on it, and looks like a Christmas tree dunked in white paint. Pine trees without snow on them look deep green; to get value out of them, they have to be photographed in direct sunlight. If the sun happens to be behind them, pump artificial or reflected light into them. The only time they serve as dark trees is when used as foreground pieces.

Icicles make very effective winter foreground pieces. Keep the light off them. Silhouette them.

CLOSE–UPS

Shoot close-ups against mountain peaks with the peaks higher than the faces, towering over the heads. It is so symbolic (Fig. 237).

MAKE–UP IN THE SNOW

As most outdoor types, especially skiers, traditionally have bronzed complexions with shiny skin, the make-up of people taking part in outdoor scenes should resemble them. If they happen to have a natural tan, use no make-up. In general it is preferred to use no make-up. Shine them up. Use no powder. Don't be afraid. You will like the results.

It is an old-fashioned, mistaken idea of the old school to have ladies' faces all powdered up, dull, and chalky white. Even in real life girls get a good tan in mountain resorts; with blond hair, blue eyes, and white teeth contrasted against the sun-toasted skin, they make very attractive pictures.

141

Fig. 234 *"White Christmas"*

Fig. 235 *"The Turn"*

FILTERS

On a clear day, the sky up in the mountains is usually a deep blue. If we photograph white snow against such a dark sky without filters, the contrast will be too great and will give the impression of night. The ideal filter for correction of this condition would be a blue filter to lighten the sky and blue the snow a bit, but the faces would photograph dark, and it would also change the wardrobe colors.

With a red filter the sky would go too dark, and it too would change the colors of the wardrobe. This is a factor to be watched when using filters of different colors. It might add difficulties to the matching and cutting of scenes. It would be confusing to have a

skier come in wearing a red sweater in one scene and in the next a white one, which is exactly what would happen if we used a red filter in one of the scenes. The ideal filter for such scenes is the *Aero 2* or perhaps a *G*. Because of the difficulty of transportation in snow, every extra pound of equipment counts. Leave the heavy filter case at the hotel; if you have *G. Aero 2, 21, 3N5,* and *5N5* filters in your pocket, you are safe.

MOONLIGHT

If you observe moonlight in the snow-covered mountains, you will find an unusual amount of visibility. One can see for miles. The light resembles daylight, but with heavier shadows. This light can easily be imitated in

Fig. 236 *Aspen, Colorado. (Photo: Tintype.)*   Fig. 237 *Aspen, Colorado. (Photo: Tintype.)*

the daytime with the proper filter, and sometimes even without it. The best time to shoot this is just before dusk, when the foreground is already in the shade, and the sun is still illuminating the background. Long shadows of skiers and trees add to the beauty of the scene. If there are any windows in the picture, cover them with tracing paper and backlight them. Turn on all practical lights in the picture. Shots against the horizon are gorgeous. The filter may be a *72* or a combination of *21* or *25* with *56*. If you have any night shots, add these to your list of filters.

TRAVELING SHOTS IN THE SNOW

It is very difficult to shoot trucking or dolly shots in the snow. One way of faking is to use a long-focus lens and pan with the skier. Another is to put the camera on a sleigh and go downhill, parallel with your skiers. If you are lucky enough to have a modern clear road, shoot from a camera-car running parallel with snow country. The trailer of the cat may come in handy on a

smooth surface. Undercrank to get required speed.

One can go down as far as 12 frames per second, and not notice it. Have the shutter wide open, or the skiers appear jumpy. Keep speeds constant or you may run into cutting difficulties. When skiers come down a slope use a high setup to get a nice design. Skiing shows up to best advantage if we can see these patterns. Little figures of skiers in the distance make an effective picture (Fig. 238). Make sure there are no other dark spots in the picture. They might confuse.

To get the floating feeling of jumpers, overcrank and use a low setup. Very attractive shots of skiers can be taken from a crevasse, with the skiers passing on top against the horizon. Have them composed in the upper half of the picture to increase the feeling of height. When shooting skiers, have them drag their poles in the powdery snow; this will raise a heavy plume of snow dust, which in backlight is so photogenic. As skiers pass snow-covered trees, have them brush against the branches, shaking snow off as they pass. A cloud of snow dust makes a good fade-in as the skiers raise it when passing in front of the camera. Backlight is ideal for this purpose.

Here the reader might ask the question, If snow pictures are so beautiful and so popular, why hasn't Hollywood made more of them? (or why isn't Hollywood making more of them?). The answer is, that the word *Snow* scares readers of possible picture material. They envision distant locations, storms, delayed schedules, and other such troubles. This may have been true in the past. It is different today. We can now make snow pictures without ever leaving the sound stage. Very few people know this. Artificial snow, process photography, and modern lighting enable us to make winter pictures for practically the same cost as any other film. Long shots of a sleigh ride on a sunny day in snow country can now be rephotographed on the stage with artificial snow, and made to appear as though the ride was through a blinding snow blizzard. More of these pictures will be seen in the near future.

Fig. 238 *Open Slopes with Deep Powder.* (*Fritz Kaeser Photo.*)

CHAPTER 8 _____

OCEAN VOYAGE

When on land we long to go to sea. And when out on the ocean for a few days, excited, we all run to the railing at the sight of land or even a lighthouse at night. Strange beings, these humans.

What is an ocean voyage? First we pack, then unpack, then pack again, and at home unpack once more. An ocean voyage costs money. You will enjoy it more than once if you take a camera along and make a pictorial record of it. Every time you look at your album or project the movie of your trip, memories will bring the trip back in its entirety with all its vivid colorings and at no extra cost.

Love, Live, Laugh, and Loaf

Whether healthy or not, I know of no better medicine than a good ocean voyage. No phone calls, no business, no cooking or dishwashing. No radios, no newspapers, no nerve-racking news. Just take it easy, nothing to worry about, all is paid for. Drink, sleep, and watch the clouds roll by while waiting for the most popular call aboard ship, "first call for dinner" (Fig. 239).

Originally I thought the chapter on exteriors would take care of all outdoor photography, but when I saw how little people know of what to do and what not to do with their cameras while aboard ship, I decided to write a few words on the subject.

Do you remember the old circus, when the clown used to appear between the acts and entertain the audience with his jokes? Chil-

Fig. 239 *"Idle Chatter"*

dren, and some grownups too, sometimes liked that better than the main attraction. This chapter is supposed to be one of these entre'actes to entertain between chapters on the more serious subjects, and at the same time give some tips on a trip by boat.

Preparation

CAMERAS

I have been asked by several people what kind of a camera I think is the ideal one for a long cruise. This question is difficult to answer. All have their advantages and also their disadvantages. The large ones are heavy to lug around, but their pictures need not be enlarged. Miniature cameras are very handy and always loaded. But some people don't like them because the size of the picture is too small. Take the in-between that has the advantage of being relatively light and of a size

146

that you might like. Make your choice. Those with bellows are harder to clean on ship and have more gadgets to watch.

FILM

Be sure you get enough film to take along, both color and black-and-white. The days when you used to go into any photo shop in Bombay, Jerusalem, or Rio de Janeiro and ask for film of any size and get it, are gone. If you rely upon buying film abroad you may be disappointed. If you intend to travel in the tropics, get tropically packed films and keep them in a cool, dry place.

Although there are many places in foreign countries where you can have your exposed films developed, it takes time, and I would advise you not to experiment. Save your exposed film and have it developed at home. Repack exposed films as they came in their airtight containers, and use Scotch tape to keep the moisture of the tropics out. Make sure that repacking is done in a dry atmosphere; any moist air sealed in with the film would be likely to cause trouble.

On board they usually have ship's photographers, but if you don't give them instructions, they usually print for the nonexistent details of the underexposed supposed-to-be-silhouette foreground, and overlook and lose the rich details of clouds or landscapes in the background. This I could never quite figure out. Be sure to take your filters and filtroscope along; you will need them both.

UNITED STATES CUSTOMS

If your camera is of a foreign make, be sure to register it at the customs and get a written receipt stating the serial numbers of lens and camera, before leaving the United States. If you neglect to do this, you may have difficulty in convincing customs guards upon your return home.

Get aboard ship in time to check and double check your baggage before the ship has left port and it is too late to claim anything.

At Sea

Get your sea legs. It takes will power, but do not eat everything on the menu just because it is all paid for. You will be sorry. . . . Strange as it may seem, your food on a trip does have something to do with good pictures. Somehow or other, if you drink only boiled milk and stay away from raw salads and other vegetables while on foreign soil, your pictures will turn out better.

Get your sun tan gradually, and take no hot showers on a freshly burnt skin. It will blister.

Watch the fish—the poor aboard ship and the rich in the water.

Watch the clouds and learn how to interpret them; their formations change from minute to minute.

Listen to the music of the waves. Stay out in the fresh air as much as possible except in torrid zones, where it is better in your air-cooled cabin.

Ladies, be sure to have an extra-strong permanent wave, for it is damp aboard ship, and the salt vapor will ruin the best of hairdos. You will spend less time curling, and less time sleeping with the iron rolling pins in your hair.

So many times when I have asked a tourist about the speed of the film in her camera, the expression on her face has changed to one we may call "Istheresuchathing?" A good many of them did not even know how to open their cameras, and blamed everything on the salesmen they bought them from, or their husbands who gave them the presents. That is what is called *the dollar line* (passing the buck).

Time and again I have seen tourists go to the trouble of getting up early at dawn to get a sunrise (Fig. 240) or the landing at a port. Sometimes they even stay up all night, for they find it easier than getting out of bed,

Fig. 240 *"Morning Prayer"*

Fig. 241

yet when it came to taking pictures they were lost, especially the ladies with movie cameras using 8 mm or 16 mm film. Many having seen me with a camera, came to me with the most unusual questions on how to do this and how to do that. Apparently they thought that paying for the camera in cash, loading it with film, winding it up, and pressing the button, are all it takes to get good pictures. Let me assure you folks, it takes more than that. Allow me to give a few hints as to what to do on an ocean voyage.

Keep your camera ready, cleaned, loaded, and handy at all times. On an ocean voyage one never knows when a good picture may present itself suddenly (Fig. 241). You run

down to your cabin and try to get in, only to find that you have locked your key inside, you look around but there is no one in sight; at last the bellboy comes; you run inside, get the camera, but by the time you get upstairs it is too late. The picture you saw is gone. Remember, the boat travels, the wind blows the clouds around, the climate changes, so does your picture, and of course the expression on your face.

Keep your camera clean. If it happens to get a good salt water spray, and aboard ship anything is possible, clean it immediately. Don't let it dry—it will corrode. Wipe your camera before putting it away. The salt accumulates and oxidizes the metallic parts. Do not touch the lens with your fingers or anything else. Use the air blower.

To keep the salt vapor off the lens have it covered with a lens cap, but do not forget to take it off when shooting!

When the ship is rolling and you walk around with your camera in your hands, be careful, you might knock it against the wall or railing. Hold onto it with both hands, especially when the wind is blowing. It might blow it out of your hands. Winds at sea are tricky.

Conditions at sea are not unlike those up in the snow-covered mountains. Reflections make it difficult sometimes to read the meter correctly. Make your exposure short to make the waves permanent (one permanent that lasts).

For filter selection, consult your filtroscope. Allow for filters when calculating your exposure. For night effects use the Wratten filter 29, or a combination of the 23 and 56. The water is blue or dark green, the sky is blue, the clouds are white—do not overcorrect with heavy filtering. The best all-around filter is the G. *Do not use filters early in the morning. The picture is moody enough without exaggerating it.*

Use diffusion only on close pictures and then only of ladies.

Taking Pictures

It is an easy thing to snap the loaded camera, give the film spool a turn, or pull out the black slip of a film pack. There is a shortage of film abroad. Don't shoot foolish pictures. A good one may come along and you will be out of film.

There are a number of possibilities for pictures at sea—from the time the gong has sounded and all visitors are chased ashore until the time you have arrived home. Below we shall give a list of some of these; you may have your choice:

The dock loaded with people waving their handkerchiefs as the band plays

People lined up on the deck near the rail, waving toward shore. Little by little the city disappears in the distance; a last look at the port and then nothing but ocean.

The gong sounds for the first meal aboard ship. Then come the uninteresting but necessary evils of unpacking, ironing, and settling down for the long voyage.

The first sunny day people will gather around the swimming pool (Fig. 242). Get your camera out. Wet your body, oil it, or smear it with vaseline to make it shiny. It photographs tan and healthy-looking.

Get low setups on deck with faces against the different shades of blue of the sky. The boat starts to rock and many people turn pale. Do not photograph people who are ill—they are sensitive about their looks. Those who tried the one day tan and got blistered all over don't make very good pictures either.

The different games start and make very interesting pictures—shuffleboard, sun bathing, deck tennis, etc. (Figs. 243, 244).

After a few days out the alarm bell sounds. Great is the excitement, for few people have read their instructions for fire drill. Everybody runs for his life belt. Babies look exceptionally cute in their little life belts. I cannot say the same for the grownups who look a bit bulky and uncomfortable, but after all

Fig. 242 *The Three Graces*

Fig. 243

Fig. 244

they were not designed for style but for emergency.

It is strange how ladies who looked old at the time of embarkation begin to look young after a week at sea.

TYPES—CRUISERS AND DESTROYERS

The different types make very good subjects for photography:

The ex-GI who has been to the Pacific and says he is used to sun, but gets burned the first day out

The English consul who has been in Colonial service brings out his shorts

The pest—there is always one. He never lets you read and can find you no matter where you hide

The children who need bringing up, but their parents are busy playing bridge

The young mother with the little baby everybody likes (the baby)

The young high-school girl on her first trip looking at the bronzed bodies of the sunburned young sailors painting the ship

The organizer—he just cannot sit down; all kinds of games, pools, horse races, Neptune initiations while crossing the Equator—always on the go.

The bore—he does not help anyone, never reads, never does anything.

The rumor manufacturer who spreads the rumors of an approaching hurricane, rigid customs declarations, spies following you, arrests, revolutions—he knows everything (he says so himself). He counts the accidents and talks only of unpleasant things. Fortunately all his prophesying does not come true.

The one who is never satisfied where he is seated in the dining room; every meal finds him at a different table.

The one to whom everything happens. He slips in the shower. His laundry is short. His bathing suit drying on deck is blown into the mean. He breaks his leg. He catches the first cold. The air conditioning is cold. The decks are hot. The meals are bad. The water tastes funny. The service is poor. He falls down the steps. His mail gets lost, he never receives a letter. He runs out of razor blades and brilliantine, never has enough towels. All the movies are bad—he knows ahead of time. He blows the fuses, his lights go out. His shower has no hot water. His beds are hard. He doesn't have enough blankets. He has too many blankets. What a character!

The sympathetic captain who, despite his age, can outdance everyone on ship. He is liked by everyone, and is a seaman when needed.

The likeable kid—the sweetheart of the ship.

The devil who breaks up all toys, makes the most noise in three languages, never lets anyone sleep, breaks everything, ruins everything, is fresh with everyone, etc. He gets sunburned, is irritating, blisters—is in the hair of all passengers.

The type who always knows the boat drills ahead of time but never really goes to the trouble of getting his life belt on. He would probably be the first one in the lifeboat in case of a real emergency.

CLOUDS

Every day is not sunny aboard ship either. Clouds begin to gather. They change and make up different formations (Figs. 245, 246).

Fig. 245 *Moonlight*

We shall not cite them by their scientific denominations or their importance in weather forecast. Learn their artistic interpretation. Watch the cloud that opens up like an invisible trap door on a plane and rains itself to nothingness.

RAIN

It is interesting to see the approach of a rainstorm in the tropics on a clear sunny day. The rain drops beat the ocean surface, and from the distance the ocean looks like a desert full of sand (Fig. 247).

SUNSETS

I have had people ask me when they saw me looking at a gorgeous sunset, what I was looking at. When I told them, they looked in that direction and shook their heads (Fig. 248). They failed to see anything (there were no dollar signs in sight . . .). The most inspiring, the most beautiful pictures there are aboard ship are the sunrises and sunsets. Have your camera handy late afternoons. Sunsets on the ocean make prize-winning pictures.

INSPIRATION

Good photographers get all excited when they see a good picture. This is only natural and a sign of latent artistic talent. Don't forget to set the diaphragm stop, cock your shutter and pull out the slide of your filmpack adapter. By the time you discover your mistake, that is, if you discover it at all, the picture that inspired you will have vanished from the horizon.

When hunting for sunsets you need to have patience. Sit it out with your camera all loaded next to you. Save your film for the best picture. If in doubt, shoot. The picture begins to be beautiful some time before the sun actually sets and is hiding behind the huge cloud formations, and lasts long after it has fallen below the horizon.

Fig. 246 *Clouds*

Fig. 247 *Rain Drops*

Fig. 248 *End of the Day*

151

Fig. 249

Fig. 250

Fig. 251

The photographs shown as Figures 249, 250, and 251 were taken within a period of ten minutes. To the layman they may all look alike but if you study them carefully you will notice the difference. All were photographed under the same conditions, same exposure, and with the same filter. Of all you may like one best. It rings all the bells. Use that. Sunsets can be photographed from the time the clouds form around the late afternoon sun, and from then on it is just a series of pictures, each more beautiful than its forerunners.

The silhouette of a profile or a dark print may change the picture. A dark foreground adds a low note to the music or tune of the picture. Just look at the same picture without the foreground. It loses authenticity and could have been taken anywhere (Figs. 252, 253, 254).

Beautiful pictures of sunsets continue long after it is dark. They look like castles and snow-capped mountains in the distance with golden rivers. Your best ideas may come when dreaming, looking at a sunset. When you awaken from your dream it is dark—dinner time. The gong awakens you. *Last call for dinner. You did not hear the first call!*

EVENING

Aboard a ship the day's activities do not end with the sunset. The fiestas, bridge parties, and other similar events offer themselves for good pictures provided your camera is equipped with a flash gun, and you brought enough batteries along.

The horse races with the excited expressions on the faces of the spectators make good pictures. There are dance parties on deck with everything decorated. The masquerade ball, the bingo party, and the like, are events aboard ship.

The masquerade ball has people dressed in different costumes. There is the parade with the captain leading, then there are the awarding of prizes, the jury, the children, the most original costumes—there is enough material for any amateur photographer. At masquerade balls people forget their adapted, civilized selves and demonstrate their real egos.

Ports look their best seen from aboard ship at night, the reflections of the lamps in the water, the signaling lighthouses, the ships sending coded messages by signal lights, the lamps of different colors. These pictures require extra-sensitive film. No matter how firmly a ship is tied to the dock there is always a little movement and vibration of the motors to ruin your pictures.

NEPTUNE

Crossing the equator is the great event of any sea voyage. Children and some grownups too are waiting to see the line on the ocean and the little red flags indicating that we have crossed the Equator; people who have never crossed it before and do so the first time will be initiated. Save film for this occasion, for you will get, if not the most beautiful, the most interesting and funniest pictures of your trip. Usually Neptune boards the ship from aft of crew quarters, and initiates the new passengers. Some of them have their hair half cut, others are dipped into the swimming pool. People are warned not to dress, but those who do are thrown into the water and painted all over with egg, salad dressing, etc. When all this is over there is a fiesta, and diplomas are issued to the victims to save them from having to go through the same thing again.

AMATEUR MOVIES OF THE TRIP

If you haven't any better stories prepared to make on board, then use the ideas listed for photographs. From the time you leave home until you return, there is ample of this material for pictures. As a matter of fact, the opportunities are better for movies than for still pictures. Check your exposure, set your diaphragm, set your focus, and have enough film for the entire trip.

Fig. 252

Fig. 253

Fig. 254

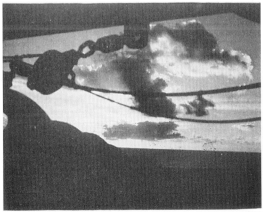

153

Fig. 255   *Meditation*

Fig. 256   *Land!*

Fig. 257

Arrival at a Foreign Port

Whatever you do on an ocean voyage, do not miss seeing the arrival of the ship at some port (Figs. 255, 256, 257). This is especially beautiful if the arrival happens to be at dawn. If the ship arrives very early in the morning, let us say about 6 a.m., you may have to get up at 4:30 or 5:00. It is not the time your alarm clock sounds off, but the hour you get on the deck with your camera ready to shoot, that counts. As the dining room is usually closed at that early hour of the morning, it is a good idea to provide yourself with a sandwich or two and some fruits the night before. For a hot drink take a thermos if you have one of your own, or the one they use for ice water, and have it filled with hot coffee the night before also. Pour the ice water out and heat the bottle before pouring the coffee into it. This will assure you of a hot drink.

You need not worry about your attire at that hour, so just throw your bathrobe on. Sometimes it is chilly and you may have to dress more heavily.

If you use filmpacks it is a good idea to have more than one filmpack adapter loaded and ready. It is usually when you have finished your filmpack or roll of film that the prettiest sunrise pictures appear on the horizon. Pictures don't wait for you.

Exposure meters come in very handy at dawn. The light fools you. It is amazing the quantity of light there is when you think that it is still dark. Keep on measuring, for it changes constantly as the sun rises. Correct exposure is of utmost importance.

To get good pictures, be different from others. Shoot the unusual. Sometimes it is foggy and not one of the passengers uses his camera. When you have different light intensities, as for instance, a dark ferryboat against the gray fog mist, or a tugboat with its smoke cutting across the horizon, you have a picture (or something like one).

PICTURES IN PORT

Good subjects include arrival of port authorities, the police commission, the passing of sailboats in the distance, and the diving of native boys for pennies in the sunlit waters. Have your camera ready with cocked shutter.

FOREIGN CUSTOMS, COSTUMES AND CUSTOM GUARDS

Customs have little to do with photography but much to do with cameras. In many countries the export and import of cameras is forbidden; you can't bring one in and you can't take one out. Upon landing, be sure to check your camera with custom officials and get a written receipt for it with the serial numbers written clearly. This certificate will be needed when you leave that country.

In some countries it is forbidden to photograph anything in public. Get permits if necessary. Keep out of naval and military zones (I thought the war was over). Other people are as proud of their countries as you are of yours; don't try to get pictures of slums, no matter how interesting they are. Natives are very sensitive about them. Stay away from such places, unless your insurance policy covers camera and skull breakage.

You can have your pick. If not included in prearranged tours, there are rubbernecks, buses, taxis and streetcars.

If you have forgotten to get foreign currency at the purser's office aboard ship, do it ashore. Before you do so inquire about the official exchange rate of the day. If some of this money is left over when returning to ship, save it for the return trip or have it re-exchanged by the purser.

In Port

Even if it is pouring rain when you go ashore at the time of landing, take your camera along. In a jiffy the sun may creep out, and if it does even for a minute you may get the prize picture of your trip. Yes, I

Fig. 258 "In Port"

know it is burdensome to carry your camera along, and you look like a tourist, and prices go up, and you have to watch it every time you stop for a beer, but it is worth it, even if you get only one good picture (Fig. 258).

Don't buy souvenirs from merchants who come aboard ship. They are much cheaper in town. Have patience until you get there.

Arrange for taxi fares in advance or you may get some embarrassing moments; these things may happen in any port of the world.

Visit the zoo, the botanical gardens, churches, temples, mosques, parks, schools, other public buildings, and race tracks.

Branches against the white of the clouds and sky make interesting silhouette lace pictures and designs. Other subjects may include a sailboat against the clouds (Fig. 259), the bay, the flag of the country or town, a storm approaching (Fig. 260), back home on your ship, the ocean and the clouds in the daytime,

Fig. 259   *"The Sailboat"*

Fig. 262   *Hindu Temple in Trinidad*

Fig. 260   *"Storm Approaching"*

Fig. 263   *Homeward Bound*

Fig. 261   *Trinidad Mainstreet*

and sky and stars at night. Don't walk bare-headed in the tropics; this is not your school campus. When in foreign places, do as the natives do. Walk slowly, or don't walk at all. Take your time, don't rush, save your energy, and you will get there sooner.

Homeward Bound

The most interesting part of any trip is the homeward bound part (Figs. 261, 262, 263). Then you may get the pictures you were not able to get before for some reason or other.

Find the receipt for your camera which you got at the customs when you left. Declare all films exposed or otherwise, developed or not.

TIPS

The question of tips is a very delicate one. Personally I don't believe in them. Tipping was a bad invention in the first place; every working human being is entitled to a living wage. But as long as we still have the custom (and I hope it will be eliminated in the near future) make your tip generous. Live and let live, goes the old saying.

CHAPTER 9 _____

VISUAL MUSIC

If we hand a baby two marbles, a shiny one in one hand and a dull one in the other, it is almost certain that he will pick the shiny one. Why? We assume that the reason is that the shiny one reflects light rays, pleasant sensations. Unfortunately, very little is known about this latent force of light, which has such a definite, strong influence upon our daily life.

To illustrate: There are days when we are blue; foggy, gloomy, smoggy days, when on every street intersection the red *Stop* signal greets us. Again, there are days of sunshine, when we are gay; we sing or whistle, and drive to town through a series of green *Go* signals.

Visual Symphony

When we look at a beautiful countryside, we like it and derive pleasure from it. We receive light sensations of different colors, different wavelengths reflected by the various objects all over the field of vision. This concert of light is similar to one played by a hundred different musical instruments, in other words, a *symphony of visual music.*

A musical symphony is an audible picture of what its composer had in mind, visualized, or actually witnessed at the time he composed it.

In photography, it is the other way around. When an artistic photographer listens to good music, he is inspired; he visualizes pictures which he paints with light, to be seen later on paper or the motion picture screen.

In photography we have not the *do-re-mi-fa* of music. What we have is various tones—blacks, grays, and whites. These different densities constitute a scale similar to the one in music. In life this scale is far longer than we can even hope to reproduce on paper, or even on the silvery motion picture screen. Pictures are reproductions of natural settings, and therefore cannot radiate like the originals; but they too, on a micro scale, vibrate, stir up emotions.

A picture, be it still or movie, may not create the magnetic spell of audible music or of its original in real life. Nevertheless, little as is known about this spell, we must acknowledge that it is powerful, or Eastman's Brownies would have never become so popular.

LIGHT SENSATIONS

In life, light waves cause sensations which differ with the brightness of the reflecting surface. In a motion picture theatre the screen reflects the light of the projection arc; and the fluctuation of illumination which constitutes the all-over picture is created by the film that passes between the light source and the screen.

If the light is projected on the screen without the film, most of it is reflected. This is the whitest part of the scale. When an opaque film passes in front of the light source, no light reaches the screen, consequently it cannot reflect any. It is jet black; this is the darkest part of the scale. It is between these two extremes that a play of various tones represents the original picture on a reduced scale. In color pictures, this sensation is much stronger, but often is exaggerated.

A picture is a reproduction of an original. It is like a phonograph record but we play it by viewing it by artificial light or sunlight. It may not have the candlepower of the original, but it retains its musical feeling. Whether by reflected daylight inside, outside in direct sunlight, or at night by artificial illumination, when we look at a picture we experience on a reduced scale a certain sensation of light representing the original light that illuminated the scene of the picture.

THE SCALE

The darkest part of the picture gives us a low feeling, that of no light, consequently that is the bottom of our visual music scale (Fig. 264). This is tone A. The sensation of the lightest part of the picture is the strongest, the top of our scale, tone J. Now take A and J and put them side by side. Although both are on the same surface, the same distance from our eyes, tone A looks much closer to us than does tone J. This establishes and proves our theory that by varying the densi-

ties of a picture, an illusion of depth and musical feeling can be created.

THIRD DIMENSION

In real life, the pleasure of visual music is enhanced by third dimension. Fortunes have been and still are being spent to put third dimension in professional motion picture photography; but to my knowledge, the closest we have come to it is an illusion of depth accomplished by the proper distribution of densities. To attain depth in any kind of photography requires no special optical attachment on the camera, nor one with which to view the picture, as does actual third-dimensional photography. The raw film in use, plus the modern processing by the laboratory, has given us a range of densities. For the purpose of demonstration, we shall use 10 different tones, starting with black and ending with white. These tones we shall call *A, B, C, D,* etc. This is our visual photographic scale of music (Fig. 265).

PICTORIAL TONES

As we look at a picture, the tone *A* of black stops us from going any further; it looks closest to us. White, tone *J*, is no tone in itself. However, it allows one's imagination to travel into the realm of distance. We shall use it to depict the spot farthest from us. The intermediate distances can best be shown by using the various tones from *A* to *J*.

I have taken tone *A* and tone *J* and have painted two pictures. Each one has a square within a square. One is black outside and white inside, and the other is reversed, white outside and black inside. Each one creates a

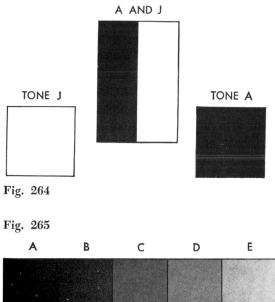

A AND J

TONE J

TONE A

Fig. 264

Fig. 265

| A | B | C | D | E | F | G | H | I | J |

different sensation to the eye. While Fig. 266 gives you no picture and less depth, Fig. 267, the one with the white square in the center, gives a decided impression of depth. There is room in it for one's imagination to travel on and on.

In lighting a picture, light should be distributed in such a fashion that the foreground is dark and the background is light. In between the two, there is space, a musical feeling of depth. Just as in music, a melody of two tones is monotonous to the ear, so in photography, two intensities of light are wearisome to look at.

If we use all of the tones modern photography can reproduce, black in the foreground and forming a frame around the picture, and white in the center of the picture, seemingly

the farthest away, all arranged in a melodious way, we have visual music with an illusion of third dimension, a picture pleasant to look at.

In sound, there are unpleasant noises; in light, there are harsh, disturbing contrasts. We avoid them.

PICTORIAL MUSIC

Visual music is a language through which the past seems to be talking to us. The Egyptians and Indians used pictures of trees, men,

Fig. 268

Fig. 269   *The Sultan's Garden*

Fig. 266

Fig. 267

Fig. 270 *Hedy Lamarr*

Fig. 271 *Paul Henreid*

Fig. 272 *The Rescue*

and other figures to express a thought, to write poetry. That is how the alphabet we use today must have originated.

People, nature, mountains, trees, flowers, birds, and other animals, lakes and rivers, ocean and boats, illuminated by light, in life or in pictures, produce psychological impressions.

A pictorial view of a countryside, or a long shot in interior photography is like a philharmonic auditorium where the picture is the orchestra. Each tree, flower, or bird represents a different visual musical instrument, emanating a different light, depending upon its color and angle of reflection. This light may change if it is a picture of storm or wind, and the light also changes with the angle.

This picture *in toto* causes a psychophysiological sensation in us which is a visual concert (Figs. 268, 269). Its construction is symphonic, like that of its musical equivalent. A beautiful feminine close-up (Fig. 270) can be compared to a violin solo, and a strong characterful picture of masculine beauty to a 'cello solo (Fig. 271). A shot of a group is a trio, etc. (Fig. 272).

In photography, as in music, tastes differ. There is no doubt in my mind that the prettiest music is sad, and the most beautiful photography is in a low key, with rich blacks. Perhaps this is the reason that, to my knowledge, no light photography has ever won the Academy Award for being the best of the year.

CHAPTER 10 _____

THE PORTRAIT STUDIO

Just as most painters stick to the conventional north light for their source of illumination, so do some portrait photographers still insist upon doing their glamorizing with the aid of retouching. Little attention, if any, is being given by either master to the lighting *per se*.

Improvements

Ask the average person who wants to have her picture taken, which she would like better, a *notan, silhouette, chiaroscuro,* or *luminart,* the latest of Hollywood's fashion lighting, the way close-ups of the glamorous stars are lit? Nine out of ten will point to the picture which is the prettiest, most life-like—luminart, the product of the Hollywood school. Notans were great for their time. Chiaroscuro was quite an improvement, and is great art, but it is luminart that goes best with the time in which we live, with the jet-propelled airplane.

If you are an artist for yourself, one with long hair, a smock and a big, flowing black necktie, you may do as you please. But if you are in business for business, you have to give your customers what they demand, the latest in style, the best in quality. It is high time to modernize your studios. Throw your old-fashioned painted backgrounds away and get the latest translite photographic ones. They have depth and allow you to take exteriors inside. Get the new Hollywood-type reflectors; they are easy to control. Have sets built to suit the nature of the picture.

When coming into a dark studio from the outside, where the eye has become accustomed to strong daylight, the change is sudden and contraction of the iris takes place. The adaptation of the eye to the new condition is gradual and slow, even on an artificially illuminated stage. This time of adjustment is just enough for one to trip over one of the many cables spread all over the studio floor. The result may be a torn ligament, or a sprained ankle; in many instances, broken bones have resulted. All are very painful. Cables on studio floors have caused more accidents than anything else.

While it is true that lamps have to be lighted with the aid of cables, for it cannot be done by radio, yet cables need not necessarily be on the floor. It is about time that we started to improve the antiquated system of illumination adapted originally from the legitimate stage. At present, the current outlets are on the floor (Fig. 273), so naturally the floor is full of booby traps. Why not have these outlets up high, out of the way, with cables leading from them which plug into the reflectors? It would be quite an improvement to reverse the present system in which each reflector carries an attached cable. With the new setup (Fig. 274), each time a reflector was added to the floor lighting, a cable could be lowered and plugged into it. This would practically eliminate cables on the floor, and it not only would save money, but would prolong the lives of artists who are so difficult to replace.

Have sets built to suit the nature of the picture. They are not as expensive as you may think. Have them built wild, that is, on wheels, so they can be moved around easily and changed to suit the occasion. Have the walls double faced, so that both sides can be used for different sets, and as many combinations as possible. With a few extra, varied types of windows and props, the setting can easily be changed. Have a clean, gay, light waiting room, with several dressing rooms. If you can afford a specialist in hairdressing and make-up, get one; if not, learn these arts yourself. Inspiring music makes waiting pleasant. Do your beautifying with lights; there is enough work as it is for the retoucher to make every-body beautiful. In spite of that, the new trend is toward realistic, shiny faces full of life.

The old motto, "Let the retoucher take care of it" sounds very much like our discarded war-cry, "Let the lab do the rest." Retouching alone cannot put feeling or mood into a portrait, and it is just as important that they be there as in any other type of picture. Character can be taken away by retouching, but not added. With sets, props, and backings, artificial trees in the background, and the eight-light system, photography can be improved considerably.

Use your studio for other purposes than just to photograph new babies and newlyweds. You too can paint with light. Get models and ideas, and create. Make photographic paintings. There is definitely a market for them. On my recent trip to South America, I was extremely pleased to find photographic enlargements instead of cheap reproductions of old paintings decorating the walls of the luxurious staterooms. There is more room for new photographic ideas. Advertising and many other fields are wide open for them. Make your place a miniature Hollywood studio, a pleasant place to come to.

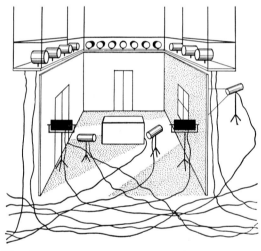

Fig. 273

Fig. 274

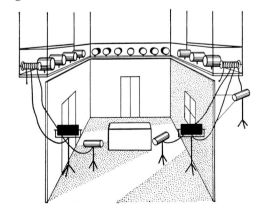

Make-up and Portrait

It is not my intention to discuss make-up. That is entirely out of my line. However, to get good photographic results, we must understand something of make-up and lighting. It often happens with portrait photographers, when they turn all lights on and are ready to shoot the picture, that they look at the model's face and notice that something is wrong. The make-up looks different in the studio than it did in the make-up room. How did it happen? The answer is very simple: The lighting conditions are not the same in the two rooms. The difference is sufficient to change the basic characteristics of the make-up. *It is absolutely essential that the lighting under which a person is to be made up, if not the same, should at least be similar to that under which she is to be photographed.* In most make-up rooms, the lighting is obsolete. The make-up table is nothing but a descendant of the original legitimate stage dressing room table, with enough light bulbs around the

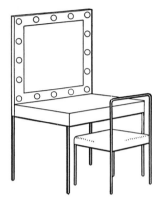

Fig. 275

mirror to blind one. In some places shadowless tubes have been added on the ceiling to modernize, but some kinds generate enough heat to make a Turkish bath of the room, especially in the summer time.

Figure 275 shows the old-fashioned make-up table. The strong lights directly face the make-up artist. These strong lights close down the irises of his eyes and everything seems dark. Hence, the tendency to lighten the make-up. Then he turns around, faces a dark wall, and the irises open up. The other side of the face is made up darker. This goes on and on. . . .

To insure proper light conditions, darken the room completely. This darkness sensitizes the eyes, enabling the artist to see the minutest details. Then place a keylight in such a position that the light reaches the model in the mirror, but not the artist's eyes. The reflection of the keylight illuminates the model's face. Get the proper meter readings of the studio, and if possible, duplicate conditions here. If arc lights are used, place a yellow filter over the keylight. When this is done place a shadowless lamp on each side of the model. This allows the make-up artist to walk around without throwing shadows on the model's face.

To change to present-day lighting facilities in your make-up room would involve an investment. But if you consider the saving of time, which is money, and also the improved photographic quality, you will find the investment justified.

CHAPTER 11

THE LABORATORY

A hidden and little heard of, but very important department of motion picture photography is the laboratory, usually referred to as the *lab*. Men who are partially responsible for the photographic quality for which Hollywood films are so famous, work here in the dark, year in and year out, without receiving fabulous salaries.

One could hardly call himself a professional photographer without having at least a working knowledge of what goes on in the laboratory. Just as a painter has to know how to mix his paints, so the successful cameraman needs to know the chemical process his film must go through before it reaches the screen. Cameramen should start at the lab.

It should be made compulsory for every candidate for the post of director of photography to go through a laboratory apprenticeship, an introductory course of film processing from the time the negative arrives at the lab, to the final stage when it reaches the public through the screen of the theatre.

When something goes wrong with the lights of your car, you start to trace the cause from the source of the current, that is, the battery, to the lamp itself. The same principle applies to motion picture photography. If the print is not entirely satisfactory, don't blame the lab right away. Find out the real reason. Start with the loading room. A thousand accidents can happen to the film between this place and the lab. Of course, accidents can happen in a lab, too, and they do.

Screen Tests

In most major studios of Hollywood, before a picture goes into production, screen tests are made of players, wardrobe, make-up, sets, etc. (Fig. 276). This is the time when the cameraman has a chance to familiarize him-

Fig. 276   *The Screen Test*

self with the characteristics of that lab's negative soup. The advantages of such tests are numerous. To mention only a few: we find out the quality of the lenses, we make certain that the camera works properly and quietly, we make certain that calibrations are correct, and most important of all, we familiarize ourselves with the faces of the stars we are about to photograph. This is the time to get together with the contact man assigned to the picture and to discuss the problems which present themselves during production.

The Contact Man

The developing, timing, and printing of an artistically photographed picture really should be supervised by the cameraman of the picture. He has read the script and worked out the light effects and changes, moods, and feelings with the director. The cameraman knows how the film should be processed, and how it should ultimately look on the screen to properly tell the story the director has in his mind. Unfortunately, he also is supposed to shoot the picture, which means that he spends the greater part of the day on the stuffy, hot, dusty, sound stage, inhaling carbon gases of the arc lights, and working with the powerful reflectors. When night comes at last, he is in no physical condition to go to the lab and supervise the developing of the negative. To facilitate matters and help him in this field, the lab appoints a *contact man,* who is a connecting link between it and the cameraman, and who sees to it that all instructions are carried out. He glances over the script and holds conferences with the cameraman.

Negative Developing

Some studios have their own laboratories; others send their negatives out to a commercial lab to be processed. Although all agree upon a certain developing formula usually furnished by the manufacturer of the raw film, each lab works a little differently from the others with its own little personally developed trade secrets and gadgets.

There are two general negative developing systems. One is called *time and temperature,* and the other works with *developing tests.* In the first, the entire negative shot during the day goes through the soup without any testing, in a certain pre-established time and temperature routine. In this system, most of the responsibilities rest on the shoulders of the cameraman. In the second, tests are made after each light change, and are notched, or are made at the end of a roll. At the lab, these test strips are torn off the roll and marked carefully. These strips are developed in normal time and then inspected. They are divided into three classes: overexposed, normal, and underlit. Those which are in the first class need less developing, the second group is normally developed, and the third have to be forced (given more developing time). Both systems have their advantages and also their disadvantages.

One great advantage of the time and temperature system is that, if the film was lit for an effect, there is no danger of ruining it. Take, for instance, the following case: The set is a large living room. It is night, with but one light in the far corner of the room. If a developing test were made of it, developed, and inspected, the dark part of the picture would, in all probability, scare the negative developer. He would be perplexed. What can he do in such a case? In order to get detail in the underlit part of the picture, he would give it more time. This would burn up the other part, and ruin the over-all effect; and the final picture would perhaps turn out to be day instead of night.

Beginners and those uncertain of themselves prefer the test developing system. If a mistake was made in the lighting, it would be caught and corrected to a certain degree by changing the developing time.

THE LIGHT TEST

The human eye is far from being perfect. Even today, with the aid of the best exposure meters, negatives made by the same cameraman on one shooting day differ in density from those of another day. To correct this difference and to even up the print, a scale was devised. This scale reads from light 1 to 22, although only every other one is printed on the *light test*. Here, too, each studio has developed its own system of printing.

As an illustration, we shall use the Cynex system. This has 22 lights. Theoretically, a

Joan Bennett

correctly exposed negative should print in the middle of the scale, or around 11 to 13. There are, however, different opinions on this subject. Some cameramen light for the center (lights 11 to 13), others prefer to overlight their negatives so that they are printed on lights 19 to 21. They claim that this gives them prints with richer blacks.

The light test is a strip of film 11 frames long. Each frame has a different number, and shows how the scene would look if printed on that light. This gives the cameraman an idea of the correct printing light, and shows if corrections need to be made. A light test is made of each scene that is marked for printing. These light tests are sent to the cameraman each morning. After he has inspected them, they are saved for future reference, in case of retakes.

RUSH PRINT

Positives are made of all the scenes photographed during a shooting day and marked for printing, and sent over to be viewed by the entire staff. These temporary prints are called *dailies* because they are viewed daily, and known also as *rushes* because they are rushed. (They are always in a hurry.)

Once having seen his rushes, the cameraman then can make his corrections, if there are any to be made. Some cameramen, after they have once found the best angles and lights for their stars, stick to that lighting scheme throughout the picture. Others change light and angle with each setup.

When an unacceptably dark print is made by selecting the wrong print light, reprints are immediately ordered. This hasty step, which costs the studios thousands of dollars annually, could be avoided if only a cameraman were consulted. The photography of a picture should be left to him alone. Photography can no more be judged by the rushes than can a musical symphony by listening to one bar of music. Just imagine listening to a bar of con-

tinuous drums. It would drive you crazy. Nevertheless, they fit in perfectly in the concert as a whole. The same applies to photography. Individual scenes may seem dark gray when seen individually, but are perfect when seen in the final photo symphony.

ARTISTIC TIMING OF THE FINAL PRINT

Once the picture is *dubbed,* that is, the sound corrected, and the music, dialogue, and other sounds united on one track, the two negatives (sound and image) are returned to the laboratory for final timing. Once again light tests are made of each scene of the picture. Moods and effects are carefully decided upon by the cameraman and contact man. The first final print is again inspected, and sometimes two or three prints are made before all lights are correct.

As the timer has not always time to read the script of the film he develops, it is not expected of him to hit the correct light. He usually selects the mathematically correct print light. It is up to the contact man to know the light effects and just what feeling each scene is supposed to have. To the average timer, the scene is night if the brackets on the wall are on, and day if the light comes through the window.

MOOD IN PRINTING

A scene printed on light 11 might be correct mathematically, but if looking at it fails to "do things" to you, if it does not give you a certain pleasure, it is just another scene. This same scene, if printed down on the scale, let us say lights 17 or 19, might turn out to be an emotional picture, a painting that rings all bells with the tremendous suggestive power of its beauty, composition, lights, and dramatic strength all combined.

Timing is an art in itself. All the creative illumination of the cameraman is lost if the timing of the negative is wrong. Negatives

169

should be timed first for mathematically correct density, second for feeling, mood. Neither one alone is sufficient. It is an ideal combination of both that makes a good print. Sometimes exceptions are made, and where mathematically it would have to be printed on light 11, it is printed on light 23 for mood.

Most final prints are made entirely too light. It is claimed that most theatres in small towns have weak projectors and need light prints. This is probably true, but with a little thought this could be remedied. Artistic prints could be made for the bigger theatres, and lighter ones for the smaller ones. Perhaps the day will come when this will be done. Until then, we must be prepared to see a picture, of which the rushes were excellent, so distorted that one cannot recognize his own work.

CHAPTER 12

DAY AND NIGHT, LADIES, WATCH YOUR LIGHT

Every woman has the right to be as beautiful as she possibly can. Hundreds of millions of dollars are spent every year in the United States alone on new dress styles, cosmetics, make-up, hairdo, permanent waves, and other beautifying means. This is perfectly all right, but how many of you ladies have ever tried to use light as a beautifier? Very few, indeed. What good are the new dress, the perfect make-up, the hairdo if, when you go out, the light in which you appear simply kills them?

Just go to the cafés, restaurants, night clubs, bars, parties in private homes, and watch those long, drawn faces, full of wrinkles, with deep-set eyes encircled by dark rings—all caused by primitive, unprepared, unplanned, murderous illumination. There are some illuminating engineers who lately have started to give thought to home illumination for decorative purposes, for the beauty of the home, but so far little has been done to beautilluminate the individual. After all, it is more important to look well oneself than to go to a place that looks well. People would much rather go out to places where *they* look the best, and not the architecture.

Great painters of the past knew of the beautifying properties of light, but many preferred to take their secrets with them. When man first invented the lamp, it was to see by during the long, tedious hours of the winter evenings. Famous ladies of history, Cleopatra and others, learned how to take advantage of light, and used that knowledge. Some of them never appeared in daylight without a protecting parasol, and at night, light conditions had previously been carefully studied, and they appeared only at those carefully selected, strategic places predesigned for the purpose of enhancing and not ruining their natural beauty. They too preferred to take their secrets along with them to better worlds. Little has been written, and less published on the subject. There are some very few fortunate individuals who have an innate understanding of light, but most persons have little knowledge of the subject.

Can light beautify? The answer is an emphatic *yes*. It certainly can. Light is an important force, an intellectual stimulus. If properly taken advantage of, it can be turned into a special and economical beautifying agent within the means of everybody. It takes no extra, expensive equipment to beautify with light. Just go out and use the light that was given to all mankind. According to scientists, there will be sunshine for another million years. Everybody is entitled to a certain amount of happiness; go out and get it. Once you have learned to master light outside, continue with your experiments inside.

We are not dealing with photographs here, but with pure light. While light is essential to photography, it is not necessary to take pictures when dealing with light.

Because many people are expected to read

this part of the book without having gone through the previous chapters, I have taken the liberty of repeating certain facts and theories about light in general. The reader is not expected to learn all in one lesson. It takes time and patience. But as you begin to notice the reward of the first lessons, you will be encouraged to continue your studies and become your own expert on lighting—your own lighting artist.

Faces

What makes nature beautiful? It is light—sunlight, moonlight, and artificial light. Take light away and what is there left? A dark, meaningless nothing. The same is true of the human face. The light that illuminates it is most important, for not all faces are alike. There are low-key faces and high-key faces; those which cannot stand daylight and those which look worse at night.

You must have noticed that some of your friends look much better at night at a party than they do at their desks in the office. The reason may be that at the office they are not in the right light. Night illumination is more becoming to their type than daylight.

There are people who after the first drink take on a tired, sleepy, old look; these people should not drink, not even beer. Again, there are those who get a tired look immediately after the sun sets; they should stay home evenings and go to bed with the chickens. Some people look better after having been out all night than do others who have had their ten hours of beauty sleep.

MAKE-UP AND LIGHT

Walk up and down on the boulevard, and you will soon notice the importance of street make-up. Once in a while you will see people stare at one particular lady, who misinterprets this unusual attention as admiration of her new dress (human nature). In reality it is her exaggerated make-up that calls everyone's

attention. In a way, the lady of attraction cannot be blamed; not all bathrooms have daylight, which is a prerequisite of daylight make-up. In all probability our little lady used artificial light for making up. Its yellowish color minimized the amount of rouge and make-up she placed on her cheeks, but once outside in broad daylight, the typical night make-up showed an overabundance of red, and appeared a bit out of place at noon. It is high time that a manufacturer of lamps came out with a good all-around make-up light. This light should have two kinds of bulbs in it—one mazda bulb with the usual yellowish light for evening make-up, and the other of a bluish color for daylight make-up. In this blue light the least bit of red is exaggerated, and there is no possible chance of overdoing the make-up.

MURDER WITH LIGHT

Before you read any further, try the following simple but eye-opening little experiment. If the room you are in happens to be light, darken it. Draw the curtains or Venetian blinds. Walk over to the mirror, turn the light on, and look at your reflection. If the lamp is in the position of the one in Fig. 277, then you have been slowly illumurdered. Yes, that too is possible. Just as light can beautify in the hands of experts, it can turn into a treacherous weapon in the hands of amateurs if thoughtlessly used. The way you look in that mirror is the way most people look in restaurants, clubs, and other places where no thought is given to their lighting.

The high lamps of today are nothing more than improved models of the old hanging kerosene lamps. Just why they had to be high we don't know; perhaps there were good reasons. If you look into the mirror you will see what we have discussed in previous chapters. A strong light coming from high creates harsh, uncomplimentary shadows on the face (Fig. 278). A high light accentuates any already existing wrinkles, and has a tendency to bring out new, normally invisible ones. We have also established previously that in the hands of experts all feminine faces can, to a certain extent, become photogenic. Whenever in the presence of others, day or night, you are constantly being photographed. Remember, love at first sight is love at first light. That first impression you make upon people is very important. Whenever possible, see to it that you are in the right light, and look your best. By properly distributing lights in your home, surrounded by well-lighted happy people, you can make it a pleasant place in which to live.

The chances are that many times in the past when you had a date, and although in reality looked lovely, when you turned on that high light and looked into that mirror, it scared you, so that you lost your courage and canceled your date. Little did you then think that it was that murderous light that made you look like a monkey.

Now let us continue our experiment. Take a few steps back, but keep on looking into the mirror. Can you notice the changes? The same light (which is now no more a high, but a front light) that made you look like your grandmother before, is now doing justice to your looks. Not only have the wrinkles disappeared, but your whole face has changed. Your eyes sparkle, you begin to smile, you look years younger. This gives you strength to live.

To illustrate the possibilities of light, we shall take two days, a weekday and a holiday, of the life of an average working girl, and demonstrate how she can take advantage of light under different circumstances. More women are murdered with bad light than with any other weapon. Let us get light-conscious.

Photographic lighting is not the only way of painting with light. There is plenty of op-

Fig. 277

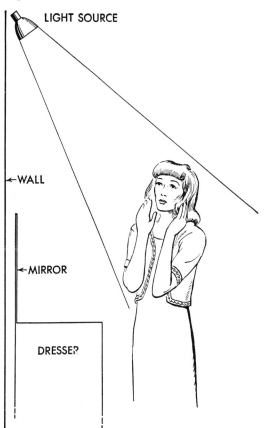

Fig. 278

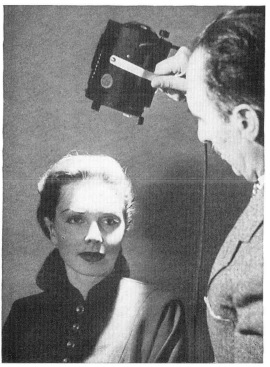

portunity to paint with light, starting right at home. Take advantage of the magnetic influence of light that makes us like or dislike people. Unquestionably light has an electromagnetic force.

PAINTING WITH BEAUTY LIGHT

In order to avoid confusion, we shall give the lights essential for beauty lighting different names from those used in lighting for photography:

Sparklight illuminates the face.

Beauty light lights the hair.

Lovelight makes the eyes shine.

Glamorlight is indirect, almost no light; it is soft, and no matter where it comes from, will do the face no harm.

Lights to avoid are the harsh light, or open light source without any shade or diffusion to break it, and the double crosslight, with its many deep shadows.

BREAKFAST TIME

If people only knew how they can look at breakfast time, they would give it a little more thought. If you haven't slept enough, you look tired. If you have slept too much, you look more tired. In any case, your face is wrinkled, and your eyes are baggy. That is where light could come to the rescue. There would be more happy marriages and fewer divorces if people would pay more attention to their morning light. Have the breakfast nook built in such a way that it takes full advantage of the warm early morning sunlight. Have some kind of curtains on your windows, so that the light is broken up. If out in the country, a tree or other plants will also help with their shadows. If the nook is artificially lit, place your lamps so that they will retouch your face.

THE LIGHT OUTSIDE

Once ready with your breakfast, we assume that you go to work. We assume—as a matter of fact, we are convinced—that you would much rather have slept a little more, or have gone shopping, or have played golf or tennis, but unfortunately, some of us have to do the work.

You step out into the open. Inside, while having your breakfast, you had better control of light conditions; even if you did not look your very best, all were in a hurry, some read the paper, and besides, it was your own family. We can allow ourselves so many things, and they may be unnoticed. Outside it is different. You are likely to meet people, so-called friends who are looking for material for talk when they arrive at their offices, early morning gossip. You cannot move the sun, and parasols are not customarily carried to business.

You may not have slept well, or may have slept too much. You may have been out the night before, and have a hangover. All these things manifest themselves on your sensitive face, and an unfavorable light only exaggerates your poor appearance. If you really want to look your best and "kill" your friends, wear a hat with a brim, for that will keep the direct, harsh sunlight off your face. Use a veil on your hat—it splits the focus, softens the vision (Fig. 279). If the sun hits you from the back, it is all right to remain on the sunny side, especially in the winter, when it feels good. But if the light crosses you double, first from its source, then reflected by the white walls, then go over to the shady side of the street. You will look better. If you have any doubts about what you have just read, when you enter the subway, streetcar, or bus, watch others. Watch their faces as the light changes on them. See how they look? Do you think that you look any better? To the layman, all lights look alike. At first, you may not detect delicate light changes; but in time as you become light-conscious and expert in observation, you will begin to notice them. Look at the illustrations and see how a normal, young, pretty face can look under different light conditions (Figs. 280, 281, 282, 283).

Fig. 279   *Claire Trevor*

Fig. 281

Fig. 282

Fig. 280   *Mary Meade*

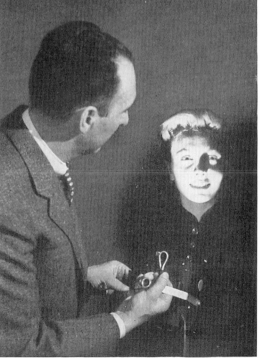

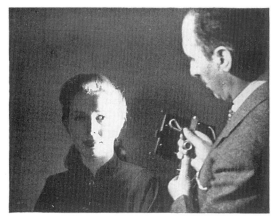

Fig. 283

LADIES' LIGHT IS MEN'S DELIGHT

When we consider that more than half of the waking hours of an average girl's life are spent at her place of employment, we realize how unfortunate it is that so little thought is given to the effect that the surroundings may have on her appearance. I have seen furniture being moved around for decorative or economic purposes, for conservation of space, but I have as yet failed to see it done to obtain a more advantageous light for the workers. Better light would make the girls look prettier, consequently feel happier. It is easier to get work out of happy people than out of gripers.

In order to illustrate what light can do, I shall relate to you a brief but true story.

Miss Z lived in a midwestern town, and was one of the many girls who graduated from the local high school whose only ambition, perhaps, was to marry the right person one day. But as she resembled a certain well-known Hollywood star, the whole town advised her to try the movies. So she packed her things, and with a few dollars came to Hollywood. She was down to her last dollar when she finally got a call for a screen test. Like most of these tests, this one too was rushed through, and the result was that all her excitement was in vain. She was just broken-hearted, and did not know where to start, or what to do. Through some friends

who felt sorry for her, she got a job in the mail department of a major studio.

From here she was promoted to become the secretary of one of the big producers on the lot. But she just cried and cried. This was not what she came to Hollywood for. Gradually all her friends left her. After darkness, light is bound to come if you wait for it. She was about to give up and wire for money to go home—a failure, when light came to her rescue. One morning a cameraman happened to pass by her office and noticed that in a certain light she looked just beautiful. In order to take advantage of that light, he suggested that they move her desk around with a window behind her, and facing the people who entered.

The next morning she was sitting in her new position. The rising sun backlit her beautiful, hitherto unnoticed, golden curls. The inpouring sunlight also hit the oil-painted, glossy wall in front of her, which lit up her face. She looked gorgeous. She looked like a new person, and the new hope put a sparkle in her big blue eyes. Her boss came in. Before, he had never noticed her as he puffed the smoke out of his big cigar and automatically reached for the morning trade papers. But this time he took a second look with that *where-were-you-all-my-life* expression on his face.

From then on everything changed, and for the better. Agents, producers, writers, and other wolves came by her office, some of them just pretending to open the door and say "Good morning," but not forgetting the wolf cry that made a general so famous. To make the story short, today Miss Z is happily married to her producer, and they have two beautiful children. In her new home great importance is given to illumination; she knows what light can do.

It is not always possible to arrange the furniture to suit your convenience. Everybody just can't be sitting with her back to the window, where the sunlight will illuminate her ash-blonde hair. All you can do is try to hit a happy medium, and not deliberately sit in a murderous light. I must repeat, time and again, stay away from the high lamp, especially in places where there are no white or light walls to fill in the pronounced shadows on the face. A high light (not to be mistaken for highlight) does no one justice.

If you have Venetian blinds on the windows of your office, or wherever you work, try to change the light by moving the blades into different positions to make them act as reflectors. See what light can do to a person. If there are several girls in the office, in spare time experiment with lighting by using one of the girls as a model, and study the different light changes on her. You can all take turns in this.

Interior Illumination of the Home

A light that is good for reading may not be ideal for writing, and vice versa. Therefore we divide the types of home interior lighting into these classes: light for reading (Fig. 284), light for eating (Fig. 285), light for celebrating, light for listening to music, and lovelight for romance (Fig. 286). No matter which of the lighting categories we deal with, different faces need different treatment. It is difficult to prescribe a certain light for one person, where many others will appear. You will have to study and find the ideal light for yourself, and stick to it as closely as circumstances will permit. I would advise the reader to go over the chapter dealing with close-up lighting, to study the different types of faces and their lighting. It might help in selecting your light. The light that is good for your type in photography should also be, in general, good beauty lighting; but because of the sensitivity of the human eye, this can be on a much lower scale.

THE READING LIGHT

When a person is reading she usually wants to be left alone and not to be looked at. There-

fore it is not only beauty we are striving for, but also comfort and ease and relaxation. The light should reach the book and not the eyes. A general light for the reader and a concentrated light for the book is recommended. If the general light is put out, leaving the concentrated one, the room is in almost complete darkness, and the wife can go to sleep while the husband continues to read, or vice versa, as the case may be. If the lamp is on a silent switch, the noise of putting it out will disturb no one. The concentrated ray should come from such an angle that even shiny pages cannot reflect the light source. This type of light is used for orchestras, illuminating the music only, and also in certain types of restaurants, where the light ray lights the table and the menu, and leaves the rest subdued.

THE EATING LIGHT

One generally does not eat alone. There are usually several people around the table, the

Fig. 284

Fig. 285 *Cathy O'Donnell and Lynn Bari, "In Love"*

family with or without guests. Without knowing who is going to sit where and when, it is almost impossible to light each chair separately. Therefore the room should be indirectly lit, in a high enough key to make it pleasant, agreeable, warm. An ultramodern touch is the addition from the ceiling of a concealed, concentrated light as recommended above for reading. This brings out the table, but does not hit the people around it. A light that may be favorable for one may be harmful for the others; hence the general soft light is recommended.

Candles are a matter of taste. However, Edison invented a light that will give the warmth of candles, but without the smoke and unpleasant odor.

The eyeball has a transparent surface which lets the incident light pass, and reflects the light source, giving it a certain luster, a certain warmth.

LISTENING TO MUSIC

If you want to listen to music and just sit back and relax, the dial of the average radio or combination radio phonograph emanates enough light to make the room cozy, and is of sufficient strength for the human eye to see by after having accustomed itself to it. There should be no strain on the eye; hence this soft light is recommended. Besides, it is ideal for you also. It throws huge but pleasant shadows on the wall, and it is not monotonous at all. It is ideally suited to music listeners.

Fig. 286   *Hedy Lamarr*

GL'AMOUR LIGHT

Here again it is you who should look well, and everything else is secondary in importance. A low-key soft light in the summer, mixed with the moonlight from outside, and the fireplace in the winter. Both are of the gl'amour type, for they register in the eyeball, but leave everything else subdued. In this type of light, all faces look well (low light is no light). This light can really be as low as photographers would never dream of daring to use.

Indirect lighting is pleasant to the human eye, not only because it is low in intensity and therefore does not strain the eye, but because it is reflected from all directions in equal proportions, surrounding the person with a warm light; it is soothing because we do not see the filament, which after all is not what we want to see, and is therefore absolutely superfluous. If colored bulbs are used, find out the person's taste for them and light accordingly, or have the lamp shades of the chosen color.

LOVE AT FIRST LIGHT

The time will come when home lighting from a beautifying angle will be as natural as having an icebox is today. Its installation will be taken care of by trained personnel. Until that time arrives, however, you will have to do your own beautylighting with whatever equipment you have available. While the lamps of today were not especially designed for that purpose, we can nevertheless, by intelligent selection and juggling around, improve conditions considerably, and improve your looks also.

If you expect a visitor whom you esteem highly and upon whom you would like to make an especially good impression, you can work miracles even with the primitive lamps. Rehearse the places where you think you will be sitting during the evening. Take a mirror and look at yourself with the present light-

ing; you may be a bit surprised at your image. Maybe you won't even recognize yourself. But don't let that discourage you. In no time this will be doctored out, corrected. In the first place, take away the light that causes the strong shadows and replace it with one that is softer, perhaps with one that has a translucent silk shade. If that does not do the trick, then kill the light before it can do the same to you. Put it out, but in a hurry. If another look in the mirror tells you that it is now too dark, put the light on again, and change your sitting position. Move it to some other place. If you still do not look well, change both the light and your place. If time allows, and it should if you want to look your best, you will have to repeat this performance with each place where you think you will sit during the evening. It is a lot of work and takes patience, but it is well worth the trouble. It will pay off in the long run.

If it is wintertime and you have a fireplace in the living room, try the following experiment. Put out all the lights in the room. This leaves the fireplace as the only light source. At first this may seem a bit radical, risqué, and you may be in doubt as to the results; but if you wait a few minutes and see how your eyes get accustomed to the low light, you will regain your courage to go on. Once again try the mirror; take a look in it. If the light from the fireplace is too strong, too contrasty, casting harsh shadows, then place the screen in front of it. This will soften its light. If you think that this light scheme is somewhat ultramodern, light a lamp in one of the distant corners of the room, but behind you. This will light up the room and your hair, but not your face; the fireplace will take care of that.

When your friend arrives, watch his facial expression. Not so much for his looks, but his surprise when he sees a new, more beautiful girl than he has known. Thus you will see the miracles that light can work.

P.S. Perhaps be prepared for pop and mom

to return from the movies, and rehearse the full light of the living room also—this only as a precautionary light.

When the caller is to be received on the porch, kill the hanging or porch light. This leaves the place in semidarkness. Leave a strong light on in the room if you have a window on the porch. This will create a romantic atmosphere in which you can look beautiful. Use frosted bulbs for fancy lighting. You can even go into the display of colored bulbs. Translucent lamp shades help a lot.

RELAXATION

When we really want to see, that is, with our psychic eyes, we close our real eyes. We put our lens caps, the eyelids, on the lenses— that stops the taking of pictures. If we want to relax—not sleep, just rest—turn out all the lights and stay in the dark. That stops your mind, the human camera within you, from taking more pictures. Sometimes we see better in the dark than in the light.

LIGHTING OIL PAINTINGS

Man was originally meant to live outside in the open spaces, with no limit to his field of vision. Then he became civilized and moved inside, curtailing his vision with the blank walls of his rooms. These walls bounce back the waves of his thoughts until they hurt. To remedy this, he goes out and spends fortunes on oil paintings. This opens up the way for his thoughts; they can travel on and on; the pictures are like windows. But then he murders the pictures with bad lighting. The reflection of the light source blocks out part of the picture. Pictures of the countryside usually are painted in the daytime. In order that such a painting may be appreciated, it should be illuminated with daylight, or if artificially lit, with reflected light.

Outdoor Lighting

Comes the Sunday, and of course you want to go out. Here, too, more attention has been paid to the dress, the color, and the model of the automobile than to the light which can ruin your looks. It seems strange that although many thousands of years have gone by, few of even our modern generation of the fair sex give any thought to illumination as a source of beauty, or are aware of the disastrous effects it can have if ignored.

Exteriors are here divided into the general categories of a walk in the woods or park, a picnic, automobiling, and a day at the beach.

A WALK IN THE PARK

Girls of yesteryear had no light worries when they went out for a walk. They had parasols that protected them against the strong direct sunlight; they acted as a sort of diffusion (Fig. 287) and their return to fashion today should be welcomed.

Outdoors the same law prevails as indoors. Stay out of the strong lights and see that your face is lit softly. Look for shady places under the trees; this diffused light is ideal. When you take a walk in the park, or in the woods, the late afternoon with the sun behind you is the time best suited for it (Fig. 288). When the sun is beginning to grow orange in color, or after it has dropped beyond the horizon in the afterglow, even front light can be very favorable to your face. The afterglow is nature's indirect light. If it lights you from in front, then you have the east with its reflected light and clouds behind you. If it is the other way around, then the light of the west outlines your head.

ON THE BEACH

When on the beach, use an umbrella or a tent to diffuse the light. It would be too complicated to light yourself outside the way you can do inside. Stay out of strong crosslights. The light at the beach is doubly strong, since it is also reflected from the sand. Therefore you must be doubly on the alert.

If there is no shade around, at least sit down where the light hits your hair and not

Fig. 287   *Mary Meade, "The Parasol"*

Fig. 288 *"The Smile"*

Fig. 289

your face. If possible, avoid walking around in the high noon (Fig. 289) light, or you will look as Figure 278 shows. If you have to walk, then for conversation find an ideal, shady place. In other words, think of the light. Be conscious of it as you are now of your attire, make-up, hairdo, or lip-rouge.

WINDOW SHOPPING

The great mistake of window illumination is the fact that there attention is concentrated too much on the window and little or none is given to the people who are going to look at it. There are store windows lit with a certain light combination that makes everyone close to it look sick. I don't know the reason for such illumination. Perhaps they want to chase the customers away, for that is exactly what they do. Have you ever seen yourself in front of such light? You will do it only once. Don't stop in front of such windows. Make them change their lighting. If anyone looks at you under those lights, he may have a wrong impression. If businessmen only knew what they are doing, they would change their lighting techniques. Faces look sickly and lips pale or a deep purple. I am sure that if anyone ever saw himself or others in such lighting he would soon escape, or slip away in a hurry. Once you have learned about light, you will stop only in front of stores where not only the window, but you, too, are well lit.

As Saturday night is usually the "out" night, don't look into the mirror when you wake up Sunday morning. You will surprise yourself. It is on such a day that you need a doctor of lights, especially if you are over sixty.

Lighting in Clubs, Bars, and Restaurants

The present lighting system in bars and clubs is just poison to the average feminine face. Lips look white, eyes deep, faces sickly. It is amazing how ladies sit around in these places, convinced that it is only the others who look badly. *Remember, you look no better than they.* Glaring walls and shiny floors help to murder your looks. I have lately visited a newly decorated place on the outskirts of Buenos Aires in Argentina. The place really looked wonderful. Where they made a mistake, however, was in using a green light for general illumination, which made everyone look seasick on land. Light, like music, has a certain rhythm. It should match the surroundings, and in this case, being artificial, it would not have been difficult to control. The palms would have been nicer painted a silver, for the moonlight was blue. Add a green light on top of this, and you can imagine the disaster of this light combination.

Candles on tables are romantic, and some people like them. The trouble with candles is that you don't see the face behind them. Besides, when they burn down too low they give the face that criminal look mentioned previously.

Fig. 290

Fig. 291

One cannot expect a restaurant to have a corrected light for every one of its customers. The best light for such a place is the indirect light, the source of which is about the height of people's eyes when in sitting position. I have seen such a place. Everybody in it looked young and gay. Of course, I realize the good Italian food and wines may have had something to do with it.

The science of lighting public places is relatively new. All owners of such places are interested in anything that is new and will improve business instead of killing it. Until the day comes when restaurants, clubs, bars, and other places of amusement are lit for the convenience of the customers, when managers are taught how to light for the beauty of their customers, you will have to be your own luminartist.

Architectural Lighting

Those who invented this type of illumination, this medium of advertising, were fully aware of the fact that this light in the dark of the night draws the attention of passers-by. What they overlooked is that this illumination, like that of motion pictures, could also be artistic. Pouring light on a building may make it light, but it does not paint a picture. It would cost the same to have it done tastefully. Study the lines of buildings, see how nature illuminates, and light accordingly (Figs. 290, 291). Try to imitate motion picture illumination, as though this too were a set. If a building has columns in front of it, leave them dark, silhouetted, and light the set behind strongly. This will make the columns stand out. A soft crosslight with stronger backlight will help the columns; it will round them up. If there is no room behind the columns, just crosslight the whole façade; this will model the columns. Don't make the entire building light, as though the sun came out suddenly. Model, leave dark spots, paint not only with light, but also with feeling.

CHAPTER 13 _____

MOTION PICTURE THEATRES

The Headache

Most theatre-goers, when coming out of a movie theatre, suffering from photopsia, think of everything as the possible cause of the splitting headache except the true one. Some blame it on the climate, or the stock market. Others suspect the food they ate. Is it the sinus, the wrong sun glasses, or was the picture that bad? Very few people even suspect the real reason. It may be any one of the following, either individually or in combination.

Let us start from the time you arrive at the theatre. In the daytime you come in directly from the bright sunlight into the dark theatre. Your eyes were light-accustomed, and the sudden light change is sufficient to cause an unpleasant effect.

Inside, you don't know what to do. You stop in the middle of the aisle, and start to look for a seat. Several times you glance at the bright screen, and back into the dark; you may grab hold of the bald head of a gentleman or upset the fresh permanent wave of a lady. People behind you, who enjoy the picture more than your silhouette, hiss, and you move on. You find a seat; you still can't see, but in you go, nevertheless. You step on feet, and brush heads. You want to sit down, and fall into the lap of a strange person. She screams, you jump. At last, you sit down. Then you hear the rustling of peanut bags. You wonder why, if they must have them, do they have to be packed in noisemaking

paper. The sound of the picture is so high that every time a musical passage comes along, it blasts your eardrums. You stuff your ears with cotton, but by then the picture is over, you are exhausted, and the "tag" is so loud that it lifts you right out of your seat.

When the fun is over, out you go. It is still daylight. You walk right into the sunlight. Your eyes are now dark-accustomed. The strong sunlight is not enough; it is reflected by the glaring pavement and the white walls of the surrounding buildings. Suddenly you notice the migraine headache. Why headaches caused by earsplitting noises of a bad picture cannot be alleviated by taking sedatives is a problem for medical science.

The Modern Theatre

The theatres of tomorrow will have different chambers for the customer to pass through and accustom himself to the different light changes, both when entering and when leaving. This will be similar to the procedure a deep sea diver goes through.

Another improvement would be to have theatres somewhat lighter than they are now. The eye glances back and forth from the screen to the dark, and by the time one leaves the theatre, the optical nerves are exhausted; a soft light around the screen would remedy this situation.

At each end of every row, an electric signal could indicate if there are any seats available.

185

Strange noises of paper rattling, gossip of the neighborhood, someone repeating the dialogue, others explaining the scene, sounds coming from different directions are enough to drive anyone crazy.

The sound is much too strong in the average theatre. There is no need for that. Prints are too light and there is too much glare on the screen. If some managers think that loud noise and white photography are "commercial," they have a few lessons to learn about mass psychology.

By eliminating these annoyances, the motion picture theatre could be made a more pleasant place to go to, and the box office would soon show the results.

CHAPTER 14

THE WORLD IS
A HUGE TELEVISION STUDIO
AND WE ARE ALL PHOTOGRAPHERS

Strange how many people claimed to be the inventors of photography, when, in reality, sensitive plates in the human head, in fact, television within the human brain, are all as old as man himself.

Have you ever thought of how important photography really is in our daily life? Without photography, we would still be monkeys or cavemen in the stone age. Learning and education would have been impossible, especially in the days before the paper and parchment, when everything had to be learned through man's photographic lenses (his eyes) and his microphonic ears.

By carving on wood and stone alone, it would have taken the world much longer to get where it is today. (Perhaps it would have been better.)

In the Spanish language, giving birth to a child is called "dar luz," to "give light." How true that is. The first thing we see upon our arrival in this world is light. Immediately we start taking pictures of everything that comes within our field of vision, and continue to do so every day, from the time we open our eyes in the morning till we close them at night, until we die. As a matter of fact, our little hidden projection rooms continue to work even after we have closed our eyes and gone to sleep.

Not only do we take pictures, but sound and smell tracks with them. This smelling idea may seem strange to you, but just try to eat something that smells or tastes like something mother used to make. Immediately, it will start rolling pictures, and it will take you back to your childhood. Perhaps this is the reason why we like certain dishes; they remind us of our youth.

The Human Camera

I am not going to dissect the human brain, for I am hardly qualified for that. I shall leave that to the medicos. Summing up in an empiric way, as far as we know, the human brain is the most completely equipped television studio there is. It cannot be compared with anything in existence. It is fully equipped with a pair of lenses, the eyes, which serve for the movie, still, and television cameras, also as radar, and for many other purposes we haven't yet discovered. Each eye has a retina, which serves both as the sensitized plate for taking pictures, and also as the television and other projection screen. Eyes change angle at will, automatically. They have automatic diffusion, lens shade (the eyebrows and lashes), built-in iris, and exposure meter.

The eye is not only the mirror of the soul, but also the lens of the human camera. Its automatic iris opens and closes according to the light it receives. The image taken is correctly exposed, so that the printing machines have little worry about evening up and correcting the final print. For instance, the entire picture of an excursion, where lights vary considerably, is taken with the iris constantly adjusting itself to light conditions. The negative is developed to one gamma, printed instantly on one light—the dream of every motion picture laboratory.

When we look at any picture, it is instantly photographed. We do not see the negative at all. It is delivered to our conscious mind in the form of a finished positive print. Invisible little gremlins wash the picture off the sensitive plate, the retina, and resensitize it for the next image.

The pictures taken are carefully classified and filed in the perfect little libraries of temperature-controlled, air-conditioned, and burglar-proof safes.

The Laboratory

The brain's processing department is what every film lab in the world would like to be. It is completely isolated from the outside world, dustproof, air-conditioned. It develops and prints, correctly following the instinctive artistic taste of the individual, and not the demands of business convenience. Its temperature is constant, and the entire system functions perfectly as long as the health of the individual is in order. The brain also has its separate little editing rooms, where pictures taken in our waking hours are edited during our rest period, our sleep, by gremlins of the gray matter. When the pictures are edited, they are mounted on separate reels, labeled, and placed in the safe for future screenings. Some pictures of importance and pleasant experiences are marked *Special.*

The entire establishment is self-supporting, manufactures its own invisible film, and all the necessary chemicals for processing. The chemicals are received from the different glands which derive their substance from the digestive system.

LEARNING

When we hear something, or see something new, we immediately set our recording apparatus in operation and take pictures. These pictures are processed and stored away. This is learning. Pages of books are thus photographed in their entirety, and put away for future reference. The bigger this library, the more of these pictures we are able to put away, and therefore the more cultured and the more learned we are.

As children we are taught the difference between good and evil, thine and mine. As these pictures serve as standards later on, the importance of a good education, well photographed and preserved, cannot be overemphasized. As we found out during World War II, training films facilitate learning enormously. The student does not have to work as hard. All the brain does is make a print of the film by simply looking at it, and storing it away. The amount of knowledge a person has depends greatly upon his photographic capacity and the quantity and quality of pictures he is able to store away properly.

MEMORY

One's earliest childhood recollection marks the beginning of the time when memory started to function properly. It is from that time that our ultra-modern photographic establishment began to take pictures and store them away in air-conditioned vaults.

The still, movie, and television cameras of today are only primitive imitations of the photo department latent in every human being, *the human camera.*

After years have passed, and we want to screen a picture, all we need to do is think of it. This presses invisible buttons, and sets all machinery in operation. *By simply thinking of it, we command the screening.* The film is immediately taken out of the vaults, sprocket holes checked, fed into the continuous projector, and projected upon the television screen.

Some people have what we call a good memory. These people have a well-functioning human camera, and can produce pictures taken years ago, at will. Others are careless, or their brains' photo departments do not function well. They have poor memories. Those whose bodies are not functioning well because certain glands do not deliver the necessary chemicals, perhaps because of wrong nourishment, should consult physicians. Some cannot help it. As children, they were "poor students," and condemned as such instead of being treated medically for what was wrong with them. These faults could have been corrected more easily in youth; later they become strongly imbedded habits, and cure becomes more difficult.

The photographic departments of some brains have only so much room. Therefore, if we fill them with unimportant matter, when space is needed for something useful, there is a *No Vacancy* sign out.

LIKES AND DISLIKES

When we meet someone for the first time, a picture of him is taken immediately and sent down to our own "police record" library. Here pictures of people we have met since our television system began functioning are filed away. A gremlin (there are lots of them on payroll) takes the picture of the new acquaintance, and going through the records at lightning speed, compares it with the pictures of similar types and characters, with whom we have had dealings in the past. When this is done a flash report comes back, and that is our first impression of the person. This is how we happen to like or dislike someone at first sight. Of course, this does not always work out correctly. We can be wrong about our impression. The first comparison is only as to looks. He may belong in one category as far as physical aspect is concerned, and

in another one when we learn more about his psyche.

No two people looking at a third person see the same picture. At the time of meeting someone our imagination goes way back into the past, in search of someone similar in looks and type. As our pasts differ, so do the pictures we see. Perhaps that is the reason why, when asking someone about the person, "Does he not look like so and so?" the answer is usually a late "No," at the same time wondering how in the world we see any similarity at all.

What Is Thinking?

Few people associate thinking with photography. In reality they are so close that we cannot tell one from the other. When a person is thinking, he is either viewing pictures of the past on his psychic screen, or, by planning the future, is creating new ones. The human television system is capable of putting thoughts into picture form, and either sending them out, broadcasting them into space in the form of telepathy, or storing them away for the future.

Some people like solitude. They want to be left alone. Apparently, they are not doing anything. In reality, they are thinking. A person who has had an interesting past has a rich library of pleasant pictures to delve into, and can pass the time away without talking to anyone. Then there are people who just cannot stay at home, or at any other place for that matter. They just cannot bear to be quiet and do not want to be alone. They crave constant excitement. Some of these people have some unpleasant pictures they cannot destroy. They keep on coming back, so they take to alcohol or dope. *Crime does not pay.*

THE PAST

There are several ways in which pictures of the past can be brought back to our memory: looking at an old photograph; thinking hard, and paging back on the calendar of life; association of some present-day occurrence with something that happened in the past. Perfumes and odors of food will take us back into the past. Words, both written and verbal, will also remind us of happenings of yesteryear. There is no better cure for insomnia than to project pictures of pleasant memories of the past, especially of our youth. It works better than sedatives, is less dangerous, and has fewer after-effects.

If we want to remember something in the future, and want to be reminded of it in due time, we photograph it the usual way; but instead of filing it away in the subconscious, it is marked "hold." A mental radio alarm is attached to it, which is set for the time we wish it to ring. To illustrate: We put a key away when going on a vacation. When we return home we want to be reminded of where we put it. Just think of it hard, with the intention of using it at a future date, and leave the rest to the gremlins.

If he has a train that leaves at a certain early hour, the average person sets the alarm clock and then cannot sleep all night for fear of oversleeping and missing it. Set your mental radio alarm, go to bed; and if you have set the alarm clock also, you will be awakened a few seconds before it begins to ring.

To forget is also a photographic process. There are two main libraries in our studio of the brain, the conscious and the subconscious. In the conscious, pictures are kept on file for a certain time, then moved down to the subconscious. As the room is limited, they move on almost constantly. Every time we photograph something new, it takes up space. As it moves down the line, pictures of less importance, which have faded, are discarded. Some people have more pleasant experiences than unpleasant. They learn to hold the good only. If it is at all possible, we destroy images of hated faces or unhappy occurrences. Some people need a change of scenery to get new

pictures which will force out and replace the old, unpleasant ones that can make one ill.

Pictures of crimes committed by a person are not easily eradicated. They stay. They make deep, indelible impressions. Conscience takes care of that.

THE ABSENT–MINDED

Certainly you must have met people who, when you talked to them, were apparently in another world. These people live up in the clouds. Some of them just cannot concentrate. They have their wires crossed. When they do think, they have to cut all other circuits off. Some blame it on bad memory; with others, it is just their own fault that they lack the necessary stamina. Perhaps it is lack of willpower. Whatever it is, their photographic departments do not function properly. They should consult a psychiatrist.

Television

Before closing this chapter, we must not forget the sound department of the brain. If we add the radio to our photo department, we have the best micro-television set devised as yet. If this is possible in man-made instruments, why could it not be in the human brain? This is no psychic phenomenon, just plain common sense. It is quite possible that a mother has her brain television set attuned to that of her son on the battlefield.

Long before Al Jolson sang "Mammy" in the first talkie, the television set of the human brain recorded and broadcast pictures with sound. When great composers looked at beautiful scenery, sound and light waves entered their brains and were transformed into music, which is the classical music of today.

There must have been times when human beings could converse and communicate with each other by merely sending out thoughts on microwaves. Today that would be very embarrassing. Imagine taking your wife, dressed in her new mink coat, to a friend's house, whose wife hasn't one. . . . Perhaps it is just as well. We would soon lose many of our friends.

This book is primarily on photography. We have included this chapter on the human camera of the brain because of its relation to photography, to encourage people who think it is difficult to learn how to take pictures. This chapter is to remind them that they have been doing it, have been making pictures since their arrival in the world, only they did not know it.

Fig. 292 *"Summertime"*